"Is there a 'legitimacy basis for the unelected'? Yes, say Erik O. Eriksen and the specialist authors in this must-read volume. In an age of scepticism about knowledge, we are reminded of the vital importance of 'public reason' as a basis for informed decision-making. We know that we cannot live without experts, but we also know we must legitimate expertise. This volume unlocks this conundrum, reinvigorating existing legal and institutional debates by re-asserting the political-philosophical foundations for legitimate action."

Michelle Everson, Birkbeck College, University of London, UK.

"Experts and expertise are under attack. They are needed but lost their aura of impartiality. This book offers a democratic understanding of experts by building on the reasons-giving requirement. Erik O. Eriksen, a master of the intersection between empirical and normative analysis, has gathered a set of intriguing contributions by excellent scholars. The result is a timely contribution to one of the most challenging issues for our democracies."

Michael Zürn, Berlin Social Science Center (WZB), Germany.

THE ACCOUNTABILITY OF EXPERTISE

Based on in-depth studies of the relationship between expertise and democracy in Europe, this book presents a new approach to how the un-elected can be made safe for democracy. It addresses the challenge of reconciling modern governments' need for knowledge with the demand for democratic legitimacy.

Knowledge-based decision-making is indispensable to modern democracies. This book establishes a public reason model of legitimacy and clarifies the conditions under which unelected bodies can be deemed legitimate as they are called upon to handle pandemics, financial crises, climate change and migration flows. Expert bodies are seeking neither re-election nor popularity, they can speak truth to power as well as to the citizenry at large. They are unelected, yet they wield power. How could they possibly be legitimate?

This book is of key interest to scholars and students of democracy, governance, and more broadly to political and administrative science as well as Science Technology Studies (STS).

Erik O. Eriksen is Professor of Political Science and former director of ARENA, Centre for European Studies, University of Oslo, Norway.

Routledge Studies on Democratising Europe

Series editors: Erik Oddvar Eriksen and John Erik Fossum, ARENA, University of Oslo, Norway.

This series focuses on the prospects for a *citizens' Europe* by analysing the kind of order that is emerging in Europe. The books in the series take stock of the EU as an entity that has progressed beyond intergovernmentalism and consider how to account for this process and what makes it democratic. The emphasis is on citizenship, constitution-making, public sphere, enlargement, common foreign and security policy, and Europe society.

Democratic Decision-making in the EU
Technocracy in disguise?
Anne Elizabeth Stie

States of Democracy
Gender and politics in the European Union
Edited by Yvonne Galligan

The European Union's Non-Members
Independence under hegemony?
Edited by Erik Oddvar Eriksen and John Erik Fossum

Expertisation and Democracy in Europe
Magdalena Góra, Cathrine Holst and Marta Warat

Towards a Segmented European Political Order
The European Union's Post-Crises Conundrum
Edited by Jozef Bátora and John Erik Fossum

The Accountability of Expertise
Making the Un-Elected Safe for Democracy
Edited by Erik O. Eriksen

For more information about this series, please visit: https://www.routledge.com

THE ACCOUNTABILITY OF EXPERTISE

Making the Un-Elected Safe for Democracy

Edited by Erik O. Eriksen

LONDON AND NEW YORK

First published 2022
by Routledge
2 Park Square, Milton Park, Abingdon, Oxon OX14 4RN

and by Routledge
605 Third Avenue, New York, NY 10158

Routledge is an imprint of the Taylor & Francis Group, an informa business

© 2022 selection and editorial matter, Erik O. Eriksen; individual chapters, the contributors

The right of Erik O. Eriksen to be identified as the author of the editorial material, and of the authors for their individual chapters, has been asserted in accordance with sections 77 and 78 of the Copyright, Designs and Patents Act 1988.

All rights reserved. No part of this book may be reprinted or reproduced or utilised in any form or by any electronic, mechanical, or other means, now known or hereafter invented, including photocopying and recording, or in any information storage or retrieval system, without permission in writing from the publishers.

Trademark notice: Product or corporate names may be trademarks or registered trademarks, and are used only for identification and explanation without intent to infringe.

British Library Cataloguing-in-Publication Data
A catalogue record for this book is available from the British Library

Library of Congress Cataloging-in-Publication Data
Names: Eriksen, Erik Oddvar, 1955– editor.
Title: The accountability of expertise : making the un-elected safe for democracy / Edited by Erik O. Eriksen.
Description: Abingdon, Oxon ; New York, NY : Routledge, 2021. | Series: Routledge studies on democratising Europe | Includes bibliographical references and index.
Identifiers: LCCN 2021002245 (print) | LCCN 2021002246 (ebook) | ISBN 9781032007625 (hardback) | ISBN 9781032007601 (paperback) | ISBN 9781003175490 (ebook)
Subjects: LCSH: Democracy—Europe. | Decision making—Political aspects—Europe. | Government accountability—Europe. | Europe—Politics and government.
Classification: LCC JN40 .A274 2021 (print) | LCC JN40 (ebook) | DDC 320.94—dc23
LC record available at https://lccn.loc.gov/2021002245
LC ebook record available at https://lccn.loc.gov/2021002246

ISBN: 978-1-032-00762-5 (hbk)
ISBN: 978-1-032-00760-1 (pbk)
ISBN: 978-1-003-17549-0 (ebk)

Typeset in Bembo
by codeMantra

CONTENTS

List of tables ix
List of contributors xi
Preface xiii

1 Introduction: making the unelected safe for democracy 1
  Erik O. Eriksen

2 Strategies for repairing legitimacy deficits 14
  Erik O. Eriksen

3 Reasoned administration: the European Union, the United States, and the project of democratic governance 34
  Jerry L. Mashaw

4 Power, money, knowledge and the European Central Bank 56
  Christopher Lord

5 Reputational threats and democratic responsiveness of regulatory agencies 81
  Tobias Bach, Marlene Jugl, Dustin Köhler and Kai Wegrich

6 Accountability and inter-institutional respect: the case of independent regulatory agencies 99
  Andreas Eriksen

7 Accountability beyond control: how can parliamentary
   hearings connect the elected and the unelected? 119
   Andreas Eriksen and Alexander Katsaitis

8 Expertise and the general will in democratic
   republicanism 137
   Kjartan Koch Mikalsen

9 Values in expert reasoning: a pragmatic approach 155
   Torbjørn Gundersen

10 Experts: from technocrats to representatives 173
   Erik O. Eriksen

Index 197

TABLES

5.1	Descriptive statistics for all articles with threats	89
5.2	Reputational profile: opinion by agency and dimension	91
5.3	Reputational dimension addressed in threats by agency	91
5.4	Logistic regression of agencies' tendency to respond to threats	92
7.1	Expected measurement outcomes depending on the authority mode in place between parliament and agency communication	124
7.2	Hearing type (I, II), title, date	130

CONTRIBUTORS

Tobias Bach is a professor at the Department of Political Science and Senior Researcher at ARENA Centre for European Studies, both at the University of Oslo. He holds a PhD from the University of Potsdam (2013).

Andreas Eriksen is a post-doctoral fellow at ARENA Centre for European Studies at the University of Oslo. He holds a PhD in the study of professions from Oslo Metropolitan University.

Erik O. Eriksen is a professor and former director at ARENA – Centre for European Studies at the University of Oslo, Norway. He holds a doctoral degree from University of Tromsø and has previously been a professor at University of Tromsø, University of Bergen and Oslo University College.

Torbjørn Gundersen is a post-doctoral fellow at the Department of Sociology and Human Geography at the University of Oslo and at the Centre for the Study of Professions at Oslo Metropolitan University, where he also obtained his PhD.

Marlene Jugl is Assistant Professor of public administration at Bocconi University. She holds an MA in public administration from the University of Potsdam and conducted her doctoral research at the Hertie School.

Alexander Katsaitis was a post-doctoral fellow at the REFLEX project at ARENA and is now an LSE Fellow in Public Policy and Administration. He holds a PhD in political science and an MSc in public policy from the School of Public Policy at University College London.

Dustin Köhler is a former research associate at the Hertie School, Berlin, Germany.

Christopher Lord is Professor at ARENA Centre for European Studies, University of Oslo, and scientific co-ordinator of the PLATO network.

Jerry L. Mashaw is Sterling Professor of Law Emeritus and Professorial Lecturer in Law at Yale University. He holds a PhD in European governmental studies from the University of Edinburgh (1969) and has previously taught at Tulane University and the University of Virginia.

Kjartan Koch Mikalsen is Associate Professor at the Department of Philosophy and Religious Studies at Norwegian University of Science and Technology, where he also obtained his PhD in 2012. He has previously been Associate Professor at Nord University.

Kai Wegrich is Professor of public administration and public policy at the Hertie School, Berlin. He holds degrees from the Free University of Berlin and Potsdam University, where he earned his PhD in 2003.

PREFACE

As the planet burns, voters run away from experts and into the arms of the demagogues. Why is that so? Why are democracies' helpers attacked and in whose name? Experts are the main target of populist opposition to the established political order. The worries about expert rule are not new. However, in contrast to worries about freedom and meaning in the age of technology and science in the 1950s and 1960s, there is now the worry that technocratic orders undermine the will of the people. The massive build-up of knowledge-based institutions and their putative power, particularly in the transnational realm, is seen as a threat to democratic self-rule. Is this criticism justified, or not? Can unelected bodies be made safe for democracy? There is a need to figure out the proper link between expertise and politics in modern democracies. What is the role of unelected expert bodies, and what can it be? In particular there is a need for a justificatory account of agencies and central banks that unavoidably wield political power. Such an account is lacking. The power of the unelected continues to be an anomaly in democratic theory.

In this book, a cross-disciplinary group of scholars analyse the functioning of and the alleged democratic problem of unelected bodies. These bodies represent an antidote to fake news and passion-driven politics. They are cognitive devices to handle the major societal challenges of today. Expert bodies are needed to save the planet, to guard against pandemics, to protect food safety and to save the Euro, but how can we know they are complying with the will of the people? The book establishes a public reason approach to address the question of how to make the unelected safe for democracy. Due to their autonomous standing and their truth-based workings, the claim of this book is that they may, in fact, be democracy's 'rescues' rather than its 'escapes'. The contributors of the book are political scientists, philosophers and lawyers who all have taken a keen interest in this theme over a long period of time. This book is the outcome of a large-scale project on the legitimacy of depoliticised bodies located at ARENA, University of Oslo, funded by The Research Council of Norway: Democracy and Expert Rule: The Quest for Reflexive Legitimacy (REFLEX) – ARENA Centre for European Studies (uio.no) (https://www.sv.uio.no/arena/english/research/projects/reflex/).

The contents of the chapters have been discussed at several stages, and at two workshops at ARENA, one in 2017 and the other in 2019. The book profited greatly from the discussions on the topic in the workshops. In addition to the contributors to this book, Marija Bartl, Lars Blichner, David Demortain, Michelle Everson, Trym N. Fjørtoft, John Erik Fossum, Cathrine Holst, Robert Huseby, Eva Krick, Jonathan Kuyper, Martino Maggetti, Joana Mendes, Asimina Michailidou, Anders Molander, Mira Scholten, Helene Sjursen and Matthew Wood attended the workshops. I am grateful for the technical assistance provided by Kaja Meeg Valvatne and Joachim Vigrestad.

Oslo, 20 December 2020
Erik O. Eriksen

1
INTRODUCTION
Making the unelected safe for democracy

Erik O. Eriksen

Introduction

The rise of unelected bodies is a conspicuous feature of modern governing and a recurrent theme in political research. Institutionalising unelected expert bodies in democratic societies testifies to a *new grammar of politics* in which the organisation of specialised forms of expertise is becoming decisive for legitimate policymaking. The new organisational complex is made up of agencies, central banks, economic regulators, risk managers and auditors, appointed with specific responsibilities and operating at arm's length from ministries and parliaments. Such bodies and networks of experts are needed for identifying viable policy options, for clarifying multifaceted problems, for resolving disputes and conflicts, and for carrying out administrative tasks, sometimes in collaboration with civil society. They are called on because the traditional institutions of representative democracy are not equipped to handle some of the major challenges facing modern societies: such challenges 'are much more amenable to action by unelected bodies' (Vibert 2007: 103). Often parliaments are not able to weigh and balance policy options when the stakes are high (Nordhaus 2008). The role and status of unelected bodies are of principal interest. They wield power but are neither elected nor directly controlled. How can they then be made safe for democracy?

Problem-solving and conflict resolution in pluralistic and functionally differentiated societies depend on knowledge-producing institutions. Modern societies are characterised both by pluralism and of social complexity. With regard to complexity, technological change and specialisation, asymmetries in competence and information require expertise to sort out what is the case on an objective basis and what the alternatives for action are. Belief in objective knowledge is what makes agreement possible; it is what unites heterogeneous publics. In the face of value pluralism and the rising degrees of conflict, non-partisan decision-making is required. Facts are not a partisan position. The unelected bodies such as agencies and central banks present themselves as apt remedies for meeting such requirements. They are even claimed to constitute *a fourth branch of government*, which due to their knowledge base and procedures can be seen as power in its own right. The reasoning of expert bodies is expected to be impartial and based on sound knowledge, respecting the virtues of professionalism, integrity, and fairness. They are expected to operate on an independent basis, taking instructions from no one. 'No one controls the agency, and yet the agency is under control' (Moe 1990: 243). Democratic control is seen as a question of institutional and procedural design. Not only are procedural rules providing cost-effective solutions to problems of noncompliance, assuring fairness and legitimacy in agency decision-making, but they also fulfil important control functions (McCubbins et al. 1987). Hence the putative normativity of the new grammar of politics.

Solving intertemporal trade-offs by being outside the electoral circle unelected bodies are pivotal democratic devices for handling collective action problems domestically. Unelected bodies are instruments to avoid bias, shirking, bigotry and blame games in policymaking and to safeguard long-term interests, such as pensions, price stability, security and the environment. They are assumed to ensure more consistent, far-sighted decision-making as well as more justifiable results (Majone 2005; Pettit 2004; Sunstein 2018).

However, unelected bodies are also vital for finding the right solutions to problems, which increasingly cross borders. The political order in Europe is rapidly developing in its administrative dimension due to the surge of regulatory powers. Complex interdependence, asymmetries and economic integration in Europe have led to a transnational build-up of administrative capabilities. The new regulatory powers deal with European standards for competition, consumer rights, privacy, health, environment protection, safety and security, and standards for income, working conditions and so on.

Many of the tasks assigned to unelected bodies are not merely technical, but of a political nature. They involve values and they affect interests and identities, rights and duties. There are collective action problems with distributive consequences to be solved, and there are regulatory decisions with consequences for rights and duties to be made. There is, however, no scientific metric according to which trade-offs between regulatory policies can be decided and according to which collective action problems can be solved. These tasks, as well as risk questions, are of a normative nature; hence, they require competence that stems from political authority. In constitutional democracies politicians are supposed to attend to ends and values – that is, 'ought-questions' – and experts to facts – that is, 'is-questions'. Experts should be 'on tap, not on top'. Nevertheless, unelected bodies are also 'on top' dealing with values and ends. Some of them are not set up to make value judgements, but more often than not these are inescapable. Inevitably, an agency discretionary decision-making involves values, judgements and perceptions, hence the danger of arbitrary rule and the quest for accountability.

Arbitrary rule refers, according to James Q. Wilson (1989: 326), 'to officials acting without legal authority or with that authority in a way that offends our sense of justice'.

Inevitably, unelected bodies deal with *values and policy ends*, not only means when they handle controversial issues. How can agency discretionary decision-making then be justified? Standard theories of agency decision-making in jurisprudence and political science offer no justification for giving agencies a role in policy-setting. They see them as more or less neutral instruments in the realisation of political goals. The assignment of broad policymaking discretion to administrative agencies is seen as an anomaly.

Thus, while necessary and indispensable, the power of such bodies raises challenges of a normative nature. If nobody controls the agency and yet it is controlled, how is it controlled? Moreover, 'who will know the knowers? No knower is knowable enough to be accepted by all reasonable citizens' (Estlund 1993: 71). This book probes the conditions under which unelected bodies can be deemed legitimate. We do so by utilising the resources of *the reason-giving perspective* to administrative decision-making, which subjects their discretionary power to the test of public reason. Accountability involves the obligation to provide reasons, to ensure that discretionary power is used in a reasoned and justifiable manner. It designates a relationship wherein obligatory questions are posed and qualified answers required. Accountability speaks to a justificatory process that rests on a reason-giving practice, in which the decision-makers can be held responsible to the citizenry, and by which, in the last resort, it is possible to dismiss the incompetent ones (Eriksen 2009: 36). Can accountability and hence the conditions of legitimacy be established on an independent basis? In this book we concentrate on European examples of depoliticised decision-making.

Background

The point of departure in the discussion of unelected expert bodies is how to reconcile modern governments' demand for knowledge with the demand for democratic legitimacy. Democratic forms of rule are expected to be better than known alternatives, and knowledge-based policies are required to fulfil this expectation. No government can make viable decisions without knowledge of facts, causal connections and interconnections as well as of risk estimates of possible negative effects of various measures. How can we reconcile this need for expertise, which places some in a privileged situation with regard to 'Truth', with democracy's requirement of popular authorisation and control of decision-makers? According to the democratic credo, only those laws that can meet with the assent of the citizens are legitimate.

More specifically, this book deals with the institutionalisation of independent expert bodies and their political role. Prototypically these bodies are 'non-majoritarian institutions' (NOMIS) with specialised authority, neither directly elected nor directly managed by elected officials (Thatcher and Stone Sweet 2002).

The rise of *depoliticized decision-making* has, in part, been justified as a response to the time inconsistency problem of politics where short-term benefits trump long-term benefits due to electoral cycles. This problem arises when a policy-maker decides one policy at one point in time, but implements a different one at a later time due to an upcoming election. NOMIS may be needed for solving problems and resolving conflicts in a rational manner. Increasingly, they are called upon to handle cross-border problems like pandemics, financial crises, climate change, migration flows and security and risk issues. Their knowledge is also needed to explain and justify policies to the general public. However, depoliticized decision-making raises the spectre of *technocratic dominance*.

In Europe, decisions affecting people's lives are made by experts in central banks and agencies as well as the European Union (EU) institutions themselves. While this is an extreme form of sectioning off certain questions from political control, it reflects a wider political dynamic privileging expert knowledge. With growing complexity comes the need for more specialised knowledge. Depoliticised decision-making is intrinsic to the rise of the *administrative state*. The seclusion of regulatory power became a distinctive ingredient of modern government that emerged during the twentieth century, first in the United States and later in Europe (Lindseth 2010). A burdensome regulatory regime, that is, statutory regulation by independent agencies, was established (Majone 1996).

Decentralised agencies have become an integral part of the way the EU operates. The first EU agencies were established in 1975. The number exploded after 2000, amounting to 44 currently. They perform regulatory, monitoring and co-ordination tasks within different policy fields. Agencies support the decision-making process by pooling the technical or specialist expertise available at both the European and national level and thereby help cooperation between member states and the EU in important policy areas. Even though agencies are "partners" to directorate generals of the Commission, the independence of staff and experts is a recurrent theme in the research on agencies. A related recurrent theme is accountability. NOMIS deal not only with information but with policy itself, and several competing accountability systems are in force. According to conventional wisdom this raises the danger of arbitrary rule. In Europe this danger has been amplified by the fact that *discretionary policy-making power* has been delegated to EU agencies (Scholten 2014: 299). As the US case raises similar disquiets as the European one, with regard to lenient delegation standards, the US model does not provide a viable solution to the European accountability problem.

However, is agency delegation a question of delegation at all, or is it rather a question of *an act of conferral*, that is, the act of conferring competences fundamental to European Union Law?[1] It is a question whether a new doctrine is in place since the EU has, in fact, conferred tasks that it did not have itself. This is, in particular, the case with the EU financial agencies in the wake of the Eurozone crisis.

Mileposts in the history of the European integration process are the establishment of the single market and the euro area. This includes the introduction of the new common currency and its progressive adoption by 19 countries, and the establishment of an EU institution governing the euro. The first step to establish the European Central Bank (ECB) was taken in 1988. The primary objective is to maintain *price stability* within the Eurozone. The Maastricht Treaty that established the ECB forbids it or any member of its decision-making bodies to take instructions from any government or EU institution in order not to compromise this objective. Increasingly it is now accused of overstepping its competencies (Tucker 2018). The core of the problem is that the ECB and many agencies do not mainly deal with the informational basis of public policy, but with policy itself.

The problem

Agencies and central banks are powerful bodies in the exercise of public authority. They are legally regulated bodies composed of selected persons with a mandate to handle joint problems through reasoned opinion. Sometimes they are authorised to inform and advise and sometimes to make binding decisions. Either way they wield power. It does not matter that some agencies will have a purely informational role because information is a key element in policymaking and policy controversy (Shapiro 1997: 276). Information in itself is a source of power as well as of counter-power. NOMIS wield public authority whilst their connections to parliaments, legislatures and elected executives are unclear (Power 1997; Vibert 2007). There is a risk that they defy democratic control, that they create political disenchantment and that they represent 'escapes' from democracy. Some claim that such seclusion of regulatory authority undermines citizens' trust and confidence in representative democracy and leads to an upsurge in populist parties (see e.g. Mair 2013; Offe 2014; Zürn 2018).

One thing is that agencies and central banks wield power in virtue of being administrative bodies. Another is that they, due to their autonomy and knowledge base, inevitably *wield political power*. They operate within large zones of discretion and are involved in the setting of goals and ends in policymaking and law-making. Hence, they are not merely exercising administrative power. In fact, 'the involvement of agencies in policy formulation is quite common, even in contexts where norms of separating policy and operations prevail' (Bach et al. 2012: 186; see also Demortain 2017). There is the danger of *self-programming* when the unelected are involved in making statutory law and the mandate that applies to themselves.

NOMIS challenge the view that the people via their elected representatives is the source of the law. They carry out much of the practical work that enables democracies to function effectively. Since they are autonomous and since their legitimacy stems from their own principles and procedures they are independent of partisan control by the elected – scored by a governing majority. NOMIS have occupied a new space between politics and the law and taken over some of the functions of the elected branch of government. In many ways they have supplanted the rational role of courts as the main interpreter of statutory law and its operationalisation and specification (Sunstein 1999). There are numerous opportunities for agency representatives and political principals to interact in policymaking processes. Being independent, NOMIS can wield its delegated powers in capricious ways. Moreover, the broad public participation that statutes facilitate is not only an instrument for civil society involvement but also one for possible manipulation and self-empowerment.

How to ensure non-arbitrariness of decision-making when unelected bodies are delegated discretionary powers and are involved in end-setting, in settling normative questions? A decision is arbitrary, and a source of *dominance*, whenever it is chosen or rejected without procedures appropriate for tracking the interests and opinions of those affected (Pettit 1997: 53). The dominated find themselves at the mercy of others (Kant 1991[1797]).

The problem of arbitrariness runs deep not only because it is hard to separate facts and values, or because of the growing awareness of epistemological uncertainties, where scientific risk assessment has come to be seen as fraught with insecurity and ambiguity.[2] The problem runs deep also because when experts handle problems, they do not merely represent facts but also their relation to norms and values. The very act of establishing knowledge involves more than the compilation of pure facts. By referring to an objective state of affairs, experts make sense of something and make claims on its behalf. They act as *representatives*. Experts create a link between facts and values when they make representative claims (more on this in Chapter 10).

When experts discover climate change and identify its putative effects, when they forbid dangerous chemicals or when they deal with a financial crisis, they relate to 'ought-questions' about what should be done. Without a value component, and without judgemental power, experts would be impotent; they would not be able to reach a decision or give pertinent advice. This raises a normative question that needs to be sorted out, because according to established standards, experts should relate to 'is-questions' only. How can we guard against arbitrary rule when it is the experts and not the elected politicians that are policy- and law-makers? How can we know they are doing *the right thing*? While political 'representation is not needed when we expect scientifically true answers', it is needed when values, judgements and decisions are involved (Pitkin 1967: 220). The scientific procedure is needed for validating truth claims, and the democratic procedure is needed for validating normative, political claims.

A convincing justification of the political role of unelected bodies is lacking. Rather, scholars have based their normative reasoning of the proper role of agencies as if they were neutral instruments for political leadership – as if they were simply transmission belts (Christiano 2012; cp. Weber 1921). Not only the instrumental agency model but also *the specification model*, which sees agencies involved in interpretation of statutory law and where 'ends can be revised via specification' (Richardson 2002: 218), suffers from shortcomings. The latter model overlooks the form of public duty towards the citizenry at large – the impartial concern for the freedom and welfare for all affected parties (Eriksen 2018, 2020a). Unelected bodies are value driven and deeply political. They go beyond instrumental means-end scheming and they wield political power. Their practice can be accounted for neither by the instrumental agency model nor by the specification model. Hence, there is a need for an alternative approach.

We need a change in approach from the prevailing principal-agent theories, which see the accountability of NOMIS as a question of how the elected can have adequate *partisan control* over expert bodies. The principal-agent model of representation presumes that the legislature delegates competence to NOMIS, which may, in principle, be revoked. As argued in Chapter 7, control for partisan advantage is inappropriate for expert bodies that are mandated to be 'non-majoritarian' and 'depoliticised'. Chapter 2 maintains that holding the agents accountable by matching their performance towards given rules will not do, since the more successful the agents are in solving problems, the more the rules will change. Conceiving of political representation as a principal-agent relationship neglects how far decision-makers actively shape opinions and decisions. Accountability processes in themselves are *sense-making*, which may create new norms and cognitions (Olsen 2017).[3] Are unelected bodies technocrats or democratic agents?

Technocrats or democratic agents

Increasingly there is a reason-giving requirement on administrative decision-making.[4] It is imposed on agencies as an intrinsic part of procedural due process. To a much greater degree than what is the case with courts, where legality constrain the rule of reasons, and with parliaments, where the reason-giving process is terminated by voting, there is a requirement to explain and justify agency decision-making. Agency processes 'may be more open to broad outside participation and more transparent and responsive to data and argument than the reviewing process of either courts or political overseers' (Mashaw 2018: 70).

The fact that experts are required to give reasons, to justify and validate their claims, points to a solution to the technocracy problem. When we realise that they are engaged in justificatory processes, we also see that there may be a legitimacy basis for the unelected. When experts seek public approval for their representation of facts, when they for example discover climate change and identify its putative effects, then their claims take the form of *public reasons* and are directed to others for recognition, justification, and validation. Claims are then tested in the wider scientific, professional, political and moral community. In contrast to the principal-agent model, which is rather static or mechanical,[5] the public reason model requires expert bodies to take part in open-ended, ongoing process of justification. From this theoretical vantage point, there is a basis for establishing the conditions under which unelected expert bodies can be *democratic agents* and not technocrats that wield unauthorised political power.

Unelected expert bodies are not exempted from democratic control. NOMIS, which highlight non-partisan control, may be a response to the time inconsistency problem of politics. By being exempted from democratic politics as a form of political competition they can solve the problem of intertemporal trade-offs. NOMIS are, however, not exempted from *democracy as a principle of justification*. This is so because democracies are more than electoral systems embedded in a unified people; they are premised on separation of powers, on judicial review, on mass media and on a functioning public sphere, which all call for the justification of the wielding of power. European agencies and central banks are *unelected bodies in democratic societies*. In Chapter 4, Christopher Lord argues that

> Independent central banks need, as it were, to be exempted from democratic politics as a form of political competition, not from democracy as a structure of justification. Problems – such as 'time inconsistency' that make it hard to optimise policy over all time periods – only require the decoupling of monetary policy from electoral cycles. They hardly justify freeing central banks from the normal obligations in a democracy to justify decisions to publics.

In this book we conceive of unelected bodies not as an anomaly, but as an integral part of modern democratic rule. They are needed to establish requisite knowledge for rational and impartial policymaking. NOMIS wield power, often simply because they know a lot more about the policy issues than the legislator that delegated competence to them. However, as they possess an independent information base and are, in principle, autonomous, as they are seeking neither re-election nor popularity, they can *speak truth to power as well as to the citizenry at large*. As their operations are based on cognitions, on claims to objective knowledge, they present themselves as potent means for handling common problems under conditions of complex interdependence; of pluralism, risk and uncertainty.

The book analyses the practice of reason giving and develops a public reason model of agency accountability. It establishes the conditions under which unelected bodies can be deemed legitimate. It questions the widespread assumption that unelected bodies cannot both be political and truth-tracking.[6] Why would affected parties accept decisions that are not perceived as correct or rational, and if so, through what process? The approach developed in the present volume is based on a revised concept of representation as well as on a move in epistemological terms *beyond decisionism*. Decisionism, which is premised on non-cognitivism, asserts that validity is determined not by the substantive content of the decision, but rather by the fact that it is made by the proper authority. Accordingly, legal positivists assert that the validity of norms depend solely on the state's sanctioning of arbitrarily set norms (see Habermas 2019: 270). In the words of Thomas Hobbes (1651): *Auctoritas, non veritas, facit legem*.

Against this position, the reason-giving perspective holds that norms have a cognitive basis, that moral judgement is truth apt and that decisions owe their legitimacy to what can be justified. Reasons, not will or power, determine the validity, and hence the legitimacy of a decision. A decision is thus not right only because it is enacted. Rightness is, as we deal with in Chapter 10, a question of normative validity, which can only be redeemed through argumentation. Whether a decision is right is a question of what can be justified, namely, what affected parties can agree on in a rational discourse. Thus, the claim that some normative questions can be settled rationally; they are 'truth apt'. In order words, the political dimension is not about polluting truth with mere preference. The aim of this theoretical proposal is squaring the circle between the epistemic and the participatory dimension of democracy by making unelected bodies safe for democracy.

The upshot is that we set out to establish a new approach to agency decision-making. In this justificatory account, NOMIS are specialised not only on means-ends calculations but also on the viability and justifiability of political ends. NOMIS are difficult to hold to account through delegation models of control. Accountability entails the obligation to justify and thus to ensure that discretionary power is used in a reasoned and justifiable manner. Accountability is, however, backward looking and is only a second criterion of democratic rule, the first being *autonomy*, to wit, the basic democratic principle that those affected by laws should also be authorised to make them. The question is whether agency accountability and hence the conditions of legitimacy can be captured in *the public reason model* (see Eriksen 2020a: 6–11, 2020b; Molander et al. 2012). In fact, such a model is reflected in actual practice. Reasons are legally requested whenever an administrative decision is subject to judicial review. The *giving reason requirement* is, as Jerry Mashaw underscores in Chapter 3, legally enshrined in Europe, in the EU and in the United States. In order to establish the public reason model of legitimacy there is a need to move beyond the electoral model of democracy, premised on regular elections and majority vote. This volume clarifies the conditions under which unelected bodies can be made safe for democracy by drawing on the deliberative conception of democracy according to which only reason giving can get political results right.

The way forward

Chapter 2 discusses *strategies for repairing legitimacy deficits*. Agencies and central banks, which prototypically act on a wide discretionary basis, cannot simply defer to the legislator's command or to instrumental rationality. NOMIS operate within large zones of discretion and they deal with values and *policy ends*, not only the means. There is thus a legitimacy problem and a danger of arbitrary rule. This chapter identifies three distinct strategies for mending the legitimacy problems of unelected bodies: the *evidence-based* strategy, the *legislator's command* strategy and the *participatory* strategy. They are all deficient. They build on unrealistic presuppositions about the relationship between expertise and politics. Hence, there is a need for an alternative.

Chapter 3 gives the contours of an alternative based on the giving-reason principle. The right to be heard and to have decisions on one's interests made fairly and impartially are embodied in modern law. Moreover, there is a moral right to justification. This chapter focusses on the right to reasons and the practice of administrative reason giving. This is a common and important feature of both EU and US administrative law. However, as the author argues, this practice is somewhat undertheorised. The chapter therefore explains why reason giving is so prominent a part of both administrative systems, how it functions juridically, and, most crucially, the rationale for demanding reasons or for providing a 'right' to reasoned administration.

Chapter 4 addresses the legitimacy problems of the *European Central Bank*. The creation of the ECB rested on strong assumptions about knowledge and the independent use of knowledge. Crucial were distinctive claims about the neutrality of money and the so-called time inconsistency problems. This chapter shows how specialised knowledge was itself expected to contribute to that taming of power relations. The development of an independent central bank within the European Union's political and legal order was supposed to go further than single-democracy central banks towards maximising the role of knowledge and minimising the role of power or preferences in monetary decisions. However, the Eurozone crisis undermined assumptions that the ECB could concentrate on a neutral use of its own specialised knowledge while largely avoiding the exercise of political power.

Chapter 5 analyses regulatory agencies' attention to stakeholders through the analytical lens of bureaucratic *reputation theory*. The chapter's basic argument is that reputation-sensitive regulatory agencies will exhibit differential response patterns to negative public judgements, depending on the kind of negative judgements and the type of actor criticising a regulator. The chapter uses data from a systematic media analysis of public judgements and regulators' communicative response, with the financial regulator and the utility regulator (electricity, railways, etc.) in Germany as empirical cases. The chapter also suggests alternative accounts, which suggest that public criticism and debate is only one channel, among many others, through which regulators are held democratically accountable.

Chapter 6 asks how accountability serves legitimacy in the case of independent agencies. It argues that the legitimacy-enhancing function of accountability presupposes procedures that express *inter-institutional respect*. This approach is developed in response to both those who believe in the sufficiency of a "system of multiple controls" and to those want to replace controls with "ethos" and "administrative culture." Mechanisms of oversight are necessary, but they must be *embedded* in an appropriate mode of interaction. The form of respect that is appropriate for accountability interaction is recognition of agency work as governed by a distinct normative domain.

The point of departure in Chapter 7 is that agencies are de facto political players in the legislative process. The chapter delivers a novel conceptual model for understanding agencies' democratic responsiveness: a model of 'mutual attunement' where accountability relations presuppose a process of working out shared understandings of the ends, means and circumstances of policy. It tests the model through a case study assessing the interaction between the European Parliament's Committee on Economic and Monetary Affairs and the European Securities and Markets Authority in the backdrop of hearings conducted between 2011 and 2017. Based on this original analytical model of social reasoning, the chapter delivers a new perspective on public accountability, and illustrates its implications for the dynamics of European economic governance.

Chapter 8 deals with expertise and the general will. It argues that reliance on political expert arrangements is internally related to democratic self-legislation. It takes issue with the claim that *epistemic asymmetry* between experts and laypersons necessarily undermines our equality in popular sovereignty – as equal 'reasoners' in political will formation processes. According to democratic republicanism, the main political function of public deliberation is to bring the impersonal force of valid arguments to bear on matters at hand. This function is not unavoidably threatened by epistemic asymmetries. Nor does our standing as political equals depend on epistemic parity in public debates. We can expect permanent tensions between the actual practice and the republican ideal, but such tensions are not fatal. Hence, the mere existence of unelected bodies is not inimical to the idea of democratic self-rule.

The following chapter (Chapter 9) analyses the proper role of moral and political values in expert bodies, namely, the role of scientists in unelected bodies. In the philosophy of science there are two incompatible normative views. *The value-free ideal* holds that moral and political values should be minimised as far as possible. *Transactionism* finds these values acceptable. Drawing on examples from the role of scientists in unelected bodies this chapter suggests a more feasible approach. It integrates insights from transactionism and the value-free ideal. The chapter defends *a set of principles* that together regulate the proper role of such values. According to this 'pragmatic view of values', scientific experts interpret, balance, and weigh epistemic, ethical, and political principles on a case-by-case basis in light of the other standards scientists face.

Chapter 10 discusses the theoretical implications of what have been established regarding the accountability of NOMIS' discretionary decision-making. In order to account for the putative legitimacy basis of unelected bodies there is a need for a revised concept of representation as well as a move in epistemological terms beyond decisionism. The point made is that experts can be 'representatives' and not 'technocrats' when properly constrained. It is the mechanism of *truth-based claims-making* that explains how the unelected can be part of a democratic practice. This approach squares the need for expertise, which positions some in a privileged situation with regard to the truth, with the requirements of democracy, that is, popular authorisation and control through elections and parliamentary and public debate.

Notes

1 According to the principle of conferral, the EU is a union of member states, and all its competences voluntarily conferred on it by its member states.
2 See Brown (2009), Eriksen (2011), Hacking (1999).
3 On agency drift, see for example Egeberg and Trondal (2017).
4 Hence the administrative law principles: participation, transparency, reason-giving, and review (Venzke and Mendes 2018: 86).
5 The agent gets a mandate, which it then more or less carries out. End of story.
6 This is particularly the case with the STS studies but is also well known from the regulatory science literature and public administration studies in general.

References

Bach, T., Niklasson, B. and Painter, M. (2012) 'The Role of Agencies in Policy-Making', *Policy and Society*, 31(3): 183–193.
Brown, M.B. (2009) *Science in Democracy: Expertise, Institutions, and Representation*. Cambridge: MIT Press.
Christiano, T. (2012) 'Rational Deliberation among Experts and Citizens', in J. Parkinson and J. Mansbridge (eds.) *Deliberative Systems* (pp. 27–51). Cambridge: Cambridge University Press.
Demortain, D. (2017) 'Expertise, Regulatory Science and the Evaluation of Technology and Risk: Introduction to the Special Issue', *Minerva*, 55(2): 139–159.
Egeberg, M. and Trondal, J. (2017) 'Researching European Union Agencies: What Have We Learnt (and Where Do We Go From Here)?' *Journal of Common Market Studies*, 55(4): 675–690.
Eriksen, A. (2018) 'Legitimate Agency Reasoning', *ARENA Working Paper*, Jan 2018. Oslo: ARENA.
Eriksen, A. (2020a) 'Political Values in Independent Agencies', *Regulation & Governance*, online first. https://doi.org/10.1111/rego.12299
Eriksen, A. (2020b) 'Accountability and the Multidimensional Mandate', *Political Research Quarterly*, online first. https://doi.org/10.1177/1065912920906880
Eriksen, E.O. (2009) *The Unfinished Democratization of Europe*. Oxford: Oxford University Press.
Eriksen, E.O. (2011) 'Governance between Expertise and Democracy: The Case of European Security', *Journal of European Public Policy*, 18(8): 1169–1189.
Estlund, D. (1993) 'Making Truth Safe for Democracy', in D. Copp, J. Hampton and J.E. Roemer (eds.) *The Idea of Democracy* (pp. 71–100). Cambridge: Cambridge University Press.
Habermas, J. (2019) *Auch eine Geschichte der Philosophie: Vernünftige Freiheit. Spuren des Diskurses über Glauben und Wissen*, vol. 2. Berlin Suhrkamp.
Hacking, I. (1999) *The Social Construction of What?* Cambridge, MA: Harvard University Press.
Hobbes, T. (1651) *Leviathan: Or the Matter, Forme and Power of a Common Wealth Ecclesiasticall and Civil*. London: Andrew Crooke, Green Dragon, St. Paul's Churchyard.
Kant, I. (1991[1797]) 'The Metaphysics of Morals', in H. Reiss (ed.) *Kant: Political Writings*, 131–175. Cambridge: Cambridge University Press.
Lindseth, P.L. (2010) *Power and Legitimacy: Reconciling Europe and the Nation-State*. Oxford: Oxford University Press.
Mair, P. (2013) *Ruling the Void: The Hollowing of Western Democracy*. London: Verso Books.

Majone, G. (1996) *Regulating Europe*. New York: Routledge.
Majone, G. (2005) *Dilemmas of European Integration: The Ambiguities and Pitfalls of Integration by Stealth*. Oxford: Oxford University Press.
Mashaw, J.L. (2018) *Reasoned Administration and Democratic Legitimacy: How Administrative Law Supports Democratic Government*. Cambridge: Cambridge University Press.
McCubbins, M.D., Noll, R.G. and Weingast, B.R. (1987) Administrative Procedures as Instruments of Political Control', *Journal of Law Economics and Organization*, 3(2): 243–277.
Moe, T. (1990) 'Political Institutions: The Neglected Side of the Story', *Journal of Law, Economics and Organisation*, 6(Special issue): 213–253. https://doi.org/10.1093/jleo/6.special_issue.213
Molander, A., Grimen, H. and Eriksen, E.O. (2012) 'Professional Discretion and Accountability in the Welfare State', *Journal of Applied Philosophy*, 29(3): 214–230.
Nordhaus, W.D. (2008) *A Question of Balance: Weighing the Options on Global Warming Policies*. New Haven, CT: Yale University Press.
Offe, C. (2014) *Europe Entrapped*. Cambridge: Polity Press.
Olsen, J.P. (2017) *Democratic Accountability, Political Order and Change*. Oxford: Oxford University Press.
Pettit, P. (1997) *Republicanism: A Theory of Freedom and Government*. Oxford: Oxford University Press.
Pettit, P. (2004) 'Depoliticizing Democracy', *Ratio Juris*, 17(1): 52–65.
Pitkin, H. (1967) *The Concept of Representation*. Los Angeles: University of California Press.
Power, M. (1997) *The Audit Society: Rituals and Verification*. Oxford: Oxford University Press.
Richardson, H.S. (2002) *Democratic Autonomy: Public Reasoning about the End of Policy*. Oxford: Oxford University Press.
Scholten, M. (2014) *The Political Accountability of EU Agencies: Learning from the US Experience*. Leiden: Brill Nijhoff.
Shapiro, M. (1997) 'The Problems of Independent Agencies in the United States and the European Union', *Journal of European Public Policy*, 4(2): 276–291.
Sunstein, C.R. (1999) *One Case at the Time: Judicial Minimalism of the Supreme Court*. Cambridge, MA: Harvard University Press.
Sunstein, C.R. (2018) *The Cost-benefit Revolution*. Cambridge: MIT Press.
Thatcher, M. and Stone Sweet, A. (2002) 'The Politics of Delegation: Non-Majoritarian Institutions in Europe' [special issue], *West European Politics*, 25(1): 1–22.
Tucker, P. (2018) *Unelected Power, the Quest for Legitimacy in Central Banking and the Regulatory State*. Princeton, NJ: Princeton University Press.
Venzke, I. and Mendes, J. (2018) 'The Idea of Relative Authority in European and International Law', *International Journal of Constitutional Law*, 16(1): 75–100.
Vibert, F. (2007) *The Rise of the Unelected*. Cambridge: Cambridge University Press.
Weber, M. (1921) *Economy and Society: An Outline of Interpretative Sociology* [reprint 1978]. Berkeley: University of California Press.
Wilson, J.Q. (1989) *Bureaucracy: What Government Agencies Do*. New York: Basic Books.
Zürn, M. (2018) *A Theory of Global Governance: Authority, Legitimacy and Contestation*. Oxford: Oxford University Press.

2

STRATEGIES FOR REPAIRING LEGITIMACY DEFICITS

Erik O. Eriksen

Introduction

'The worst financial crisis in global history' commenced in the United States but hit Europe and the Eurozone economies hard.[1] The European Central Bank (ECB) has been widely credited with saving the euro, which was on the brink of collapsing. What seems remarkable, however, is the ECB's unrelenting insistence on recipient countries honouring their debts, rejecting any other solution (Tooze 2018: 360). The insolvent countries, not the banks, paid the price. This brings up the pertinent question of in whose interest's central banks and *non-majoritarian institutions* (NOMIS) in general, act, and whether they represent a threat to democracy.

While indispensable, the discretionary power of NOMIS raises challenges. There is a risk that NOMIS defy democratic control, that they create political disenchantment and that they represent 'escapes' from democracy. Some claim that such delegation undermines citizens' trust and confidence in representative democracy and leads to an upsurge in populist parties (see e.g. Caramani 2017; Mair 2013). This is because NOMIS appear to wield increasing public authority while their connections to parliaments, legislatures and elected executives are unclear (Power 1997; Slaughter 2004; Vibert 2007). They are *expert bodies* with some grant of specialised authority, neither directly elected nor directly managed by elected officials (Thatcher and Stone Sweet 2002). Such bodies operate with large zones of discretion and inevitably deal with values and *policy ends*, not only means. Sometimes NOMIS are authorised to inform, advise and even make collectively binding decisions. Due to their autonomy and knowledge base, NOMIS inevitably *wield political power*.[2] Policymakers rely on agencies' expertise to set policies. Agencies advise and help sort out the basis for statutes. Since NOMIS are involved in setting political ends and not only in means-end scheming, there is an obvious danger of arbitrary rule or *dominance*; that it is the experts and not the people or their representatives that govern. A decision is arbitrary, and a source of dominance, whenever it is taken or rejected without reference to the interests, or opinions of those affected (Pettit 1997: 53). Arbitrary rule means being at the mercy of others' will and is the essence of injustice.[3] The core of dominance is dependence on others' unauthorised discretion to affect citizens' rights and duties. Can expertise-based decisions be reconciled with lay participation and mass democracy – and, if so, how?

NOMIS qualify decision-making by fact gathering and by validating data for policymaking. They pursue long-term interests and are supposed to apply principles and procedures ensuring accuracy and to observe the law, not merely the elected politicians. For example, the time-inconsistency problem of monetary policy may justify setting longer-term goals and leaving the execution to an independent central bank or other authorities (Kydland and Prescott 1977). In NOMIS, objective knowledge enjoys a strong, if occasionally rebuttable conjecture. Belief in objective knowledge is a *conditio sine qua non* for democracies, as it is what unities heterogeneous publics. But when it comes to practical decision-making, it is difficult to rely only on objective knowledge. Some types of knowledge are embedded in contested theories (about the good society, about the economy, about justice, about norms etc.), and some types involve predictions about the effects of proposed policies on complex human systems. Objective knowledge is hard to obtain and an insufficient guidance for action. In effect, experts must draw on extra-scientific types of knowledge when dealing with practical questions – when they make decisions about what to do.

There are different proposals for mending the putative legitimacy problems of NOMIS, both those related to stricter separation of facts and values and those related to stricter political control. These proposals can be more or less well-suited to alleviate the problem, but they share a deficiency in that they do not adjust for the fact that the NOMIS are involved in norm setting and policymaking and not solely in technical implementation. Is then more participation an alternative? After all, the legitimate exercise of political authority requires justification to those bound by it.

This chapter assesses ways to mend the legitimacy problems of NOMIS. In order to clarify the multifaceted nature of the problem and the dilemmas involved, it distinguishes between three ideal typical approaches to the problem of depoliticised decision-making. They amount to strategies for repairing legitimacy deficits reflecting the authority relations of legitimate government. Political decisions should be defensible on scientific, legal and popular accounts. This chapter examines whether legitimacy can be restored by establishing purely scientifically based independent bodies – *the evidence-based strategy*; by establishing proper delegation rules – *the legislator-command strategy*; or through including lay people – *the participatory strategy*. These strategies all highlight important normative concerns that need to be addressed. However, all are deficient with regard to providing solutions. They are mistaken about the nature of unelected bodies and do not adjust for the fact that they necessarily are power wielding entities.

I start by briefly discussing the predicaments that the NOMIS' mode of administration and the risk agenda pose for democratic self-rule. In Part II, I set out three strategies for handling legitimacy deficits and address their shortcomings.

Part I: Legitimacy deficits of epistocratic orders

The rise of *the administrative state* populated with NOMIS raises questions as to their implications for democratic legitimacy and accountability.

Statutory regulation

The administrative state based on the seclusion of regulatory power became a distinctive ingredient of modern government that emerged during the twentieth century, first in the United States and later in Europe (Lindseth 2010; Tucker 2018). It all started with central banks in the 1920s as part of the economic reconstitution after First World War. The idea was, according to the League of Nations, that central banking 'should be free from political pressure, and should be conducted solely on lines of prudent finance' (Tucker 2018: 12). However, the 1929 stock market crash and the Great Depression stripped central banks of power, and they did not regain pre-eminence until the 1990s when the International Monetary Fund and the World Bank recommended independent central banks to the emerging-market economies. The effect was deregulation, liberalisation and privatisation – the 'neoliberal turn'. It meant, however, not the end of governmental control, but now in the form of a burdensome regulatory regime, that is, statutory regulation by independent agencies (see Majone 1996).

In the context of European integration, the central bank is an important institution. The first step towards creating the European Central Bank (ECB) was the decision, taken in 1988, to build an Economic and Monetary Union: free capital movements within Europe, a common monetary authority and a single monetary policy across the euro area countries. The ECB was established with the primary objective to maintain price stability within the Eurozone. Once the Bank was established in 1998, its Governing Council fixed its monetary policy to an inflationary target. Price stability is defined as a year-on-year increase in the Harmonised Index of Consumer Prices (HICP) for the euro area of below 2 per cent. Central banks are generally independent from direct political control; the ECB is even more so. The ECB is a special case of depoliticised governing in a multi-state setting that is often accused of epistocratic dominance and expansion of competence (see e.g. Tooze 2018; Weisbrot 2015). Why do the ECB and not the parliament set the inflationary target, why is the target set to 2 per cent and why is inflation only measured with reference to consumer prices? (Menéndez 2020). Another pertinent question, as posed by Ingo Venzke and Joana Mendes (2018: 76), is, 'Should the European Central Bank take decisions on outright monetary transactions, given that such decisions can have a far-reaching impact on matters of economic policy?' In Europe, there is a massive development of the regulator capacity, with newly fortified powers to oversee and control diverse public affairs.

Agencies have proliferated both at the national and the European level as a consequence of an increase in the EU's competences but not in budgets. Agencies are not confined to economic and financial issues. Since the Single European Act in 1986, the EU has become very active in the area of risk regulation. Health and safety regulation of products within the European Single Market is a high-priority issue. Initially the EU Commission was not allowed to delegate legislative power to other bodies, according to the *Meroni doctrine*. However, this would be improbable in view of the growing complexity of EU competencies and regulatory tasks.[4] The first EU agencies were established in 1975, and the number exploded after 2,000, amounting now to 44.

Decentralised agencies have become an established part of the way that the EU operates. They perform regulatory, monitoring, and coordination tasks within different policy fields. It can be distinguished between agencies dealing with production and dissemination of information, and those with advisory, assistant and administrative decision-making functions (Chiti 2009: 1395). They all contribute to the implementation of important Union policies, thus allowing the institutions, in particular the Commission, to concentrate on core policymaking tasks. Agencies support the decision-making process by pooling the technical or specialist expertise available at European and national level and thereby helping to enhance the cooperation between Member States and the EU in important policy areas. On the other hand, their independence and discretionary policy-making power give rise to accountability problems. Even though agencies are 'partners' to directorate generals (DG) (the Commission), the independence of staff and experts are recurrent themes in the research on agencies. Often, the constituent regulations do not make it clear 'from which actors exactly agencies' employees, boards and/or committees are intended to be independent: only from politicians or also from national ministries and agencies and/or perhaps also from industry and organized interests?' (Busuioc and Groenleer 2014: 181; see Everson et al. 2014; Mendes and Venzke 2018). Miroslava Scholten notes that '[a]t this moment determining who holds EU agencies to account and how becomes a rather challenging exercise when 35 agencies are held to account in more than 30 different accountability regimes' (Scholten 2014a: 305).

Another recurrent theme is the question of what powers and what type of discretion can be delegated to agencies. In the controversy over the applicability of the *Meroni doctrine* (Chamon 2014), the CJEU in the 1981 *Romano case* reiterated that the Council could not delegate the power to adopt acts 'having the force of law' to agencies (Guiseppe Romano v. Institut national d'assurance maladie-invalidité 1981). The Court prohibited the delegation of such powers to an agency. The Treaty foresaw the delegation of legally binding powers to the Commission only.

A new doctrine

In the vast literature on agencies and agencification, there is increasingly the question of whether they have been assigned policymaking discretionary powers. Over a longer period of time, quasi-legislative powers have been conferred to the agencies. It has been argued that the *Meroni-Romano doctrine* does not fit with practical realties. A series of treaty reforms that have taken place since 1958 have demonstrated the necessity to update the doctrine. Notwithstanding the necessity to revise the doctrine to fit with practical realties, the delegation of legislative powers is not allowed, at least according to Locke's famous doctrine:

> The power of the legislative, being derived from the people by a positive voluntary grant and institution, can be no other than what that positive grant conveyed, which being only to make laws, and not to make legislators, the legislative can have no power to transfer their authority of making laws and place it in other hands.
>
> Locke ([1690]1963: §141)

However, such delegation of law making authority has, in fact, taken place. The discretion assigned to agencies at times is of a normative, political nature (see Scholten 2014b; Scholten and Van Rijsbergen 2014; see also Moloney 2019: 103ff). The competence to take legally binding measures of general application powers were in 2010 assigned to the three new EU financial agencies (the European Banking Authority (EBA), the European Insurance and Occupational Pensions Authority (EIOPA) and the European Securities and Markets Authority (ESMA)). As the *ESMA-short selling ruling* attests to, a new doctrine is in place:

> [T]he *ESMA-short selling* case (Case 270/12), which was decided explicitly in relation to an EU agency and within the realities of the new treaties [...] shows that [...] the Court did formulate a new delegation doctrine in relation to EU agencies: EU agencies can be the recipients of executive discretionary powers if this discretion is limited.
>
> Scholten and van Rijsbergen (2014: 390)

The ESMA-short selling ruling states that *EU agencies can be assigned powers to take legally binding decisions of general application*. EU agencies have thus been given policymaking, discretionary powers, exactly the type of powers that the Court prohibited. This is a delegation situation that is not limited to the ESMA case, but applies to EU agencies in general to a lesser or larger degree. Nor is it just a European phenomenon. In the United States, there has been a heated debate over the issues of legislative powers given to agencies, in particular the Environmental Protection Agency (EPA), which is a federal executive agency. The Clean Air Act directed the EPA to regulate emissions from power plants if the agency found the regulation 'appropriate and necessary' (Mashaw 2018: 118). The EPA is empowered, on the basis of Section 109(b)(1) of the Clean Air Act, to promulgate and revise air quality standards from time to time, more specifically 'to establish uniform national standards at a level that is requisite to protect public health from the adverse effects of the pollutant in the ambient air' (cited from Scholten and van Rijsbergen 2014: 397). This attests to the EPA's normative power, namely, power to affect citizens' choice situation, their rights and duties.

When a legislator assigns to agencies competences that it does not possess itself, there is a problem of accountability and a question of the delegation model itself.

> [T]the tasks that the EU legislator has been giving to EU agencies are not the tasks that it has had itself. EU agencies have been usually assigned tasks that have been previously exercised by national authorities, the Commission or the Council. [...] Conferral of powers seems, therefore, to describe better the process of giving powers to EU agencies by the EU legislator.
>
> Scholten and van Rijsbergen (2014: 402)

The principle of conferral is a fundamental principle of EU Law. According to the principle of conferral, the EU is a union of member states, and all its competences are voluntarily conferred on it by its member states.[5] But when competences, which the EU itself is not in possession of, are delegated, there is a problem. Neither legal nor electoral control mechanisms are fit to handle this problem, because parliaments cannot hold discretionary executive power to account, and courts cannot review rule compliance when the agencies are allowed to establish the rules themselves. In contrast to the strict delegation model, the conferral of powers requires new regulation.

> The conferral of powers [...] raises the questions of what powers (and how much discretion) can be conferred upon an entity, when and how the conferral takes place (within what procedural and substantive limits) and who holds the recipients of the conferred powers to account and how. This is especially the case when a constitution or a treaty is silent on these matters. In contrast to delegation, the conferral of powers requires a legal framework to be in place in order to realize the conferral.
>
> Scholten and van Rijsbergen (2014: 402)

This debate on the power of NOMIS is not merely a concern of academic interest.

Contestation and protest

Unelected bodies are under attack due to contestation and politicisation (Hooghe and Marks 2015). Often, they are accused of being undemocratic, of making biased decisions, of not being neutral and pursuing their own professional interests or those of the privileged elites. There is a problem of *trust* and there are legitimacy deficits. It is, the story goes, 'faceless bureaucrats' – experts and professionals – with a dubious political mandate that make decisions with harsh consequences, about the interest rates and public finance, about security and terrorist precautions and about product, health and food safety standards. The critique is often focussed on depoliticised bodies, which are seen to overtax the democratic procedure, hence spurring populist opposition and Euro-scepticism (Crouch 2011; Kuyper 2016; Mair 2013; Michelsen and Walter 2013; Pollitt and Talbot 2004).

The widespread outsourcing of government functions to unelected bodies entails advantages with regard to gathering and presenting information, analysing evidence and linking decision-making to the current state of knowledge. Yet it also privileges those who possess certain forms of expertise and the executive branch of government. When experts are kept on a longer leash, the room for *discretion and manoeuvre* is high. According to critics, the focus on efficiency and outputs entails a shift from norm-based politics to pragmatic problem-solving – a shift that diverts attention from the power bases of non-majoritarian institutions (Bartl 2015; White 2015). Depoliticised bodies, including courts, are the beneficiaries of this shift.

The rise of 'depoliticized decision-making' has, been justified as a response to the time inconsistency problem of politics where short-term benefits trump long-term benefits due to electoral cycles. The conventional justification of the NOMIS is that expert judgements are needed to ensure rational decision-making; to choose the right means to realise political ends. From time to time, monetary, financial, security and military policy need to be isolated from partisan politics in order to enable considered judgements. It is in everybody's interest that complexity is handled intelligently. Expert competence and administrative advice are needed to enable collective goal attainment and problem-solving, to ensure consistency, long-sightedness and rationality in policymaking (see Majone 2005; Pettit 2004). No government can make viable decisions without knowledge of facts, causal connections and interconnections as well as knowledge of risk estimates and the possible negative effects of measures. There is, however, the danger that the serving administrative-scientific machinery becomes the real master. The complexity of public policies in advanced democracies 'threatens to cut the policy elites loose from effective control by the demos', effectively creating a *quasi-guardianship* (Dahl 1989: 335).

The new risk agenda

NOMIS deal with tricky issues and wicked problems to which there often is no single correct answer. Regulatory problems in the EU prompted new regulatory competences and the establishment of independent bodies on a whole range of fields, as we have seen. Compound monetary and financial policies with consequences for public revenues, taxes and citizens' income are handed over to central banks. Agencies deal with delicate security and military policies with deep ethical and moral implications. Even though these independent bodies are not set up to make value judgements, this is in practice inescapable. Some bodies in areas such as health and safety, embryology and genetics are also required by their mandates to base their advice on ethical norms (Vibert 2007: 45).

Developments within the scientific community itself, such as the continued specialisation and differentiation of science into different sub-disciplines, have made scientific consensus, even on the purely factual aspects of an issue, all the more fragile, and in important areas quite unlikely. Due to a growing awareness of epistemological uncertainties, scientific risk assessment is now seen as burdened with *insecurity and ambiguity*.[6] It is hard, if not impossible, for scientists to establish 'reliable and consensually accepted measurements for certain risks, which could act as clear guidance for decision-making' (Krapohl 2008: 35). This is clearly demonstrated in the questions of GMOs, monetary policy, immigration, security and economic crisis management. Disagreement prevails among experts, and scientific conclusions are often politically charged.[7] The claim is that 'science is not made scientifically' – that values and facts are inextricably entangled. For Foucault (1980: 131) and his followers, power and knowledge are intertwined. 'Everything is political' claims Bruno Latour (cited in Brown 2009: 187).

However, if science is politicised, if it is seen as a kind of politics, how can we know that epistemic agents are right? If facts and values are interwoven, if there are no scientifically true answers, on what basis can decision-makers be held to account? If *expertise* is fraught with uncertainties and is socially fabricated, as the critics hold, then what prevents the power holders from constructing it however they like (see Brown 2009: 202)? Ambiguity on this point has led to the allegation that the science and technology studies (STS) domain is responsible for the emergence of *post-truth politics*:

> By revealing the continuities between science and politics, science studies opened up the cognitive terrain to those concerned to enhance the impact of democratic politics on science but, in so doing, it opened that terrain for all forms of politics, including populism and that of the radical right wing.
> Collins et al. (2017: 581)

The predicament is that epistemological conflicts create a situation where science loses its functional authority. When experts face experts, they often no longer serve to disencumber political discourse, but instead constitute *a strategic resource* that can be utilised by political decision-makers and interest groups. But without trust in objective knowledge it becomes impossible to justify shared programs of political action. It becomes impossible to establish a common ground for reaching agreement. A post-truth democracy, one which would have to seek agreement on a non-cognitive basis, would no longer be democratic (Habermas 2005: 150).

Many have protested against the technical way of understanding risks and demanded broader involvement and lay participation. Experience- and practice-based knowledge are called for as well. Because judging whether a certain level of risk is acceptable or not cannot be determined scientifically, risk assessments cannot be left to epistemic agents alone. The 'deconstruction of science' and reactions to the *scientisation* of risk questions demonstrate their intricate nature. Risk assessments involve values, judgements and perceptions. In many areas, it becomes more difficult to leave questions regarding technological risks solely to the problem-solving capacity of expertise. When the division between science and politics becomes more obscure, a broader set of premises for decision-making is called for. The fact that, in a constitutional state, such risk assessment has never been delegated in its entirety to expert bodies is further evidence of the value-ladenness of the issues.

Part II: Legitimacy repairing strategies

Democratic legitimacy would seem to require that political authority is involved in NOMIS in some way, hence the problem of reconciling the epistemic and the participatory dimension of democracy.

Squaring the circle on NOMIS

NOMIS represent a challenge to democracy because they recognise some forms of knowledge as expertise and exclude alternative, competing forms, and because they operate within large zones of discretion. The assumption is that NOMIS ensure more consistent, far-sighted decision-making as well as more justifiable results. But it is not clear how this type of reasoning can be reconciled with non-arbitrary decision-making, and thus how and when NOMIS can be legitimate, namely, acceptable for affected parties. Can NOMIS be justified on democratic terms or are they simply a more refined mode of *epistocratic governance*?

The tension between expertise and participation is mirrored in the procedural complex of modern democracies as they are premised on separation of powers, knowledge-based administration, judicial review and independent central banks. There are procedures for including affected parties as well as experts. Both are needed to ensure rational and non-arbitrary decision-making. Accountability entails the obligation of decision-makers to provide justification in order to ensure that discretionary power is used in a reasoned and legitimate manner. Accordingly, decisions need to be perceived as rational and reasonable. The presumption is that decisions that affect peoples' interests and values must be based on shared and commonly assessable and objective knowledge if they are to be acceptable. At the same time, the democratic principle requires the participation of affected parties. How to square the circle between the epistemic and the participatory dimension of democracy?

Standard theories of agency decision-making in jurisprudence and political science offer no justification for agencies' role in policy-setting, the assignment of broad policymaking discretion to administrative agencies (Seidenfeld 1992: 1515).

Different research traditions have contributed to the field and have suggested different cures. In order to get a grasp of the principled problems involved, I will address the basic assumptions that can be identified in the mainstream research traditions. I identify three principally different ways – three strategies – for repairing the legitimacy problems, that is, to ensure non-arbitrary decision-making. The strategies are derived from the authority relations of legitimate government in constitutional democracies, according to which decisions should be in line not only with the popular will but also with verifiable knowledge and legal norms.

The following three ideal typical strategies stand out: *the evidence-based strategy*, *the legislators' command strategy* and *the participatory strategy*. They highlight principally different solutions to the legitimacy problem of depoliticised decision-making and hence help us to discern the dilemmas and concerns involved.

The evidence-based strategy

This strategy holds that establishing bodies on a purely scientific basis will enhance the legitimacy of the relationship between expert advice and politics. Rigorously established evidence informs policy decisions. Building on the idea of a strict separation between facts and values, this strategy aims at developing and clarifying the scientific basis for political action by removing manipulated, anecdotal or cherry-picked knowledge. 'Evidence-based' can mean many things, but essentially involves a system for rigid control of the quality of knowledge. Alternatives are established and ranked on the basis of the rational assessment of their consequential merits. In a political context, the idea is 'to move away from policy based on "'dogma"' to *sound evidence of what works*' (Boswell 2009: 3). NOMIS, in this strategy, are conceived of as instrumental entities organised outside of and independent of government. Through a clearly delimited, documented and justified knowledge base, independent knowledge-providers will be able to provide decision-makers with precise, objective knowledge to use as they wish. This strategy is premised on the epistocratic argument that *wise men* can reason rationally and there is no need to gather a group of those who will be affected by the decision.[8] It envisions the restoring of value neutrality based on instrumental agency.

Max Weber ([1920]1978) is the towering figure of the theory of bureaucracy and *agency instrumentalism*: the citizens by their representatives set the basic aims through legislation that the agencies are to implement in a value-neutral manner. Administrative bodies are transmissions belts, so to say. Weber counterpoised the role of the expert to that of the politician. Politicians employ value-neutral knowledge provided by experts, namely, knowledge as to which means are most suitable for reaching a specific political value, end or goal; for ranking alternatives and for assessing consequences and possible by-products of choices. Politicians attend to ends and values – that is, to 'ought-questions' – and experts to facts – that is, to 'is-questions'. Experts should be 'on tap, not on top'. In line with this, Thomas Christiano (2012: 42) claims that 'citizens rule over the society by choosing the aims for society and experts, along with the rest of the system, are charged with the tasks of implementing these aims with the help of their specialized knowledge'.[9]

By distinguishing between evidence-based and value-based judgements, NOMIS in the evidence-based strategy seek to clarify the empirical and normative premises for political decision-making and to insulate issues for independent action. The independence of NOMIS stems from the fact that they operate outside hierarchy and are not directly accountable to politicians or voters. They act on the basis of strict professional norms such as 'expertise, professional discretion, policy consistency, fairness or independence of judgment' (Majone 2005: 37). Majone, who advocates for delegating policymaking power to non-majoritarian institutions – not to directly elected or accountable agencies – acknowledges the ensuing questions of accountability and legitimacy, but maintains that these could be solved by sectioning off particular policy areas in line with the *Pareto optimum* criteria.

Sectioning off particular issues as pragmatic, efficiency issues presuppose the ability to separate facts and values. Facts are seldom incontestable, however. They are infused with values and cognitive frames and remain open to interpretation and reinterpretation.[10] In political controversies, truth claims are often interwoven with moral and counterfactual claims (Tetlock 2005: 4). For example, when experts advise politicians on whether to vaccinate against pandemics, this has less to do with the actual facts than with the perception of responsibility and socially defined standards of health. 'Controversy studies' have problematised the knowledge claims of experts (Timmermans 1999), and shown that the public construction of science is wrong (Collins and Pinch 1993) and that the law's construction of science is arbitrary and misguided (Jasanoff 1995).[11]

Due to the contingent nature of facts, evidence is hardly ever unequivocal or unambiguous (see Williams 2002: 125). More often than not, facts and values are hard to separate. The production, selection and transmission of knowledge are hardly neutral and rely on *extra-scientific support factors*. Evidence-based methods do not improve our ability to predict which policy will be effective and which will lead to bad results (Cartwright and Hardie 2012). And lastly, who determines the content of extra-scientific input in decision-making? This model does not ensure non-arbitrariness. In fact, the Weberian transmission-belt model of administration does not fit the world of delegation of regulatory competences. Agencies enjoy qualitative higher degrees of autonomy compared to that of bureaucracies. Also because disagreement prevails among experts, democratic legitimacy would seem to require that political authority is involved in some way.

The legislators' command strategy

To restore trust, one may call on the democratic chain of legitimation and establish bodies more firmly subjected to democratic control. The *legislators' command strategy* holds that politicians – or the democratic constitution – lay down the rules and procedures for unelected bodies so that the *principals* can firmly supervise and control the *agents*. The principal-agent model of representation presumes that the legislature delegates competence to NOMIS, which may, in principle, be revoked. Such delegation can come with a powerful set of controls imposed by political bodies, to ensure that NOMIS remain within the remit of the mandate. As a response to the deficiencies of the traditional rule-of-law model with regard to control of these new bodies poised between law and politics, a new discipline, *constitutional economics*, has been developed (Buchanan 1990; see McKenzie 1984).

The tools available to politicians are institutional design based on incentives, fixed rules and contracts, oversight and control mechanism. The legislature both authorises the actions of NOMIS and confines and delimits their range of operations through the provisions set out in the basic rules – the constitution – as well as through a set of institutions that permit each of the principals to exercise veto power. Constitutional rules amount to *collective auto-paternalism* when designed to advert dangers arising from our own (predictable) judgemental failures due to akratic (licentious) behaviour (Elster 1979: 65–67, 77–85, 88–103; Holmes 1988: 195ff). Pre-commitments are aimed at either restraining future passions, protecting long term self-interest, preventing *hyperbolic discounting* of the future or preventing future changes of preference.

Fixed rules help to discipline the representatives as well as pre-commit politicians to certain policies. It is hard to commit others unless one-self is committed. *Self-binding* solves the credibility problem. Some see the whole rationale for delegation to NOMIS in the 'need for credible commitment, so that government sticks to the people's purposes rather than departing from them for short-term gain, electoral popularity, or sectional interest' (Tucker 2018: 12).

However, would this strategy solve the legitimacy problem? Credibility also has to do with being responsive to voters' current demands not only their long-term interests. Would people accept this kind of paternalistic *auto-paternalism*? Besides, why should long term be identified with the public interest, and, what is more, who knows what the people's long-term interests might be? We (or anybody) do not have infinite knowledge about future social and objective circumstances, nor are we fully transparent to ourselves.

Constitutional rules raise the problem of what should be constitutionalised and what should be left to political discretion as well as the problem of *formalism*. Despite constitutional principles that define what can be left to political discretion, it is hard to foresee the need for regulation or to establish all the rules that may be required to deal with an evolving set of problems. Lacunae and gaps will appear, requiring new regulation (cp. Crozier 1963).

In general, accountability through legislatures' control is difficult because rational decision-making requires decisional autonomy and flexibility, especially when ends are ambiguous and statues and legal prescriptions are vague and open for interpretation. Control through delegation is increasingly difficult due to the *de facto* autonomy and the large discretion zones of decision-making bodies necessary to facilitate rational decision-making. NOMIS require the free assessment of information and reasons, beyond what can be foreseen by the principal. Sometimes, agents must amend ends and divert from statues in order to reach a rational solution or a common position in case of conflict. What is more, 'The reasonableness of means and ends are not separate issues, and the understanding of ends is discovered in the process of developing and applying means' (Mashaw 2018: 121). *Preference and agency drift* as a result of the discretionary power of decision-making bodies are well known, as is the danger that experts are co-opted by think tanks and parties (Caramani 2017: 60). Karen Alter (2009) asks the pertinent questions: When does delegation turn into abdication? When are the 'principals' captured?

Holding the 'agents' accountable by matching their performance towards given rules will not do, since the more successful 'agents' are in solving problems, the more the rules will change (Sabel and Zeitlin 2010). Conceiving of political representation as a principal-agent relationship neglects how far decision-makers actively shape opinions and decisions. Accountability processes in themselves are sense-making, which may create new norms and cognitions (Olsen 2017). They open up for new forms of arbitrariness. Internationalisation/globalisation compounds the problem, as there is an asymmetry between what the individual delegates are authorised to and what is needed to make needed decisions and prudent compromises. In the transnational context, there are several principals and several accountability lines. The legislature often lacks competence or capacity to supervise and control.

The mere speed of developments makes governance through legislative measures alone obsolete. The response has been to develop broader *frame-legislation* in which the more fine-grained regulative measures are delegated to more permanent surveying entities inside or outside the administrative apparatus. Through this, a higher degree of flexible regulatory measures and alertness to new developments can be achieved than with strict legal regulation. However, this raises the stakes for democratic authorisation and accountability. How could the decision-makers ever be under democratic control when the formal lines of authorisation and control are not intact?

The participatory strategy

Plato famously argued that the knowers, the wisest, should rule because of their knowledge of *the good*. But even though experts can save the planet, win battles, protect refugees and solve the euro crisis, epistocracy is wrong.[12] It fails not only because scientific knowledge is fallible and often contested; experts err and may be mistaken about facts as well as norms. Epistocracy is wrong also because it entails a danger of dominance; the use of power that does not track the interests or opinions of the citizens. In a democracy, nobody has privileged access to what is good or just. Epistocracy is not the answer. In order to find out what is equally good for all, it is required that everyone has their say. Participation is needed to avoid dominance and the *pitfall of false impartiality:* Judges may defy neutrality, and existing laws may be biased or wrongly institutionalised.

The third strategy holds that the participation of lay citizens is necessary for dealing with legitimacy problems because expertise involve values, which depoliticised bodies cannot handle adequately on their own. Where science cannot supply correct or complete answers, there is need for bringing in the people. Including lay persons serves to encourage civic or community involvement and provides a link to the citizenry (Barber 1984). Participation furnishes the value-based judgements of expert bodies with democratic authorisation (Anderson 2011). It is the method to counter technocratic governance and epistocratic dominance (Zürn 2018: 77ff). According to science and technology studies, 'the technical is political, the political should be democratic and the democratic should be participatory' (Moore 2010: 793). Moreover, following John Dewey (1927), many proponents of deliberative democracy focus on the co-constitution of issues and polities and see enlarged cooperation as a response to problematic situations.[13] Participation and deliberation are requirements for *experimental inquiry* – for pragmatic problem-solving within most fields of action in modern societies. The EU has sought to enhance legitimacy by extended participation and active involvement of civil society (European Commission 2001; Official Journal of the European Union 2012, Art. 11). *Partnership arrangements* entail a commitment to additional consultations with civil-society actors such as NGOs, interest groups and 'social partners' but have left civil society split between professionalism and citizen contiguity (Kohler-Koch and Quittkat 2011: 167ff). In the EU, the Open Method of Coordination involving wide consultation, as well as the co-decision procedure, where the consent of both the Council and the European Parliament is required, reflects this strategy (see Stie 2013). Moreover, agencies themselves are not established solely when there is a need for an independent assessment based on specific expertise but also when the execution of legislation requires discretionary power and the participation of civil society is deemed necessary. Statutes often allow for broad participation, but the extent and model of participation are politically controlled (see Majone 2005: 87; McCubbins et al. 1987; Scholten 2014a: 302).

Participation is an important means for defining, but also for contesting the collective will of society (Pettit 2001). However, such a strategy runs the risk of oversimplifying problems, of bias and of lending artificial and false justification. Biased hearing prevents rational policies and civic engagement risk been absorbed into technocratic policymaking (Brown 2009; Fukuyama 2014). There are (wicked) problems that lend themselves neither to precise scientific assessment, nor to easy solution by lay participation. It is because problems are ill formed in the first place – they do not have an unambiguous right answer – that citizens and politicians call on expertise. Moreover, who do lay people stand, speak or act for; who do they represent, themselves, the people or a section of the people? Participation may either prove itself to be *illegitimate* because participants are asymmetrically privileged over non-participants, or *superfluous* as democratic legitimacy would require 'the quality of macro-deliberation in the broad public sphere' (Lafont 2015: 20).

Participation does not, in and of itself, ensure sound and legitimate decisions, although it is the basic democratic norm. Also with lay participation, decisions may be based on the wrong questions, falsely grounded interests and biased perceptions and deliberations. Problems of tacit knowledge, of groupthink, of ideology, of mass-movement manipulation, 'activism' and extremism prevail in informal settings. Further, participation is not an end in itself. It is there to ensure that power is wielded in a legitimate manner. As we cannot know the will of the people before the hearing the citizens, there can be no democracy without democratic procedures. Participation, by itself, does not warrant non-arbitrariness in depoliticized decision-making. It would be *participation by invitation* and involve only a section of the people – a group, a set of stakeholders.

The upshot is thus that all three strategies come with serious shortcomings. They do not prevent dominance and cannot provide justification for the role of agencies in policymaking. Neither the transmissions belt model of instrumental agency, in which agencies merely carry out statutory laws in a neutral manner, nor the standard model of constitutional economics based on principle-agent theory, nor the model of participatory governance provide an adequate justificatory account of the open-ended grants of discretion that characterise depoliticised decision-making.

Conclusion

Taken together these strategies raise pertinent concerns and dilemmas of depoliticised decision-making and they identify dimensions that are critical for NOMIS legitimacy. When we cannot expect scientifically true answers, participation and representation are needed. But when representative bodies are structurally incapable of controlling NOMIS and increased participation does not yield better or approximately correct answers, we need an alternative approach to establish the legitimacy conditions of unelected expert bodies.

The institutionalisation of NOMIS goes to the core of modern democracies, premised on separation of powers, knowledge-based administration, judicial review and independent central banks. In order to establish the legitimacy basis of depoliticised decision-making, to give a justificatory account of NOMIS, there is need for a new approach. The point of departure in this endeavour is that NOMIS serve to cash in the epistemic claim of modern democracies – that they are there to produce rational, reasonable or good results. However, to understand their democratic role one must see NOMIS not solely as agents obeying and specifying political directives, but rather as representatives making claims and reasoning on the basis of politically given premises. This new approach is based on *the reason-giving principle*, which also is, as we shall see, entrenched in modern administrative law.

Notes

1 Revised version of paper read at SSRC-DFG Workshop on *Polarization, institutional design and the future of representative democracy*, Berlin, Harnack Haus, 5–7 October 2017. Another version was read at the *REFLEX Workshop on the legitimacy of depoliticized decision-making* 16–17 November 2017, ARENA, Oslo, Norway. I am grateful for comments provided by the participants, and particularly to Jonathan Kuyper and Rainer Schmalz-Bruns.
2 It does not matter that 'EU agencies will have purely informational roles because information is a key element in policy-making and policy controversy' (Shapiro 1997: 276).
3 Arbitrary rule refers, according to James Q. Wilson (1989: 326), 'to officials acting without legal authority or with that authority in a way that offends our sense of justice'.
4 See the ruling in the European Court of Justice, the *Meroni doctrine,* which arose from cases C-9/56 and C-10/56, and relates to the extent to which EU institutions may delegate their tasks to regulatory agencies.
5 According to the Bundesverfassungsgericht (BVerfG), 'As long as, and in so far as, the principle of conferral is adhered to in an association of sovereign states with clear elements of executive and governmental cooperation, the legitimation provided by national parliaments and governments complemented and sustained by the directly elected European Parliament is sufficient in principle' (see BVerfGE 89, 155). DFR – BVerfGE 89, 155 – Maastricht (unibe.ch).
6 See Brown (2009), Fischer (2009), Hacking (1999), Jasanoff (1995), Latour and Woolgar (1986), Weingart (1999).
7 One expert is, however, a layman in relation to another expert.
8 See Plato (2003), Estlund (2008: 7, 22, 30–31, 40, 277–278) for the 'epistocratic' position.
9 See also Christiano (1996: 195ff, 239).
10 The influence of heuristics, of cognitive dissonance and framing is well known (Kahneman 1997; Tversky and Kahneman 1974).
11 See also Turner (2001).
12 Even the strongest case in favour of epistocracy fails (Viehoff 2016; cp. Lippert-Rasmussen 2012).
13 See the works of Cohen and Sabel (1997), Bohman (2007), Dryzek (2006). For critique, see Eriksen (2011).

References

Alter, K. (2009) *The European Court's Political Power: Selected Essays*. Oxford: Oxford University Press.
Anderson, E. (2011) 'Democracy, Public Policy, and Lay Assessments of Scientific Testimony', *Episteme*, 8(2): 144–164.
Barber, B. (1984) *Strong Democracy: Participatory Politics for a New Age*. Los Angeles: University of California Press.
Bartl, M. (2015) 'Internal Market Rationality, Private Law and the Direction of the Union: Resuscitating the Market as the Object of the Political', *European Law Journal*, 21(5): 572–598.
Bohman, J. (2007) *Democracy across Borders: From Dêmos to Dêmoi*. Cambridge: MIT Press.
Boswell, C. (2009) *The Political Uses of Expert Knowledge*. Cambridge: Cambridge University Press.

Brown, M.B. (2009) *Science in Democracy: Expertise, Institutions, and Representation*. Cambridge: MIT Press.

Buchanan, J.M. (1990) 'The Domain of Constitutional Economics', *Constitutional Political Economy* 1(1): 1–18.

Busuioc, M. and Groenleer, M. (2014) 'The Theory and Practice of EU Agency Autonomy and Accountability: Early Day Expectations, Today's Realities and Future Perspectives', in M. Everson, C. Monda and E. Vos (eds.) *European Agencies In between Institutions and Member States* (pp. 175–200). Alphen aan den Rijn: Kluwen Law.

Caramani, D. (2017) 'Will vs. Reason: The Populist and Technocratic Forms of Representation and Their Critique to Party Government', *American Political Science Review*, 111(1): 54–67.

Cartwright, N. and Hardie, J. (2012) *Evidence-Based Policy: A Practical Guide to Doing It Better*. Oxford: Oxford University Press.

Chamon, M. (2014) 'The Empowerment of Agencies under the Meroni Doctrine and Art. 114 TFEU: Comment on United Kingdom v. Parliament and Council (Short-selling) and the Proposed Single Resolution Mechanism', *European Law Review*, 39(3): 380–403.

Chiti, E. (2009) 'An Important Part of the EU's Institutional Machinery: Features, Problems and Perspectives of European Agencies', *Common Market Law Review*, 46(5): 1395–1442.

Christiano, T. (1996) *The Rule of the Many*. Boulder, CO: Westview Press.

Christiano, T. (2012) 'Rational Deliberation among Experts and Citizens', in J. Parkinson and J. Mansbridge (eds.) *Deliberative Systems* (pp. 27–51). Cambridge: Cambridge University Press.

Cohen, J. and Sabel, C. (1997) 'Directly-Deliberative Polyarchy', *European Law Journal*, 3(4): 313–342.

Collins, H. and Pinch, T. (1993) *The Golem of Science*. Cambridge: Cambridge University Press.

Collins, H., Evans, R. and Weinel, M. (2017) 'STS as Science or Politics?' *Social Studies of Science*, 47(4): 580–586.

Crouch, C. (2011) *The Strange Non-Death of Neoliberalism*. London: Polity Press.

Crozier, M. (1963) *The Bureaucratic Phenomenon*. New Brunswick: Transaction Publishers.

Dahl, R.A. (1989) *Democracy and Its Critics*. New Haven, CT: Yale University Press.

Dewey, J. (1927) *The Public and its Problems*. New York: Holt Publishers.

Dryzek, J. (2006) *Deliberative Global Politics*. London: Polity Press.

Elster, J. (1979) *Ulysses and the Sirens*. Cambridge: Cambridge University Press.

Eriksen, E.O. (2011) 'Governance between Expertise and Democracy: The Case of European Security', *Journal of European Public Policy*, 18(8): 1169–1189.

Estlund, D.M. (2008) *Democratic Authority: A Philosophical Framework*. Princeton, NJ: Princeton University Press.

European Commission (2001) 'European Governance: A White Paper', COM (2001) 428 final. Brussels, 25 July.

Everson, M., Monda, C. and Vos, E. (eds.) (2014) *EU Agencies In between Institutions and Member States*. Alphen aan den Rijn: Wolters Kluwer.

Fischer, F. (2009) *Democracy and Expertise*. Oxford: Oxford University Press.

Foucault, M. (ed.) (1980) *Power/Knowledge*. New York: Pantheon.

Fukuyama, F. (2014) *Political Order and Political Decay: From the Industrial Revolution to the Globalization of Democracy*. New York: Farrar, Straus and Giroux.

Guiseppe Romano v. Institut national d'assurance maladie-invalidité (1981) ECR 1241, Case 98–80. Available at: https://eur-lex.europa.eu/legal-content/EN/TXT/?uri=CELEX%3A61980CJ0098.

Habermas, J. (2005) 'Religion in der Offentlichkeit: Kognitive Voraus-setzungen fur den "Offentlichen Vernunftgebrauch" Religioser und Sakularer Burger', in J. Habermas (ed.) *Zwischen Naturalismus und Religion: Philosophische Aufsatze* (pp. 119–154). Frankfurt am Main: Suhrkamp.

Hacking, I. (1999) *The Social Construction of What?* Cambridge, MA: Harvard University Press.

Holmes, S. (1988) 'Pre-commitments and the Paradox of Democracy', in J. Elster and R. Slagstad (eds.) *Constitutionalism and Democracy* (pp. 195–240). Cambridge: Cambridge University Press.

Hooghe, L. and Marks, G. (2015) 'Delegation and Pooling in International Organizations', *Review of International Organizations*, 10(3): 305–328.

Jasanoff, S. (1995) 'Procedural Choices in Regulatory Science', *Technology in Society*, 17(3): 279–293.

Kahneman, D. (1997) 'New Challenges to the Rationality Assumption', *Legal Theory*, 3(2): 105–124.

Kohler-Koch, B. and Quittkat, C. (2011) *Die Entzauberung partizipativer Demokratie*. Frankfurt am Main: Campus.

Krapohl, S. (2008) *Risk Regulation in the Single Market: The Governance of Pharmaceuticals and Foodstuffs in the European Union*. Basingstoke: Palgrave Macmillan.

Kuyper, J.W. (2016) 'Systemic Representation: Democracy, Deliberation, and Non-Electoral Representatives', *American Political Science Review*, 110(2): 308–324.

Kydland, F.E. and Prescott, E.C. (1977) 'Rules Rather Than Discretion: The Inconsistency of Optimal Plans', *Journal of Political Economy*, 85(3): 473–491.

Lafont, C. (2015) 'Deliberation, Participation, and Democratic Legitimacy: Should Deliberative Mini-Publics Shape Public Policy?' *The Journal of Political Philosophy*, 23(1): 40–63.

Latour, B. and Woolgar, S. (1986) *Laboratory Life: The Construction of Scientific Facts*. Princeton, NJ: Princeton University Press.

Lindseth, P.L. (2010) *Power and Legitimacy: Reconciling Europe and the Nation-State*. Oxford: Oxford University Press.

Lippert-Rasmussen, K. (2012) 'Estlund on Epistocracy: A Critique', *Res Publica*, 18(3): 241–258.

Locke, J. ([1690]1963) *Second Treatise of Civil Government* (P. Laslett, ed.). Cambridge: Cambridge University Press.

Mair, P. (2013) *Ruling the Void: The Hollowing of Western Democracy*. London: Verso Books.

Majone, G. (1996) *Regulating Europe*. New York: Routledge.

Majone, G. (2005) *Dilemmas of European Integration*. Oxford: Oxford University Press.

Mashaw, J.L. (2018) *Reasoned Administration and Democratic Legitimacy*. Cambridge: Cambridge University Press.

McCubbins, M.D., Noll, R.G. and Weingast, B.R. (1987) 'Administrative Procedures as Instruments of Political Control', *Journal of Law, Economics, & Organisation*, 3(2): 243–277.

McKenzie, R.B. (ed.) (1984) *Constitutional Economics: Containing the Economic Powers of Government*. Lexington, MA: Lexington Books.

Mendes, J. and Venzke, I. (eds.) (2018) *Allocating Authority: Who Should Do What in European and International Law?* Oxford: Hart Publishing.

Menéndez, A. (2020) 'Austerity through the Rule of Numbers: Dominance through the Combination of a Legal and an Economic Discourse', Paper presented at EU3D Workshop, 23 January 2020, mimeo.

Michelsen, D. and Walter, F. (2013) *Unpolitische Demokratie. Zur Krise der Repräsentation*. Frankfurt am Main: Suhrkamp.

Moloney, N. (2019) 'The European Supervisory Authorities and Discretion: Can Functional and Constitutional Circles Be Squared?' in J. Mendes (ed.) *EU Executive Discretion and the Limits of Law* (pp. 85–117). Oxford: Oxford University Press.

Moore, A. (2010) 'Beyond Participation: Opening Up Political Theory in STS', *Social Studies of Science*, 40(5): 793–799.

Official Journal of the European Union (2012) The Consolidated Versions of the Treaty on European Union (TEU) and the Treaty on the Functioning of the European Union (TFEU). 2012/C 326. Available at: http://eur-lex.europa.eu/legal-content/en/TXT/?uri=CELEX%3A12012M%2FTXT [accessed 4 June 2019].

Olsen, J.P. (2017) *Democratic Accountability, Political Order and Change*. Oxford: Oxford University Press.

Pettit, P. (1997) *Republicanism: A Theory of Freedom and Government*. Oxford: Oxford University Press.

Pettit, P. (2001) *A Theory of Freedom*. Cambridge: Polity Press.

Pettit, P. (2004) 'Depoliticizing Democracy', *Ratio Juris*, 17(1): 52–65.

Plato (2003) *Plato's Parmendies* [trans. S. Scolnicov]. Berkley: University of California Press.

Pollitt, C. and Talbot, C. (eds.) (2004) *Unbundled Government: A Critical Analysis of the Global Trend to Agencies, Quangos and Contractualisation*. London: Routledge.

Power, M. (1997) *The Audit Society: Rituals of Verification*. Oxford: Oxford University Press.

Sabel, C.F. and Zeitlin, J. (2010) *Experimentalist Governance in the European Union: Towards a New Architecture*. Oxford: Oxford University Press.

Scholten, M. (2014a) *The Political Accountability of EU Agencies: Learning from the US Experience*. Leiden: Brill Nijhoff.

Scholten, M. (2014b) *The Political Accountability of EU and US Independent Regulatory Agencies*. Leiden: Brill.

Scholten, M. and Van Rijsbergen, M. (2014) 'The ESMA-Short Selling Case: Erecting a New Delegation Doctrine in the EU upon the Meroni-Romano Remnants', *Legal Issues of Economic Integration*, 41(4): 389–406.

Seidenfeld, M. (1992) 'A Civic Republican Justification for the Bureaucratic State', *Harvard Law Review*, 105(7): 1511–1576.

Shapiro, M. (1997) 'The Problems of Independent Agencies in the United States and the European Union', *Journal of European Public Policy*, 4(2): 276–291.

Slaughter, A.M. (2004) *A New World Order*. Princeton, NJ: Princeton University Press.

Stie, A.E. (2013) *Democratic Decision-making in the EU: Technocracy in Disguise?*. Abingdon: Routledge.

Tetlock, P.E. (2005) *Expert Political Judgment*. Princeton, NJ: Princeton University Press.

Thatcher, M. and Stone Sweet, A. (2002) 'The Politics of Delegation: Non-Majoritarian Institutions in Europe', *West European Politics*, 25(1): 1–22.

Timmermans, S. (1999) *Sudden Death and the Myth of CPR*. Philadelphia, PA: Temple University Press.

Tooze, A. (2018) *Crashed: How a Decade of Financial Crises Changed the World*. London: Allen Lane.

Tucker, P. (2018) *Unelected Power, the Quest for Legitimacy in Central Banking and the Regulatory State*. Princeton, NJ: Princeton University Press.

Turner, S. (2001) 'What Is the Problem with Experts?' *Social Studies of Science*, 31(1): 123–149.

Tversky, A. and Kahneman, D. (1974) 'Judgment under Uncertainty: Heuristics and Biases', *Science*, 185(4157): 1124–1131.

Venzke, I. and Mendes, J. (2018) 'The Idea of Relative Authority in European and International Law', *International Journal of Constitutional Law*, 16(1): 75–100.
Vibert, F. (2007) *The Rise of the Unelected*. Cambridge: Cambridge University Press.
Viehoff, D. (2016) 'Authority and Expertise', *Journal of Political Philosophy*, 24(4): 406–426.
Weber, Max ([1920]1978) *Economy and Society*. Los Angeles: University of California Press.
Weingart, P. (1999) 'Scientific Expertise and Political Accountability: Paradoxes of Science in Politics', *Science and Public Policy*, 26(3): 151–161.
Weisbrot, M. (2015) *Failed: What the 'Experts' Got Wrong about the Global Economy*. Oxford: Oxford University Press.
White, J. (2015) 'Emergency Europe', *Political Studies*, 63(2): 300–318.
Williams, B. (2002) *Truth and Truthfulness: An Essay in Genealogy*. Princeton, NJ: Princeton University Press.
Wilson, J.Q. (1989) *Bureaucracy: What Government Agencies Do and Why They Do It*. New York: Basic Books.
Zürn, M. (2018) *A Theory of Global Governance*. Oxford: Oxford University Press.

3

REASONED ADMINISTRATION

The European Union, the United States, and the project of democratic governance[1]

Jerry L. Mashaw

Introduction

There are broad similarities between conceptions of 'good administration' in the United States and in the European Union (EU). These similarities are combined with considerable variations, both in the understanding of the scope of these 'rights' or 'expectations' and the institutional context within which they are articulated and enforced. On the European side of the Atlantic, article 41 of the Charter of Fundamental Rights – incorporated as article II-101 of the (as yet unratified) Treaty Establishing a Constitution for Europe – provides a similar definition of the 'Right to good administration':

1. Every person has the right to have his or her affairs handled impartially, fairly and within a reasonable time by the institutions and bodies of the Union.
2. This right includes:
   a. The right of every person to be heard, before any individual measure which would affect him or her adversely is taken;
   b. The right of every person to have access to his or her file, while respecting the legitimate interests of confidentiality and of professional and business secrecy;
   c. The obligation of the administration to give reasons for its decisions.
3. Every person has the right to have the Community make good any damage caused by its institutions or by its servants in the performance of their duties, in accordance with the general principles common to the laws of the member states.

Every person may write to the institutions of the Union in one of the languages of the Treaties and must have an answer in the same language (Official Journal of the European Union 2000).

These principles of good administration are surely familiar to American lawyers as well. The right to be heard and to have decisions on one's interests made fairly and impartially are embodied in the Due Process Clauses of the US Constitution and in a wide range of statutes, including the Administrative Procedure Act (APA) (1946). The right of access to government information is guaranteed by the Freedom of Information Act (2000). In addition, the rights to petition administrative institutions, to receive responses to those petitions, and to obtain reasons for administrative decisions are guaranteed both by the APA[2] and numerous judicial determinations. The right to compensation for damage caused by administrative officials is defined largely by American common law, whereas the government's liability for damages is structured by statutes such as the Tucker Act (28 U.S.C. § 1491, 2000) and the Federal Tort Claims Act.[3]

Nevertheless, when pursuing any of these principles in more detail, one would find some significant differences in US and EU practices. Although richly embellished by judicial interpretations, American lawyers can generally point to a text: the US Constitution, the APA, or some more specific statute as the source of a particular right to good administration. In the European Union, the treaty articulating a number of these rights remains to be ratified, and that ratification effort may stall indefinitely (Tempest 2007). 'Good administration' is, up to now, often a function of judicial decisions[4] and agency codes of behaviour. Access to information in the Freedom of Information Act is a general right to most government documents,[5] not, as in the European Union, just those relating to a person seeking access to his or her own file (Official Journal of the European Union 2004, Article II-101 (2)(a)). Moreover, the exceptions to the Freedom of Information Act are spelled out in great detail and backed by an expedited enforcement procedure. On the other hand, a right to damages for official misconduct, error, or nonfeasance begins in the United States from a premise of governmental immunity. Compensation is permitted only to the extent that statutes specifically waive the government's immunity from suit.[6]

Exploring the many similarities and differences in the 'right to good administration' in the European Union and the United States is the task of many books, not the task of one chapter. This chapter focusses therefore on the right to reasons and the practice of administrative reason giving. This is a common and important feature of both EU and US administrative law and, I will argue, a somewhat under-theorised one. This chapter therefore seeks to explain why reason giving is so prominent a part of both administrative systems, how it functions juridically, and, most crucially, what the reasons are for demanding reasons or for providing a 'right' to reasoned administration. In the course of that exploration, I hope to show that the reasons most commonly advanced for reason giving in both the EU and the US systems tend to ignore reason giving's most fundamental function – the creation of authentic democratic governance.

Reason giving as a social practice

In a recent book, Charles Tilly sets out to explain the reason for reasons (Tilly 2006: ix). According to Tilly's view, which, as he explains, has a long intellectual history, reason giving is an entirely relational enterprise (ibid.: x, 14–15. Reasons are given to negotiate, establish, repair, affirm, or deny relationships (ibid.: 19–20). Moreover, the type of relationship (that exists or that is claimed to exist) determines the type of reasons that are appropriate and, therefore, potentially acceptable or persuasive (ibid.: 15). Tilly demonstrates with many arresting examples how various reasons work relationally, that is, to justify our behaviour depending upon the type of relationship involved and whether our purpose is to establish, affirm, negotiate, or repair relations with others.[7]

This relational account is perfectly understandable, indeed illuminating, when placed in the context of the relations of administrative officials with those to whom they might give reasons. When carrying out their administrative tasks, officials have relationships of at least three types: relations with other officials, the general public affected by administrative actions or policies, and particular individuals or firms who are the specific addressees of administrative orders or the direct or personal beneficiaries of administrative decisions.

Consider first an administrator's relationship with other officials. Those would include relationships with hierarchical superiors in the administration, political controllers (legislatures, parliaments, ministers, or elected chief executives), legal controllers (courts), and coordinate officials (officials at essentially the same level in the same or other agencies). With respect to the first three of these relationships, administrators have a particular sort of reason to offer reasons if requested. Hierarchical superiors, political controllers, and the judiciary have the power to impose unpleasant consequences on administrators who fail to explain themselves successfully. And coordinate officials are unlikely to provide co-operation (or withhold complaint) unless provided with an acceptable explanation of why they should do so. To be sure, the types of reasons one official gives to another are likely to vary. Although 'my immediate supervisor told me to do so' may be sufficient for the head of the bureau, it is not likely to satisfy a parliamentary investigating committee, an official in a coordinate agency or coordinate national administration, or a court reviewing the legality of official action. Yet, in each case, officials have strong prudential reasons to give reasons. They need to supply justifications, or at least excuses, to avoid or mitigate unpleasant consequences, or to solicit co-operation or acceptance.

For present purposes, we might describe these official-to-official reason-giving relationships as 'bottom-up' (to bureaucratic, political, or legal controllers) and 'side-to-side' (to co-ordinate officials). They proceed according to the power relationships established by law and custom among official actors. They facilitate control, accountability, and co-ordination amongst institutions that have been placed in certain relationships to each other in what we might loosely call the constitutional arrangements of a particular polity, whether national or supranational.

The power relations between officials and the general public, or officials and particular individuals or firms, are rather different. Acting within their jurisdiction or authority, administrative officials exercise consequential legal power. Private parties are accountable to or dependent upon them, not the other way around. The relationship is 'top-down'. Why should officials give reasons to non-officials rather than simply issuing edicts or orders? To some degree, the answer might parallel that suggested for coordinate officials. Explanations may assist officials in obtaining public co-operation and in avoiding complaints or lawsuits, which have their own unpleasantness even if the officials are ultimately found to be blameless. And the degree to which the officials feel the need to solicit co-operation or avoid complaint may determine the specificity and style of their explanation. Or, alternatively, political or legal controllers might demand that reasons be given to otherwise powerless citizens as a way of facilitating bottom-up monitoring or oversight. What better way for these controllers to assure that officials accountable to them are behaving properly than to require transparency in decision-making with respect to private parties who have an interest in calling official error or malfeasance to account?[8]

In some sense, the simple difference between bottom-up, side-to-side, and top-down relations may explain why it is thought necessary to provide a right to reasons in the latter case. A right to reasons facilitates hierarchical, legal, and political accountability. As we shall see, most of the reasons for reason giving articulated by courts or legal commentators are precisely of this consequentialist sort. They explain the reasons for reasons in terms of maintaining appropriate institutional relationships in the legal order, or as a means of policing official behaviour. But this observation gets somewhat ahead of the story. Before turning to what courts and commentators say about reasons within the legal orders of the United States and the European Union, we should consider a quite different explanation for reason giving.

This second account denies that reason giving can be fully understood in consequentialist terms. A good example is a recent essay by John Gardner on the concept of responsibility (Gardner 2006). Gardner does not deny that reason giving is often relational or that much of it is designed to justify or excuse behaviour in contexts in which we might anticipate unpleasant consequences (ibid.). But, on Gardner's view, this relational account does not go very deep into the reasons for reason giving (ibid.: 221). He contrasts this 'Hobbesian' consequentialist view with what he styles as an 'Aristotelian' one (ibid.: 221–222). On this account, to be a rational being is to have reasons for our actions; without reasons for our actions, our lives make no sense to us (ibid.: 221). According to Gardner's account, '[w]e cannot but want there to have been adequate reasons why we did (or thought or felt) what we did (or thought or felt) (ibid.)'.

The implication for Gardner is that although we might give differing reasons depending upon social contexts and social relations, there is certainly no necessity that we do so (ibid.: 228–229). Hence, the relational account is at best incomplete. Moreover, to make rational sense of our lives, this tailoring of reasons to particular relationships may have unhappy consequences (ibid.: 229–230). It makes us appear incoherent to ourselves. Indeed, tailoring our reasons differently for different purposes, particularly if we are thinking of justifications or excuses, tends to deny that we had some reason that explains ourselves to ourselves. And to deny that is to deny, in some sense, that we are responsible actors with rational life plans. In carrying out this Aristotelian project, we want to give a good account of ourselves. It is that sort of accounting or reason giving that affirms our own rationality and our status as responsible moral agents.

But what does this account of reason giving have to do with reasoned administration or the right to reasons as a part of a right to 'good administration'? Just this: to be subject to administrative authority that is unreasoned is to be treated as a mere object of the law or political power, not a subject with independent rational capacities. Unreasoned coercion denies our moral agency and our political standing as citizens entitled to respect as ends in ourselves, not as mere means in the effectuation of state purposes. This sort of explanation begins to illuminate why we might think of reasoned administrations as an individual right, indeed a fundamental individual right, not just as a contingent feature of accountability regimes.

I will come back to this reason for reason giving towards the end of this chapter, but first, we should take a look at the reasons for reasons that are common in the jurisprudence and literature of administrative law in the United States and European Union. As we shall see, the common reasons generally track Tilly's relational, consequentialist description with little attention to Gardner's more fundamental explanation.[9] In so doing, American and European administrative law tend to treat the right to reasons as a contingent right, one that is parasitic on other substantive or procedural rights or institutional arrangements. I will argue that this approach fails to explain not only why reason giving is ubiquitous as a human practice but why reason receiving should be instantiated as an important and independent human right. I shall argue further that recognising this more fundamental grounding for reason giving has important implications for the ongoing project of democratic governance in unavoidably administrative states.

Reasons and law

Reasons in American administrative law

The right to reasons in American administrative law is conventionally understood as parasitic on other rights or on the necessities of effective judicial review. In the world of American administrative law, rights to hearings and reasons are sharply divided between cases involving individual claims of right and situations in which administrative action takes place by general rule or regulation.

Individual hearing rights in American administrative law are grounded in either the Due Process Clauses of the US Constitution or in particular statutes as supplemented by the APA. It has been long established that the Constitution makes no independent requirement for hearings, including reason giving, where general rules or regulations are at issue.[10] Indeed, as a constitutional matter, not all administrative decisions in individual cases are protected by hearing rights or rights to reasons. Those protections are limited to actions affecting individual interests that fall within the Supreme Court's evolving definition of 'life, liberty, and property' under the Due Process Clauses of the Fifth and Fourteenth Amendments.[11] Of course, Congress may, and does, provide for hearings that would not be demanded by the Constitution. When a statute requires that actions be taken only on the basis of a record made at a hearing, the APA provides a standard set of formal hearing requirements (5 U.S.C. § 554, 2000). Whether the hearing is required by the Constitution or by a statute supplemented by the APA, the giving of reasons is one of the standard features of the hearing right itself.

In a celebrated article, Judge Henry Friendly (1975) identified 11 features that might be regarded as essential to a fair administrative hearing: (1) an unbiased tribunal, (2) notice of the proposed action and the grounds asserted for it, (3) an opportunity to present reasons why proposed action should not be taken, (4) the right to call witnesses, (5) the right to know the evidence against oneself, (6) the right to have a decision based exclusively on the evidence presented, (7) the right to counsel, (8) the making of a record, (9) the availability of a statement of reasons for the decision, (10) public attendance and (11) judicial review of the final decision (ibid.: 1279–1295).

All of these legal protections are meant to ensure that when significant individual interests are at stake, the government acts only on the basis of reliable evidence and within its proper authority. In one of the most famous cases on due process of law in the United States, *Goldberg v. Kelly* ([1970] 397 U.S. 254), the Supreme Court explained the requirement of reason giving in wholly instrumental terms (ibid.: 271). In two brief sentences, the Court said,

> Finally, the decisionmaker's conclusion as to a recipient's eligibility must rest solely on the legal rules and evidence adduced at the hearing. To demonstrate compliance with this elementary requirement, the decision maker should state the reasons for his determination and indicate the evidence he relied on, though his statement need not amount to a full opinion or even formal findings of fact and conclusions of law.
>
> *Ibid.*

In short, reason giving is meant to ensure that the hearing itself is not a charade. Reasons must be linked to the legal rules and evidence that were a part of the hearing record. Reasons help to ensure that the individual's rights to contest, present evidence, make legal arguments, and so on have been respected in making a final judgement on the case.

Moreover, these hearing rights are themselves viewed essentially in instrumentalist terms. The leading case on due process in the United States, *Mathews v. Eldridge* ([1976] 424 U.S. 319), sets forth a 'balancing' formula for determining whether particular procedures are required as a part of a hearing process (ibid.: 334–335). According to the *Eldridge* Court,

> [O]ur prior decisions indicate that identification of the specific dictates of due process generally requires consideration of three distinct factors: first, the private interest that will be affected by the official action; second, the risk of an erroneous deprivation of such interest through the procedures used, and the probable value, if any, of additional or substitute procedural safeguards; and finally, the Government's interest, including the function involved and the fiscal and administrative burdens that the additional or substitute procedural requirements would entail.
>
> *Ibid.*

In short, due process requirements of procedural protection, including the requirement of reason giving, are part of a social welfare calculation that weighs and balances the importance of the individual's substantive claim, and the likely contribution of any particular procedural requirement to the accurate determination of that claim against the government's interest in effectiveness and efficiency. The right to reasons where individual interests are concerned is therefore dependent upon (1) the legal status of that interest (i.e. whether it qualifies as a substantive right protected by the Constitution, statute, or common law) and (2) the contribution that the provision of procedural protections, including a right to reasons for the decision, will make to an accurate determination of that claim of right. Or so it would seem.

One can find in American jurisprudence, however, a somewhat more general ground for reason giving that is not parasitic on individual rights to a hearing. In any case subject to the APA,[12] which covers the vast majority of federal administrative decisions having legal effect, a reviewing court is instructed to reverse the administrative determination where the actual choice made was 'arbitrary, capricious, an abuse of discretion, or otherwise not in accordance with law' (5 U.S.C. § 706(2)(A), 2000). To make that finding, or reject it, the reviewing court must know the agency's basis for its decision, as the Supreme Court put it in yet another iconic case, *Citizens to Preserve Overton Park, Inc. v. Volpe* ([1971] 401 U.S. 402): '[t]o make this finding the court must consider whether the decision was based on a consideration of the relevant factors and whether there has been a clear error of judgment' (ibid.: 416). The problem in the *Overton Park* case was that the secretary of transportation, in making a location decision for an interstate highway, had not provided a contemporaneous statement of the reasons for his choice (ibid.: 408). The Supreme Court recognised that there was no statutory or constitutional requirement of contemporaneous reason giving that applied to this sort of decision (ibid.: 409). Yet the Court declined to approve a review based upon affidavits from the secretary and other administrative officials concerning the reasons for their decision (ibid.: 419). In the Court's terms, '[t]hese affidavits were merely "*post hoc*" rationalizations, which have traditionally been found to be an inadequate basis for review' (ibid.).

Under these circumstances, the Court felt it necessary to remand the case to the district court for a plenary inquiry into the secretary's decision, including, if necessary, calling the secretary and other officials to testify concerning their rationale (ibid.: 420). The Court closed with this suggestion:

> The District Court is not, however, required to make such an inquiry. It may be that the Secretary can prepare formal findings [...] that will provide an adequate explanation for his action. Such an explanation will, to some extent, be a '*post hoc* rationalization' and thus must be viewed critically. If the District Court decides that additional explanation is necessary, that court should consider which method will prove the most expeditious so that full review may be had as soon as possible.
>
> *Ibid.: 420–421*

On this view of reason giving, reasons are necessary whenever an administrative decision is subject to judicial review. Moreover, because judicial review is meant to determine the real reasons for the action, it should proceed, wherever possible, on the basis of contemporaneous reasons explaining both the factual and legal bases for the administrative determination. And, from a practical standpoint, any administrator who does not want to spend his or her time in court testifying about past decisions would be well advised to provide a contemporaneous statement of reasons when a decision is made. For, if that is done, another well-known decision, *United States v. Morgan* ([1941] 313 U.S. 409), provides that reviewing courts should make no further inquiry into the mental processes of administrative decision-makers (absent some special showing of corruption or bad faith) (ibid.: 422).

American jurisprudence on the making of general rules has elaborated on this notion of administrative reason giving as a requirement in aid of judicial review. Section 553 of the APA contains the relatively innocuous requirement that, when making rules or regulations having binding effect on private parties, the agency must provide notice of its proposal, an opportunity for affected parties to comment, and 'a concise general statement of their basis and purpose' in the order issuing the rule or regulation (5 U.S.C. § 553(b)–(c). 2000).

This language lay relatively dormant in the APA until the late 1960s and early 1970s when Congress passed a series of health and safety statutes concerning motor vehicle safety, occupational safety and health, and environmental protection that were themselves almost empty of substantive legal requirements.[13] These new statutes gave federal administrators extremely broad discretion to develop general regulations governing virtually every industry and occupation in the United States. Resistance to this relatively novel exercise of federal power was to be expected, and litigation about these rule-making activities proceeded apace. In one of the first cases to come before the Court of Appeals for the District of

Columbia, the US court that reviews much federal administrative rule-making activity, Judge McGowan cautioned against an 'overly literal reading' of the APA's requirement of a 'concise general statement':

> These adjectives must be accommodated to the realities of judicial scrutiny, which do not contemplate that the court itself will, by a laborious examination of the record, formulate in the first instance the significant issues faced by the agency and articulate the rationale of their resolution. We do not expect the agency to discuss every item of fact or opinion included in the submissions made to it in informal rule making. We do expect that, if the judicial review which Congress has thought it important to provide is to be meaningful, the 'concise general statement of [...] basis and purpose' mandated by [the APA] will enable us to see what major issues of policy were ventilated by the informal proceedings and why the agency reacted to them as it did.
>
> *Motor Vehicle Manufacturers Ass'n v. State Farm Mutual Automobile Insurance Co. 1983*

Since the *Automotive Parts* decision, a focus on an agency's reasons for a regulation has become the hallmark of judicial review of rule-making activity under the APA. Courts routinely return decisions to administrative agencies on the ground that the rationale provided is inadequate to explain some critical fact or issue that the agency was required to consider.[14] Indeed, one of the Supreme Court's most famous cases supporting a so-called hard look standard of judicial review, *Motor Vehicle Manufacturers Ass'n v. State Farm Mutual Automobile Insurance Co.*, rejects the rescission of a rule by the National Highway Traffic Safety Administration because of the agency's failure to consider amending its rule rather than rescinding it (*Motor Vehicle Manufacturers Ass'n v. State Farm Mutual Automobile Insurance Co.* ([1983] 463 U.S. 29, 51) In the Court's words, '[n]ot having discussed the possibility, the agency submitted no reasons at all' (ibid.: 50). Lack of adequate discussion alone was sufficient for a finding that the agency's determination was arbitrary under the APA (ibid.: 50–51).

The requirement that agencies give understandable and relatively complete reasons for rule-making as well as for decisions in individual hearings does more than facilitate judicial review. It also increases the power of participants in informal rule-making processes to force agencies to consider problems and issues that they raise by submitting comments concerning the agency's proposals. Hence, a demand for reason giving is also in some practical sense a demand for responsiveness to the submissions of affected parties. It therefore reinforces their rights of participation as provided by the APA. The judicial demand for reasons to facilitate judicial review reinforces participatory rights concerning general regulations in the same fashion that reason giving protects individualised hearing rights concerning particularised decisions.

Reason giving as a requirement of administrative law in the United States is thus a common – but a contingent – enterprise. With respect to individual cases, reason giving is parasitic on the requirement of a hearing, and the entitlement to a hearing is itself a function of a right to defend some particular substantive legal entitlement. With respect to general regulations or rule-making, reason giving is demanded as a facilitator of judicial review. It is also a *protector* of judicial review in a constitutional system dedicated to separation of powers. It allows judicial review of policy choices for reasonableness, a practice made problematic by the Supreme Court's aggressive use of 'substantive due process' to strike down New Deal legislation in the 1930s, while insulating the judiciary from the charge that it is inappropriately second-guessing the political branches of government. The judicial demand for *reasons* has become a legitimate procedural version of an otherwise illegitimate substantive demand for *reasonableness*, as judicially determined.

The proceduralisation of rationality – the conversion of the demand for non-arbitrariness into a demand for understandable reason giving – rephrases the question of whether the agency's action is reasonable in some substantive sense as a demand that the agency demonstrate a reasoning process. The demand for reasons and yet more reasons, at least rhetorically, keeps the court within its appropriate domain. The agency may make policy choices, so long as it explains how its exercise of discretion is connected to its statutory authority and to the technical facts that have been developed through the rule-making proceeding. That this 'restrained' judicial posture may in fact disable or seriously impede regulatory activity is merely an ironic, unintended consequence of the maintenance of the American understanding of the court's role within its constitutional, legal structure.[15]

Reason giving in the law of the European Union

The obligation of the administration to give reasons for its decisions, as set out in the European Charter of Fundamental Rights and incorporated into the proposed European Constitution, has been elaborated in the European Code of Good Administrative Behaviour ('ECGAB') (European Ombudsman 2005). The ECGAB supplements and explains the obligations set out in the Charter (ibid.: 7). According to article 18 of the ECGAB, the requirement of reason giving applies to decisions 'which may adversely affect the rights or interests of a private person' (ibid.). In addition, decisions should not be based on 'brief or vague grounds, or which do not contain individual reasoning' (ibid. 20); this requirement suggests that the right to receive reasons is contemplated for circumstances described in the preceding Parts, involving individualised adjudication, rather than the enunciation of general rules or regulations. Nevertheless, article 253 of the Treaty Establishing the European Community ('EC Treaty') demands the following:

> Regulations, directives and decisions adopted jointly by the European Parliament and the Council, and such acts adopted by the Council or the Commission, shall state the reasons on which they are based and shall refer

to any proposals or opinions which were required to be obtained pursuant to this Treaty.
Official Journal of the European Union (2002, Article 253)

As in the United States, the case law and scholarly writing suggest almost exclusively instrumental grounds for these reason giving requirements: the necessity to permit judicial monitoring of institutional decision-making and the need to facilitate the capacities of individuals to contest official determinations that are contrary to their interests.[16] Indeed, two decades ago, the European Court of Justice ('ECJ') bundled these two instrumental grounds together. In *Union Nationale Des Entraineurs et Cadres Techniques Professionneles du Football (UNECTEF) v. Heylens* ([1987] E.C.R 4097), the Court held,

> Effective judicial review, which must be able to cover the legality of the reasons for the contested decision, presupposes in general that the court to which the matter referred may require the competent authority to notify its reasons. But where, as in this case, it is more particularly a question of securing the effective protection of a fundamental right [the right of free movement] conferred by the Treaty on Community workers, the latter must also be able to defend that right under the best possible conditions and have the possibility of deciding, with full knowledge of the relevant facts, whether there is any point in their applying to the courts. Consequently, in such circumstances the competent national authority is under a duty to inform them of the reasons on which its refusal is based, either in the decisions itself or in a subsequent communication made at their request.
> *Ibid.: 4117*

In many ways, this approach directly parallels what we might call the 'double instrumentalism' of the American due process jurisprudence. A right of defence ('hearing' in the US vernacular) is essential where fundamental rights are at stake, and reasoned decision-making is critical to an effective right of defence.

In a recent article, Lord Millet explains the genesis of the requirement of reason giving in EU law as derivative from or inspired by member states' administrative laws (Millett 2002: 311). In France, for example, administrators generally have wide discretion in making administrative decisions, they are held to a duty of care and reasonableness in their decision-making, which according to Millet 'would be unenforceable in the absence of [...] [an additional] duty to give reasons' (ibid.: 314). Millett thus emphasises the contribution of reason giving to judicial review for reasonableness (ibid.). But a requirement of reasoned administration is common to the administrative systems of many member states.[17] And other authors also emphasise its contribution to the right of defence and to transparency.[18] Because reason giving contributes to the general transparency of official decision-making, it also to that degree facilitates oversight and accountability to political actors and the general public, not just to courts and litigants.

Although it is not possible here to make a detailed comparison between the jurisprudence of U.S. and EU courts (the ECJ and the Court of First Instance) concerning the demands of reason giving, the cases reveal many similarities.[19] As in the United States, reasons need not cover every detail of the contested proceeding but must be sufficient to show how the major issues of fact and law were resolved.[20]

And like their American colleagues, EU judges have tended to proceduralise rationality, that is, to demand more careful attention to articulation of the bases for decisions precisely where they are most within the technical expertise of the administrative authorities. In this way the judges can hope to assure conformity to law without invading the political or policy discretion reserved for administration.[21]

Hence, it seems fair to say that in both American and European Union jurisprudence, the right to receive reasons is a sort of derivative right. It facilitates individual decision-making about whether to contest official decisions, protects rights to individualised adjudication, and promotes the monitoring activities of both political and legal institutions. And reasons in both systems have a special value in maintaining vigorous judicial review along the treacherous boundary between law and policy. From this perspective, the fundamental value of reason giving is political and legal accountability. The requirement that administrative officials give reasons is merely a crucially important means to that end.

A revisionist account of reason giving

As suggested earlier in this chapter, there is more to reason giving as an aspect of good administration than is suggested by these instrumental accounts. Indeed, there are clues that this must be true in the positive law of both the European Union and the United States. Article 253 of the EC Treaty requires reasons for general acts (Official Journal of the European Union 2002, Article 253),[22] even though there is no right to judicial review of all general decisions in the European Union,[23] and general acts do not implicate the individual right to defence. Similarly, the Supreme Court has interpreted § 555(e) of the APA, although in a concurring opinion, to demand reasons in some cases where no right to hearing or to judicial review of the decision's substance is available (*Heckler v. Chaney*. [1985] 470 U.S. 821, 841–842). What more, then, is at stake when we demand reasoned administration?

At an abstract level, just this: reason giving is fundamental to the moral and political legitimacy of the American and European legal orders. To be sure, the United States does not suffer quite the same 'democratic deficit' that exists in the European Union. Therefore, it might be superficially plausible to argue that the legitimacy of administrative decision-making in the United States is a function of (1) the electoral accountability of Congress, which creates, structures, funds, and monitors administrative institutions; and (2) the elected president, who appoints and removes high administrative officials. On this view, administrative legitimacy lies in tracing administrative authority to the mandate of democratically elected institutions. But this electoral connection is notoriously thin. Administrators have enormous discretionary authority, and the exercise of that authority cannot be explained and legitimated as, in any realistic sense, the direct expression of the will of the people's representatives.[24]

As Max Weber noted long ago, the legitimacy of bureaucratic action resides in its promise to exercise power on the basis of knowledge (Roth and Wittich 1968, cited in Mashaw 2001: 23). Administrative legitimacy flows primarily from a belief in the specialised knowledge that administrative decisionmakers can bring to bear on critical policy choices. And the only evidence that this specialised knowledge has in fact been deployed lies in administrators' explanations or reasons for their actions. 'The statute made me do it' is sometimes an adequate explanation for a ministerial, that is, nondiscretionary, administrative act. But, in a much wider class of cases, the acceptability or legitimacy of an administrative decision will hinge not just on the authority or jurisdiction provided by a statute or treaty but on the reasons provided for exercising that authority or jurisdiction in a particular way – either in deciding individual cases or in promulgating general norms.

So far, so good. But what makes reason giving legitimating? The answer I think relates back to the Aristotelian view of responsibility, that is, the human capacity both to have and to give reasons for one's behaviour, which I earlier associated with John Gardner's account of responsibility.[25] That vision of reasoning and reason giving has particular moral force in a democratic polity. For in a democracy, the basic unit of social value is the individual: persons are viewed from a Kantian perspective as ends in themselves, and governments are democratically legitimate to the extent that they seek to carry out the collective desires of the citizenry. Those desires are, of course, only vaguely and imperfectly expressed through electoral processes and representative institutions, which themselves, of necessity, delegate large amounts of discretionary authority to unelected officials. But in a polity where the individual is the basic unit of social value, the fundamental reason for accepting law, or any official decision-making, as legitimate is that reasons can be given why those subject to the law would affirm its content as serving recognisable collective purposes.

To be sure, there may be much disagreement and dispute about which public policies are preferable, and which decisions affecting individual interests are justified. Nevertheless, a law or decision with which one disagrees can be recognised as acceptable or legitimate only because it is explicable as a plausible instance of rational collective action. Reason giving thus affirms the centrality of the individual in the democratic republic. It treats persons as rational moral agents who are entitled to evaluate and participate in a dialogue about official policies on the basis of reasoned discussion. It affirms the individual as subject rather than object of the law.

This is not to argue, of course, that the instrumental grounds for reason giving that courts and commentators routinely provide are unimportant. It is to suggest, instead, that there is a deeper ground for reason giving in a democracy and therefore a reason for treating a right to reasons as a fundamental, rather than as a contingent or derivative, human right. Authority without reason is literally dehumanising. It is therefore fundamentally at war with the promise of democracy, which is, after all, self-government.

This view of reason giving as an aspect of good administration is, I think, more than an academic or philosophical quibble about the grounds of a common practice. Whether one views reason giving as instrumental to other rights, or to the monitoring functions of political and legal institutions, or as a fundamental aspect of democratic governance, has implications for the reach and strength of the right in a democratic legal order.

The first implication is that if reason giving, or the right to receive reasons, is not a right parasitic on the protection of hearing rights, legal entitlements or the facilitation of judicial review, it is a general one that should be demanded outside of those particular contexts. As I have noted, the generality of the right to reasons is already recognised by the broad statements of article 253 of the EC Treaty and by the language of § 555(e) of the APA. The latter provides not only for reasons in connection with general rules but also demands 'prompt notice' of the denial in whole or part of any written application or petition by any interested person 'in connection with an agency proceeding', including a statement of the grounds for denial (5 U.S.C. § 555(e), 2000).

Yet these broad statements cannot be taken completely at face value. Article 253 applies to actions of EU institutions that have the force and effect of law.[26] The same is true of the United States' APA, where reason giving is specified only for administrative hearings determining individual rights or the issuance of regulations having the effect of law.[27] And, although it is sometimes given a broader application, the requirement in APA § 555(e) for reason giving with respect to applications, petitions, or requests applies only to the extent that those petitions are 'made in connection with any agency proceeding' (5 U.S.C. § 555(e)). 'Agency proceeding' is a defined term in the APA which refers only to agency processes of rule-making, adjudication, and licensing (ibid, § 551(12)).

These limitations have not gone unchallenged. Justice Marshall, for example, dissenting in *Board of Regents of State Colleges v. Roth*, stated boldly, 'In my view, every citizen who applies for a government job is entitled to it unless the government can establish some reason for denying the employment' (*Bd. Of Regents of State Coll. C. Roth.* [1972] 408 U.S. 564, 588). Marshall objected to the notion that because applicants or employees without tenure had no legal 'right' to their jobs, the Due Process Clause of the Fourteenth Amendment had no application to their situation (ibid.: 588–589). Justice Marshall seemed to take the position that the language 'life, liberty or property' in the Constitution was merely a placeholder for any significant human interest (ibid.). For him, the Due Process Clause was 'our fundamental guarantee of fairness, our protection against arbitrary, capricious, and unreasonable government action' (ibid.: 589). And to the argument that it would be too burdensome to always give reasons, Marshall replied, 'The short answer to that argument is that it is not burdensome to give reasons when reasons exist' (ibid.: 591).

Commentators, myself included, have also objected to the Supreme Court's instrumentalist conception of due process and reason giving. In a somewhat apoplectic vein, I wrote some years ago that limiting due process protections, including the right to reasons, to situations in which legal entitlements were at stake, produced both an incoherent jurisprudence and bizarre assignments of constitutional value to individuals' interests (Mashaw 1987: 437). As I said then and believe now,

> Such an approach is functionally inadequate to address the problems of governmental or bureaucratic discretion that the due process clause was meant to address. [Providing hearings only to protect pre-existing legal entitlements] gives legal protection, or at least due process attention, where some legal protection already exists, while excluding due process concern where a legal regime seems to permit official arbitrariness. Although many have a taste for irony, few would choose Kafka or Ionesco as constitutional draftsmen.
>
> *Mashaw (1987: 437)*

The current position in the United States is particularly disadvantageous for persons who are the potential beneficiaries of state regulatory action against others, or persons who suffer indirectly from official actions concerning another party's legal rights. In general, persons who seek the enforcement of existing regulatory provisions against violators who are injuring their interests, or who would be benefited by the exercise of dormant official regulatory authority, have no right either to a hearing before the responsible officials (*O'Bannon v. Town Court Nursing Ctr.* [1980] 447 U.S. 773, 775), or to judicial review of their refusal to act (*Heckler v. Chaney.* [1985] 470 U.S. 821, 832). And, so long as the requirement of reasoned decision-making is parasitic on either hearing rights or the facilitation of judicial review, these potential beneficiaries or indirect victims have no right to reasons either.[28] 'Standing' requirements in the United States also tend to deny judicial review to anyone not having been directly and concretely affected by state action.[29] This denial of access to judicial review, which is almost always available to directly regulated parties, further reduces the capacity of potential beneficiaries to engage regulatory authorities in reasoned discourse about their policies.

A similar analysis would seem to apply in EU law.[30] To be sure, there is broad language in some decisions suggesting that the 'right to good administration' implies a general requirement of responsiveness to complaints and requests that the Commission use its enforcement power, including the requirement that the Commission's response be sufficient to give the court an adequate basis for judicial review.[31] A closer reading, however, suggests that these obligations are contingent on a finding that the particular Treaty provision under which action is requested imposes an obligation on the Commission to take appropriate measures. And although one senses a general disposition in the European jurisprudence to take a more favourable view towards judicial review of inaction by enforcement authorities, American courts have also been willing to put aside standing and reviewability concerns where particular statutes seem to impose more specific obligations on enforcement officials.[32]

There may, of course, be good reasons for limiting rights to hearings and rights to judicial review. All such rights run risks of providing legal opportunity for the harassment of officials or of others over whom those officials have some authority. Formal hearings and judicial review are also expensive and time-consuming legal enterprises. But, as Justice Marshall suggested, reason giving alone does not necessarily burden administration or provide opportunities for harassment through legal adversarialism.[33] Accommodations to practical necessities can be made. Article 18 of the ECGAB, for example, recognises that its broad requirement that reasons be given any time a decision affects the 'interests' of private persons may have to be modified where individualised reason giving produces significant administrative burdens (European Ombudsman 2005: 59). Yet, even there, article 18 demands that where large numbers of people are affected similarly by a decision, an official must supplement a standardised statement of reasons with a detailed explanation if requested by particular individuals (ibid.).

These practicalities of legal enforcement suggest a second implication of treating reason giving as a general and fundamental right rather than as an instrumental one. The legal order should understand this right both as a 'hard law' right, sometimes enforceable in court, and as a 'soft law' right to be promoted through other means. Courts may decline to enforce legal rights to reasons in order to maintain a necessary separation between judicial and administrative judgement, that is, between legal constraints and administrative discretion. Courts cannot intervene in every dispute between individuals and government authorities while maintaining their own legitimacy as deciders. Responsible administration, however, reaches beyond those requirements that are judicially enforceable, and administrators can police themselves. Internal institutional codes of conduct and the oversight and publicity functions of audit institutions are two devices for internal monitoring and enforcement of the right to good administration. The Ombudsman in the European Union, and the departmental offices of inspectors general and the Government Accountability Office in the United States, are examples of the latter. The European Code of Good Administrative Behaviour for EU administrative officials exemplifies the former.

Perhaps because of the very nature of its legal order, which is based importantly on consensus and progressive co-ordination of legal norms, the European Union may be somewhat ahead of the United States in recognising the importance of these 'soft law' regimes. With limited exceptions (such as the Office of the Taxpayer Advocate in the Internal Revenue Service), the United States has never created ombudsman offices for federal administrative agencies or departments, and the operations of the offices of inspectors general and of the Government Accountability Office are directed more towards uncovering corruption or systematic programmatic failure than in promoting standards of good administration governing the relationship of officials to individuals. The European Union's interest in pressing forward the idea of 'good administration', including reason giving, through a host of techniques that are internal to administration rather than imposed by external legal guardians perhaps also reflects the general historical development of European administrative law, which has never been so judiciocentric as administrative law in the United States.

Finally, understanding reason giving by official institutions as fundamental to human rights in a democracy and as a part of the dynamic project of developing democratic government, suggests that reasoned administration should be understood both as a goal and as a right. It is a goal that Americans and Europeans have long shared. The organisation of state power in ways that produce a non-alienating and authentic democratic dialogue has been a dream of American republican theorists since the American Revolution. The same objective is deeply embedded in European social theory of the sort now most prominently represented perhaps by the writings of Jürgen Habermas.[34] Reasoned administration is not only fundamental to our understanding of ourselves as independent moral agents but to the future of the democratic project itself.

To be sure, there are many visions of democracy; not all are 'dialogic' in their ambitions, and those that are may be too demanding for most twenty-first-century contexts. Thomas Jefferson famously viewed the protection of democracy as demanding that virtually all government be conducted at an exquisitely local level.[35] If Jefferson's localism seems quaint in a globalising world, Jürgen Habermas's 'ideal speech situations' may be realisable only in the virtual world of the Internet.[36] Moreover, the protection of individual moral agency may be thought to be realised more through the 'checks and balances' of Madisonian-style democratic institutions than through the direct participation of individuals in public decision-making,[37] and these three possibilities hardly scratch the surface of the variations to be found in democratic theory.[38]

Nevertheless, when unelected officials, whether judges or administrators, make collective decisions, visions of democracy that rely on the will of the electorate as the legitimating claim are contextually irrelevant. We must either have some other view of democratic governance or declare all such decision-making democratically illegitimate. The alternative to will-based democratic theories are theories based on some vision of public reason. How 'rational' is understood, through what devices it should be expressed, how demanding systems of rational accountability should be and so on are all deeply contestable issues of institutional design. But this much seems clear: administration without reason cannot meet the challenge of defending its democratic legitimacy.

Notes

1 This chapter was first published in Yale Law School's *Faculty Scholarship Series*, 1179.
2 See 5 U.S.C. § 555(e).
3 See for example 28 U.S.C. §§ 1346, 2674, 2680.

4 Klara Kanska suggests that the rights included in article 41 of the Charter of Fundamental Rights and article II-101 of the Treaty Establishing a Constitution for Europe are a somewhat incomplete compilation of the separate rights developed by the Court of Justice and the courts of the member states (Kanska 2004). See also Millett (2002). (dating this process of development to Joined Cases 7/56 & 3/57–7/57, *Algera v. Common Assembly.* [1957] E.C.R. 39).
5 See 5 U.S.C. § 552.
6 See for example *United States v. Mitchell.* [1983] 463 U.S. 206.
7 See generally Tilly (2006), explaining how reasons work in four categories: conventions, stories, codes, and technical accounts.
8 Indeed, some literature on positive political theory in the United States suggest that this monitoring feature of private rights is the major explanation for procedural safeguards such as the APA. See McCubbins et al. (1987, 1989).
9 See Tilly (2006): 14–15. See generally Gardner (2006).
10 Compare *Londoner v. Denver.* [1908] 210 U.S. 373, 386 (holding that a small group of plaintiffs in a taxation proceeding were denied due process of law when a local board adjusted their tax liabilities on individualised grounds but without providing them with a hearing), with *Bi-Metallic Inv. Co. v. State Bd. of Equalization.* [1915] 239 U.S. 441, 445 (finding that individuals have no constitutional right entitling them to a hearing before a local taxing commission when changes in their tax liabilities result from a general increase in taxable property rates).
11 See e.g., *Perry v. Sindermann.* [1972] 408 U.S. 593, 599; *Bd. of Regents of State Coll. v. Roth.* [1972] 408 U.S. 564, 569–570.
12 See 5 U.S.C. § 701, 2000.
13 See for example National Traffic and Motor Vehicle Safety Act of 1966, Pub. L. No. 89-563, 80 Stat. 718 (recodified at 49 U.S.C. §§ 30101–30170 (2000)); Occupational Safety and Health Act of 1970, Pub. L. No. 91–596, 84 Stat. 1590 (codified as amended at 29 U.S.C. §§ 651–678 (2000)); National Environmental Policy Act of 1969, Pub. L. No. 91–190, 83 Stat. 852 (1970) (codified as amended at 42 U.S.C. §§ 4321–4347 (2000)).
14 See for example *Motor Vehicle Mfr. Ass'n v. State Farm Mut. Auto. Ins. Co.* [1983] 463 U.S. 29.
15 See for example Mashaw and Harfst (1987).
16 Klara Kanska (2004: 320) asserts,

> [A]ccording to the case law of the Courts, the duty to state reasons has two objectives: it is necessary in order to ensure that the individual has an opportunity to consider whether it is feasible to challenge a given measure, and it serves to ensure that the Court can exercise its powers to review the legality of the measure.

Bo Vesterdorf (1998: 904) echoes this view:

> The statement of reasons [...] must provide information to all persons interested in the measure and ultimately the reasoning must be sufficient to allow the Community Courts to ascertain whether or not the Community measure has been adopted ultra vires.

17 Dr. Juli Ponce (2005: 556) provides the following examples:

> The 1947 Italian Constitution establishes that Italian agencies must be organized so as to achieve administrative impartiality and *buon andamento*. The last words have been considered by many Italian scholars to be a duty of good administration (*buona amministrazione*) [...] The current Spanish Constitution of 1978 is especially interesting. It provides in Articles 31 and 103 that public administration must act with objectivity and impartiality, in accordance with the *principles of effective action, efficiency, economy and coordination*; it also establishes *a prohibition of arbitrariness*.

Similar provisions can be found in other countries.

18 For example, Bo Vesterdorf (1998: 906) states,

> Inadequate reasoning means *insufficient transparency*, because the consequence is, firstly, that the parties affected by the measure are unable to determine whether the measure is issued on a sound legal basis or whether it could be challenged before the courts and, secondly, that the courts are unable to examine whether the arguments on a given point are well-founded.

See also Kanska (2004: 320) (asserting that 'motivation of decisions promotes transparency of administrative actions').

19 A detailed comparison of US and EU jurisprudence up through 1992 can be found at Shapiro (1992).

20 The ECJ does not require European institutions to discuss every item of law or fact 'which may have been dealt with during the administrative proceedings'; however, 'the reasons on which a decision adversely affecting a person is based must allow the Court to exercise its power of review as to the legality of the decision'. Joined Cases 43 & 63/82, *VBVB & VBBB v. Comm'n*. [1984] E.C.R. 19, 58–59, 1 C.M.L.R. 27, 81 (1985); see Case 322/81, *NV Nederlandsche Banden-Industrie Michelin v. Comm'n*. [1983] E.C.R. 3461, 3500, 1 C.M.L.R. 282, 319 (1985), *cited in* Joshua (1991); see also Bignami (2005: 345).

> [K]nowing the grounds for a Commission decision is one thing, obtaining a reply on every objection of fact, policy, and law is another thing. The European Courts require only that the statement of reasons be complete enough to enable the parties to determine that the administration acted according to law or that they must go to court to vindicate their right to a government of laws and not of men.

Asimilar principle appears in EU member countries' practices. For example, Julian Joshua cites several British cases in this regard. See *R v. Sec'y of State for the Home Dep't, ex parte Swati*. [1986] 1 All E.R. 717 (A.C.); *Greater London Council v. Sec'y of State for the Env't*. [1985] 52 P. & C.R. 158 (A.C.); *Norwest Holst Ltd. v. Dep't of Trade*. [1978] 3 All E.R. 280, 296 (A.C.); *Elliott v. Southwark London Borough Council*. [1976] 1 W.L.R. 499, 508 (A.C.); *Metro. Prop. Holdings Ltd. v. Laufer*. [1975] 29 P. & C.R. 172 (Q.B.); *Howard v. Borneman*, [1974] All E.R. 862 (A.C.). In addition, Joshua (1991: 88) notes,

> Where there is a duty to give reasons, they have to be intelligible and adequate and deal with the substantial points at issue, but they neither have to set out the full reasoning process of the decision maker nor record all the evidence given or submissions made.

The ECJ supported this principle in Case T-323/99, *Industrie Navali Meccaniche Affini SpA (INMA) & Italia Investimenti SpA (Itainvest) v. Commission*. [2002] E.C.R. II-545, finding it unnecessary to address,

> all the relevant facts and points of law, since the question whether the statement of reasons meets the requirements of Article 253 EC must be assessed with regard not only to its wording but also to its context and all the legal rules governing the matter in question.
>
> ibid. II-562 (citing Case C-56/93, *Belgium v. Comm'n*. [1996] E.C.R. I-723)

21 Jürgen Schwarze (2004: 105) comments, 'The rigorous control of administrative procedure is particularly intended to counter-balance the far-reaching discretionary powers of the executive'.

22 See Kanska, (2004: 319–320); see also Vesterdorf (1998: 903) (emphasizing former EC Treaty article 190's – now article 253's – requirement to give reasons). Reason giving in the European context has also been influenced substantially by the European Convention for the Protection of Human Rights and Fundamental Freedoms, Nov. 4, 1950, Europ. T.S. No. 5, 213 U.N.T.S. 221, and its reasons requirement. See Dyzenhaus and Taggart (2007: 144–145). Dyzenhaus and Taggart (2007: 145) also

23 See Case 25/62, *Plaumann v. Comm'n.* [1963] E.C.R. 95, 1964 C.M.L.R. 29, 35–37. Although the *Plaumann* decision has been much criticised, the ECJ has reaffirmed its view of standing to review general orders of the Community. See Cornelia Koch (2004). In many cases, a claimant will be able to contest the national measures that implement a Community regulation in national courts on the ground that the regulation being implemented is itself illegal (ibid.: 816). Such a case can then produce a referral to the ECJ for a determination of the legality of the Community norm (ibid.). The ECJ, however, has declined to accept an appeal based on the claim that no national review possibility existed and that the denial of standing would therefore constitute a denial of justice. See Femke de Lange (2003: 841–842).
24 See Rubin (2001: 728, 782) for a more detailed inquiry into the comparative 'democracy' of the European Union, the United States, and Swiss federations. See generally Zweifel (2003) (comparing the 'accountability and independence of merger regulation in the European "regulatory state"' with those of the United States and Switzerland).
25 See Gardner (2006).
26 See Official Journal of the European Union (2002, Article 253) (requiring reasons for '[r]egulations, directives and decisions adopted jointly by the European Parliament and the Council, and such acts adopted by the Council or the Commission').
27 See 5 U.S.C. §§ 553–554 (2000).
28 For a recent general treatment of this topic, see Mendelson (2007: 403–433).
29 See *Lujan v. Defenders of Wildlife.* [1992] 504 U.S. 555, 562.
30 In particular, the requirement that individuals have both a concrete and individualised interest in Community decisions will often exclude beneficiaries of regulatory regimes or other protective regimes because they will not be able to distinguish themselves from the general public, or a broad class of beneficiaries, who are also protected. For a recent case excluding beneficiaries on grounds of standing, see Case C-321/95P, *Greenpeace & Others v. Commission.* [1998] E.C.R. I-1651, 1998 3 C.M.L.R. 1, discussed in Gérard (1998). See also supra note 64 and accompanying text (discussing how the ECJ has followed the *Plaumann* formula, refusing to broaden an individual's standing on matters of general application).
31 See for example Case T-54/99, *max.mobil Telekommunikation Serv. GmbH v. Comm'n*, [2002] E.C.R. II-313, II-333.
32 See *Dunlop v. Bachowski.* [1975] 421 U.S. 560, 566.
33 See *Bd. of Regents of State Coll. v. Roth.* [1972] 408 U.S. 564, 591.
34 See infra note 90.
35 See Letter from Thomas Jefferson to Governor John Tyler (26 May 1810), reprinted in *The Life and Selected Writings of Thomas Jefferson* 604–605 (Adrienne Koch & William Peden eds., 1944); Letter from Thomas Jefferson to Joseph C. Cabell (Feb. 2, 1816), *id.* at 660–662
36 This possibility is explored in Froomkin (2003).
37 See Rossi (1997).
38 For one overview among many on democratic theory, see generally Shapiro (2003) (exploring democratic theory in relation to the nature of power and domination).

References

Administrative Procedure Act 1946 (U.S.C.). Available at: https://www.justice.gov/sites/default/files/jmd/legacy/2014/05/01/act-pl79-404.pdf [accessed 25 November 2020].
Bignami, F. (2005) 'Creating European Rights: National Values and Supranational Interests', *The Columbia Journal of European Law*, 11(2): 241–354.

de Lange, F. (2003) 'European Court of Justice, Unión de Pequeños Agricultores v. Council', *Review European Community & International Environmental Law*, 12(1): 115–118.

Dyzenhaus, D. and Taggart, M. (2007) 'Reasoned Decisions and Legal Theory', in D.E. Edlin (ed.) *Common Law Theory* (pp. 134–167). Cambridge: Cambridge University Press.

European Ombudsman (2005) *The European Code of Good Administrative Behaviour*. Luxembourg: Office for Official Publications of the European Communities. Available at: https://www.ombudsman.europa.eu/en/publication/en/3510 [accessed 18 December 2020].

Freedom of Information Act 2020 (U.K.) Available at: https://www.legislation.gov.uk/ukpga/2000/36/enacted [accessed 25 November 2020].

Friendly, H.J. (1975) 'Some Kind of Hearing', *University of Pennsylvania Law Review* 123(6): 1267–1317.

Froomkin, M. (2003) 'Habermas@Discourse.Net: Toward a Critical Theory of Cyberspace', *Harvard Law Review*, 116(3): 749–873.

Gardner, J. (2006) 'The Mark of Responsibility (With a Postscript on Accountability)', in M.W. Dowdle (ed.) *Public Accountability: Designs, Dilemmas and Experiences* (pp. 220–242). Cambridge: Cambridge University Press.

Gérard, N. (1998) 'Greenpeace and Others v. the Commission – C 321/95P', *Review of European Community & International Environmental Law*, 7(2): 209–211.

Joshua, J.M. (1991) 'The Right to Be Heard in EEC Competition Procedures', *Fordham International Law Journal* 15(1): 16–91.

Kanska, K. (2004) 'Towards Administrative Human Rights in the EU: The Impact of the Charter of Fundamental Rights', *European Law Journal*, 10(3): 296–305.

Koch, C. (2004) 'Commission of the European Communities v. Jégo-Quéré & Cie SA., Case C-263/02', *American Journal of International Law*, 98(4): 814–819.

Mashaw, J.L. (1987) 'Dignitary Process: A Political Psychology of Liberal Democratic Citizenship', *University of Florida Law Review*, 39(2): 433–444.

Mashaw, J.L. (2001) 'Small Things Like Reasons Are Put in a Jar: Reason and Legitimacy in the Administrative State', *Fordham law Review*, 70(1): 17–36.

Mashaw, J.L. and Harfst, D.L. (1987) 'Regulation and Legal Culture: The Case of Motor Vehicle Safety', *Yale Journal on Regulation*, 4(2): 257–316.

McCubbins, M.D., Noll, R.G. and Weingast, B.R. (1987) 'Administrative Procedures as Instruments of Political Control', *Journal of Law, Economics & Organization*, 3(2): 243–277.

McCubbins, M.D., Noll, R.G. and Weingast, B.R. (1989) 'Structure and Process, Politics and Policy: Administrative Arrangements and the Political Control of Agencies', *Virginia Law Review*, 75(2): 431–482.

Mendelson, N.A. (2007) 'Regulatory Beneficiaries and Informal Agency Policymaking', *Cornell Law Review* 92(3): 397–452.

Millett, L. (2002) 'The Right to Good Administration in European Union Law', *Public Law*, 47(2): 309–313.

Official Journal of the European Union (2000) Charter of Fundamental Rights of the European Union. 2000/C 364. Available at: https://www.europarl.europa.eu/charter/pdf/text_en.pdf [accessed 17 December 2020].

Official Journal of the European Union (2002) Treaty Establishing the European Community (consolidated version). 2002/ C 325 135. Available at: https://eur-lex.europa.eu/legal-content/EN/TXT/PDF/?uri=OJ:C:2002:325:FULL&from=EN [accessed 18 December 2020].

Official Journal of the European Union (2004) Treaty Establishing a Constitution for Europe. 2004/C 310. Available at: https://eur-lex.europa.eu/legal-content/EN/TXT/?uri=OJ:C:2004:310:TOC.

Ponce, J. (2005) 'Good Administration and Administrative Procedures', *Indiana Journal of Global Legal Studies*, 12(2): 551–588.

Rossi, J. (1997) 'Participation Run Amok: The Costs of Mass Participation for Deliberative Agency Decisionmaking', *Northwestern University Law Review*, 92(1): 173–250.

Roth, G. and Wittich, C. (eds.) (1968) *Max Weber, Economy and Society: An Outline of Interpretive Sociology*. New York: Bedminster Press.

Rubin, E.L. (2001) "Getting Past Democracy', *University of Pennsylvania Law Review*, 149(3): 711–792.

Schwarze, J. (2004) 'Judicial Review of European Administrative Procedure', *Law & Contemporary Problems*, 68(1): 85–105.

Shapiro, I. (2003) *The State of Democratic Theory*. Princeton, NJ: Princeton University Press.

Shapiro, M. (1992) 'The Giving Reasons Requirement', *University of Chicago Legal Forum*, 1992: 179–220.

Tempest, M. (2007) 'Q&A: The EU Constitution', *The Guardian*, 18 June.

Tilly, C. (2006) 'Why and How History Matters', in R.E. Goodin and C. Tilly (eds.) *The Oxford Handbook of Contextual Political Analysis* (pp. 417–437). Oxford: Oxford University Press.

Vesterdorf, B. (1998) 'Transparency – Not Just a Vogue Word', *Fordham International Law Journal*, 22(3): 902–929.

Zweifel, T.D. (2003) 'Democratic Deficits in Comparison: Best (and Worst) Practices in European, US and Swiss Merger Regulation', *Journal of Common Market Studies*, 41(3): 541–566.

4
POWER, MONEY, KNOWLEDGE AND THE EUROPEAN CENTRAL BANK

Christopher Lord

Introduction

The relationship between knowledge and democracy is one of the oldest problems of politics. Plato (360 BC [1955]: 249–250) famously argued that allowing the many, rather than the knowledgeable, to make decisions would be like allowing the sailors, instead of the navigator, to decide the direction of a ship. While, however, Plato worried about making knowledge safe from democracy, his own solution – that philosophers should rule – is a warning that democracy also needs to be safe from those who believe that knowledge confers some special claim to decide.

The puzzle of how to base government on both knowledge and democracy remains unresolved. Instead, contemporary democracy lurches between technocracy and populism (Bickerton and Accetti 2017): between technocratic belief in expertise and populist belief in a pure will of the people (Müller 2017; Weale 2018) unmediated by evidence, expertise or knowledge. Technocracy fallaciously assumes that some choices can be value free or, at least, that expert choice of means in the framing of policy and law can be separated from public control of ends (Richardson 2003: 15). But means also involve choices of what is good or right (Sen 2002: 12); and, in a democracy, choices of what is good or right need to be contested and decided through processes in which all citizens count equally regardless of their expertise (Habermas 2015). In contrast, populists fail to understand that the will of the people is only ever the will of a majority with a responsibility to justify itself that can only be met with some attention to knowledge if democracy's choices are not to be every bit as absurd as not listening to what the navigator has to say about steering the ship.

So, how might we identify forms of government – of collective self-rule – that are based on both knowledge and democracy? A logical starting point might be to explore where democracy and knowledge presuppose one another. If it turns out there are 'epistemic justifications' for democracy – ways of justifying democracy, in part, by its contribution to knowledge – it would be hard, as Gerald Gaus puts it, 'to overestimate how important' that would be for democracy. No longer would 'democracy be an uneasy mix of 'fairness' and 'rule by collective stupidity' (2011: 271, 273). Difficulties in combining popular control with knowledge-based decisions would be, at least, somewhat offset by the contribution of democracy to knowledge.

Democracy might be important for knowledge either (a) because democracy helps produce knowledge in general or (b) because democracy helps produce forms of knowledge and mutual understanding needed for minimal standards of rights and justice that are, in turn, needed for basic standards of democracy or (c) because there are normative commitments common to both knowledge and democracy. I explore and distinguish those three epistemic arguments for democracy more fully elsewhere (Lord 2017). It will, however, help with subsequent discussion of this chapter if I say a bit more about (a) and (c).

It was, of course, John Stuart Mill (1972 [1861]) who identified the deep connection between the equal democratic freedom of all to challenge claims in public debate and the development of knowledge. First, he invites us to assume that a particular belief turns out to be false. In that event we lose the opportunity to weed out that false belief from our total stock of knowledge – and all the other false conclusions that follow from falsely holding that belief – if it is not open to challenge. Second, he invites us to believe that a claim turns out to be true. We will still, Mill argues, lose out if we cannot challenge that belief in public debate. For how else can we know that the belief is true – and why it is true – unless that belief has survived every attempt to disprove it in free and testing discussion? Yet there is a third possibility, perhaps the most common of all, namely, that few beliefs are the whole truth. Rather, truth is scattered between many individual claims. Knowledge is once again the loser in the absence of free, equal and therefore democratic discussion. The equal openness of each of our beliefs to be challenged by any other belief is what helps us integrate all our beliefs into a coherent body of belief.

Indeed, Robert Talisse (2009: 121) has argued that 'only in a democracy can an individual practise proper epistemic agency' at all. Epistemic norms and democracy share a commitment to the equality of persons and opinions. Without those equalities how can we be sure that our beliefs are based on epistemic norms and not on uneven distributions of power over processes of acquiring beliefs? Hence, Jürgen Habermas (2003: 107) identifies how inclusiveness and equality are both democratic standards and conditions for the reliable acquisition of knowledge. As he puts it, knowledge requires the following: (i) publicity and inclusiveness: no one who could make a relevant contribution with regard to a controversial activity should be excluded; (ii) equal rights to engage in communication: everyone must have the right to speak to the matter at hand; (iii) exclusion of deception and illusion: participants have to mean what they say; and

(iv) absence of coercion: communications must be free of restrictions that prevent the better argument being raised or from determining the outcome of the discussion. Indeed, Talisse ingeniously argues that only agreement on epistemic standards, and not agreement on moral standards, can ground shared commitment to democracy. While, moreover, people are divided by their moral beliefs, they do have common obligations as knowledge seekers (Talisse 2009) – such as those set out in (i) to (iv) – that are also democratic standards (see also May 2011).

The foregoing arguments made by Mill, Habermas and Talisse plainly identify where democratic and epistemic principles require one another. But they do not tell us what forms of collective choice or institutional design are most likely to deliver requirements common to knowledge and democracy. Among many important attempts to address the relationship between knowledge and democracy within an actual process of institutional design and evolution, the case of the European Central Bank (ECB) is of special interest. The ECB's design rested on strong assumptions about knowledge and the independent use of knowledge. Yet those assumptions were far from devoid of democratic principle. Then, of course, the ECB also goes beyond the question of how expertise and democracy should relate to one another within a single state. The ECB is the central bank for a multi-state, multi-democracy and multi-*demoi* political order that exercises its powers from beyond the state.

Hence, in the expectation that the ECB is a useful case in how expert knowledge and democracy can relate in a supranational political order, this chapter proceeds as follows. The "Introduction" section argues that monetary union was an attempt to tame power relations in the political management of money. The "Money, power and knowledge in the creation of the euro" section shows how the ECB was supposed to contribute to that taming by maximising the role of knowledge and minimising the role of power or preferences in monetary decisions. The "More knowledge than power or preferences" section shows how the ECB has only demonstrated how central banking is unavoidably an exercise of political power. The "The elusiveness of purely epistemic central banking" section concludes by considering implications for combining knowledge and democracy in monetary policy beyond the state.

Money, power and knowledge in the creation of the euro

Money is a creation of political power and law. States usually enforce a monopoly on their own preferred forms of money, not least by only meeting their own obligations in that money, and by insisting that others can only meet their obligations and pay their taxes in what the state defines as money (Wray 2019). But as well as being the creation of political power, money begets more power. Of course it is a truism that resources confer power. But I mean much more than that, namely, that powers over technical features that define money – as a medium of exchange, a unit of account, and a store of value – are sources of further power. As well as power over what counts as money, power over the price of money (interest rate), power over the quantity of money and power over access to money in the form of credit are important forms of the powers *of* states and of power *within* and *between* states. Money creation is a key component of state formation. States with credible central banks that can backstop them by acting as lenders of last resort or by just helping them to borrow most efficiently in volume and at low cost are not just less likely to default. They can also afford to develop the full range of powers and policies of modern states. Small wonder then that technical knowledge in the management of money is, as we will see, decisive to geopolitical competition between states. Even the French Revolution depended on a technical innovation in the creation of money. Before they were over-issued, *assignats* – banknotes secured on the land of the king and the clergy – successfully financed the early stages of the revolution (Harris 1930).

Then, of course, what counts as money and who has access to it is critical to the distribution of power in economies and societies. One of the reasons why the poor usually stay poor, and the rich usually stay rich, is the hard-to-eradicate problem of capital market failure. Asymmetries of information between borrowers and lenders make it hard to create capital markets in which everyone has access to all forms of credit that would advance their life chances (Stiglitz and Weiss 1981).

While, however, technical decisions over what counts as money, on what terms, are ways in which some can enforce their will or shape opportunities available to others, money also covers the full spectrum of 'public good' and 'public bad' characteristics. At the benign end of the spectrum, money can be a positive externality network good. The more people use a particular form of money, the more useful it is to all of them. At the malign end of the spectrum, money can be a common resource pool. People can deplete the credibility of a particular form of money in ways that create huge costs for others.

Thus, power creates money, and money creates power. Yet, crucially, the two-way relationship between money and power is mediated by knowledge and expertise. It might have been thought that power over the silver mines of the Americas in a world of metallic money would give Spain the advantage in its epic struggle against the independence of the Netherlands (1555–1648); or even that France, as initially the richer of the two, would win out in its many wars against the United Kingdom (1688–1815). But Amsterdam and London led in developing the financial expertise needed to develop stock trading, bond trading and modern forms of banking; and those proved the real trumps in the financing of government and therefore in geopolitical power games (Ferguson 2008).

Then, of course, if knowledge in the technical management of money is so important to political power, it is also important to the justification of power (Beetham 2013: 5), and, indeed, to justice, legitimacy and democracy as first questions of politics. If access to finance, and laws that govern access to finance, affect life chances, then they are also important to how, as Rawls (2003: 4) put it, the whole structure of laws, public policy and opportunities 'fits together' as a more or less 'fair scheme of co-operation'. If money has important 'public good' and 'public bad' characteristics, then any 'ideal of democracy as one in which individuals can as equals determine the terms of their collective conditions of living together' (Bohman 2007) will be incomplete if publics cannot control institutions and laws that determine the definition, price and quantity of money, since, to repeat, those things are crucial to any 'collective terms of living together'. Of particular importance here is public control of central banking. It is not without reason that libertarians have a near obsession with identifying where it might be possible to do without central banks. Central banks can be powerful forms of domination, not least in creating perverse incentives in which the financial system as a whole can take a free ride on bail-outs at huge expense to publics (Tucker 2018). For non-libertarians, however, the only solution is not to do without central banks, but rather to identify the normative and empirical conditions where it might be possible to have central banking without domination. As we will see, debates about the ECB have much to tell us about that problem.

Indeed, monetary union is potentially a new departure that requires us to rethink and re-investigate our understanding of relationships between money, power, knowledge and democracy. Combining these things within the EU's political order is likely to be different to combining them within a single state. Given the crucial distinction between 'democratically justified' and 'purely technical epistocracies' (Holst 2011: 6–7) the question of how to achieve an independent, yet democratically justified, form of central banking will plainly need rethinking where the central bank is not that of a single democracy, but rather a central bank shared between many democracies within a political order with uncertain prospects of developing common representative institutions and democratic politics of its own. For sure, the Eurozone adopted at European level a form of independent central banking that was fashionable at national level.

Yet monetary union does much more than up-load an established model of central banking. By moving together to create a shared central bank within the EU's non-state, multi-state, multi-democracy and multi-*demoi* political order, the 11 and now 19 member state democracies that created monetary union also transformed independent central banking. Departure from the normal relationship between statehood and central banking – one state, one central bank – is precisely, for its critics, what makes Europe's Monetary Union absurd, unsustainable, and dangerous. In contrast, that departure is precisely, for its defenders, what justifies the Euro (see for example Issing 2008a). With the help of other unusual characteristics of the EU's political order, a multi-state, multi-democracy monetary union would create new possibilities for enhancing the role of knowledge, and constrain the use of power and preferences, in monetary policy. To understand all that the remainder of this section examines how monetary union was both the product of concerns over power relations and an attempt to tame them.

Andrew Moravcsik (1998) has argued that monetary union was based on convergent commercial interests and not on geopolitical transformations brought about by the end of the cold war and the reunification of Germany. He clearly has a point that the road to monetary union began well before 1989. Yet monetary union was essential, nonetheless, to the new power settlement in Europe after 1989. As Kenneth Dyson and Kevin Featherstone (1999: 261, 271) have remarked, EMU was perceived by the German 'security community' as 'making European unification irreversible'. The binding of Germany into an irreversible process of European integration was then, in turn, seen as essential to reassure Germany's neighbours that Germany could be reunified – and Germans could live like others in a single national democratic political community – without pursuing unilateral policies (*Sonderweg*) that disregarded others.

However, geopolitical power interacted, as it so often does, with considerations of political economy. From 1979 members of the European Community developed arrangements for managing their currencies through the exchange rate mechanism (ERM) of the European Monetary System (EMS). The ERM, though, had the unintended consequence of contradicting the core aim of using European integration to multilateralise powers so that member states could not dominate one another. Instead of sharing power over monetary decisions the ERM evolved – through market preferences rather than institutional design – into a system of German policy leadership in which the Bundesbank effectively set 'monetary policy for the whole system' (Giavazzi and Giovannini quoted in James 2012: 207, see also Gros and Thygesen 1998).

For sure, the Bundesbank exercised that power at arm's length from the German Government and with a stubborn independence from the latter that was, in turn, supported by public opinion. The Bundesbank was also a reluctant policy leader in an arrangement that satisfied no one. Other member states had to live with monetary policies that the Bundesbank – under the terms of its own mandate – could only base on West German economic conditions and not those of the European Communities as a whole. Yet, even then, an exchange rate commitment involved some cost to the Bundesbank's policy autonomy (Frattiani and Von Hagen 1991). Hence, as early as 1982, its President, Karl-Otto Pöhl, told the Committee of Central Bank Governors (COG) that, even for the Bundesbank, a 'complete monetary union' could be better than an ERM that delivered 'neither stability nor independence' (quoted in James 2012: 182).

Indeed, monetary union responded to power imbalances in the international, and not just the European, monetary order. The collapse of the Bretton Woods system in the early 1970s eroded a form of 'embedded liberalism' (Ruggie 1982) in which states could largely choose their own economic policies within a context of interdependence. Instead, there was often disagreement on how 'burdens of adjustment' should be distributed where the economic policies of the United States and other participants in the international system conflicted. French governments, in particular, concluded that the European Community needed monetary integration to 'increase its weight' in shaping any reform of the international monetary system (quoted in Dyson and Featherstone 1999: 152).

However, the euro was not just a response to changes and concerns in power relations. It itself changed power relations. Most obviously, it removed a core power of its participating states: to issue their own money and change its value. As the ECB's founding chief economist, Otmar Issing (2008b: 2, 20), has remarked, 'for sovereign states to cede their authority in the monetary sphere to a supranational institution, while retaining a greater or lesser degree of autonomy in other policy areas, is historically unprecedented. [...] The transfer of responsibility for monetary policy from the national central bank to a supranational institution, the ECB, and the related loss of sovereignty represent a fundamental change in the structure of the state.'

Still, most participating states arguably stood to lose less policy *autonomy* than formal *sovereignty*. Small states – with only thinly traded currencies – often had limited monetary policy autonomy anyway in globalised markets. States other than Germany would conceivably have more autonomy by being represented in ECB decisions based on shared economic conditions, rather than, as seen, following Bundesbank policies. Moreover, such questions of how to achieve stability, autonomy, and, indeed, non-domination between democracies in monetary questions – of currencies, interest rates and access to financial capital – were themselves part of a more general problem of democratic politics within any interdependent monetary order. Danni Rodrik (2011: 200) has identified what he calls 'a trilemma of the world economy' in which 'we cannot have hyperglobalisation, democracy and national self-determination all at once'.

Yet that predicament was first identified in the discussion of monetary integration in Europe and from the study and practice of the ERM. The economist Tommasso Padoa-Schioppa (1987) – who was later rapporteur for the Delors Committee that began the design of the ECB – identified what he called an 'inconsistent quartet' of free trade, capital mobility, managed exchange rates and autonomy in making monetary policy. That problem was later reformulated as what Issing (2008b: 7) has described as an 'uneasy triangle' in which 'only two of the three goals of stable exchange rates, free movement of capital and monetary policy autonomy can ever be attained at the same time.' That meant EC members – who were already on their way to removing capital controls as part of the single market – would either have to give up stable exchange rates (Rogoff 1985a) or autonomous monetary policies.

Small wonder, then, that some believed that they had little autonomy to give up in forming a full monetary union (James 2012: 322). Indeed, a monetary union could, arguably, even allow member state democracies to increase autonomy in non-monetary policies (Issing 2008b). Europe's economic constitution for those in the single currency would be one of monetary centralisation, fiscal decentralisation and regulatory condominium (market regulation decided at both Union and national levels). Giving up their own currencies could – in some ways and under some conditions – even make national fiscal policies and market regulation more effective through the admittedly paradoxical effects of self-binding and pooling of powers.

Yet the main point of monetary union was not a cunning attempt to increase autonomy through self-restraint; rather, monetary union was supposed to be a straightforward taming of power relations. Indeed, it aimed at a double taming of power relations through a new way of achieving the old strategy of using integration to constrain European states from arbitrarily dominating both one another and their own publics (Weiler 1997). 'Member state democracy' on 'member state democracy' domination would be constrained, as seen, by multilateralising power over monetary policy. Domination of publics by their own elected governments would also be constrained if core justifications for independent central banking were correct.

To explain, I now reconstruct assumptions of democratic theory that were implicit in the economic theory of central banking. The core economic argument for independent central banking rests on the so-called neutrality of money. According to those who believe in the neutrality of money, there is no enduring benefit to be had from manipulating the quantity of money. Over the medium term, output and employment will be much where they would have been in the absence of policy intervention. The only thing that will be different is that inflation will be higher (Lucas 1972). While, however, the 'neutrality of money hypothesis' implies that short-term attempts to manipulate the supply of money to achieve outcomes other than price stability is a pure welfare loss to voters, it can allow elected politicians to create an illusion of improved output and employment at the time of their re-election. Worse still, since it is known that elected politicians can behave in this way, even elected politicians who are motivated solely by a wish to manage the economy with reasonable competence will be unable to achieve the best possible trade-offs between employment and growth on the one hand and inflation on the other (Barro and Gordon 1983; Kydland and Prescott 1977). Financial markets will demand higher interest rates – and workers will demand higher pay – to cover the risk that elected politicians might just turn out to be less honest and motivated than they seem, or that they might just succumb at the last moment to an electoral incentive to manipulate the economy to their short-term advantage.

If this argument is correct, the strongest democratic case for independent central banking might run as follows: transferring responsibility for monetary policy from elected politicians to an independent central bank would allow publics to achieve a combination of outcomes – lower inflation and higher growth and employment – that is both desirable from most points of view and unattainable through normal majoritarian politics. If the public really is to be able to govern itself by choosing its own policy and laws it would be absurd to argue that citizens should not have some democratic means to decide for themselves to delegate powers away from a majoritarian process that has no chance of achieving what are better outcomes from most points of view towards one that has some chance of achieving those outcomes. Moreover, such a delegation would also be a benefit to the democratic process itself, since it would remove an opportunity for governments to manipulate the terms of their own re-election by managing the economic cycle so that it coincides with the political cycle. This implied independent central banking is a form of monetary-democratic constitutionalism that publics might want to choose to prevent their own governments cheating on them and to safeguard the democratic process itself. An important question, however, is what would be needed for an epistemic-monetary-democratic constitutionalism; or, in other words, for a form of central banking that would maximise the role of knowledge and minimise the role of power or preferences in decisions. The next section shows how the constitutional design of the ECB was supposed to answer this question.

More knowledge than power or preferences

Locke (1924 [1690]: 163) famously objected that Hobbes supposed men 'are so foolish that they take care to avoid what mischiefs may be done to them by polecats or foxes, but are content, nay, think it safety, to be devoured by lions.' A monetary union that tamed *inter*-state power by multilateralising monetary policy and tamed *intra*-state power by constitutionalising monetary policy would not tame power relations if a European central bank itself became a source of technocratic domination (Howarth and Loedl 2005). To be a part of the solution and not of the problem, an independent European central bank would also need to contribute to a taming of power relations. Just how it was supposed the ECB would be able to use its specialised knowledge without arbitrarily exercising power – or hardly exercising power at all – requires an understanding of the epistemic community that shaped the ECB; of the institutional design of the ECB; and of arrangements for its political and legal responsibility.

Epistemic Community. It cannot be supposed that key actors in the agreement of monetary union – right up to Chancellor Kohl and President Mitterrand – had a full understanding of the theoretical debates that led most democracies to adopt independent central banking between the 1970s and 1990s. Kohl and Mitterrand arrived at the conclusion that a European central bank would have to be very like the Bundesbank more through an understanding of bargaining power than monetary theory. The Bundesbank would oppose any European central bank that was not at least as independent as itself. German public opinion would side with the Bundesbank and any German government would either have to veto monetary union or soft-pedal on its implementation.

Yet that same calculation of bargaining power persuaded member states to delegate much of the design of the ECB to those whose thinking was closely shaped by prevailing theory of central banking. If the Bundesbank had a de facto veto on any monetary union then why not involve it in the design of a European central bank of its own choosing? The ECB largely developed out of a Committee of Central Bank Governors (CoG) that had been the crucial component of any monetary co-ordination through the European Communities since the 1960s (James 2012). The national central governors went on to form the largest component of the ECB's Governing Council. The ECB's statute was largely written by the central bank governors before being adopted with only minor changes in wording into proposed changes to the EU Treaties agreed by the Maastricht European Council in December 1991.

All that, in turn, had important effects on how it was believed expert knowledge and democratic standards would align in the case of the ECB. The CoG was more than a part of an 'epistemic community' (Verdun 1999) whose members largely subscribed to the normative and causal theories of independent central banking described above. The CoG also had specific knowledge of the likely effects of applying general principles of independent central banking to a monetary union formed initially out of 11 member state democracies of the European Union, each with its distinct monetary transmission mechanism (i.e. means of transmitting monetary policy changes into outcomes), and each with its distinctive banking and financial system. Indeed, the central bankers also had a unique understanding of what had become a two-level problem in which national monetary conditions were, in turn, hard to understand without knowledge of previous co-ordination at the European level and continuing plans to remove capital controls and create a single financial market. The CoG had years of experience in managing realignments, currency interventions and interest-rate changes through the ERM. If they had not depended on the Bundesbank not opposing monetary union, governments would surely have depended on the expertise of the CoG to make the transition to a single currency. But in doing so much to shape the ECB's statute and its subsequent operationalisation, just what kind of a central bank – and, to use David Estlund's (2008: 7) phrase, just what kind of 'rule by knowers' – did Europe's 'epistemic community' of central bankers create? The next sub-section answers this question.

Institutional design. During discussions in the 1980s of options for the further monetary integration of the European Communities the solution that eventually emerged – a single currency managed by a European central bank – was often described as a corner solution. It was, in other words, in the most supranational corner of all solutions available. In the opposite corner was no monetary integration, and therefore a disintegration and renationalisation of existing co-operation through the ERM and EMS into uncoordinated and free-floating national currencies. Various forms of partial monetary union existed in between the aforesaid solutions: a common currency that would be used in parallel with national currencies without replacing them; a permanent fixing of national currencies against one another that would keep those currencies but put them under the common management of a central bank; or even competing currencies that could, at their most Hayekian, challenge public monopolies over the creation of money.

The parallel currency, in particular, was rejected because it entailed divided responsibility for the management of monetary policy. Nervousness about dividing responsibility for monetary policy reflected the most distinctive challenge in creating a European central bank in a multi-state, multi-national, multi-*demoi* political order. Still, there were unifying principles to the EU's political and legal order which could, conversely, be used to develop a more independent form of central banking than that was possible within a single-state democratic system. One such is the supremacy of EU law created under Union Treaties that can only be changed with unanimous agreement of member states. Designing a monetary union within the EU's Treaties created an unusually independent central bank, rightly described by the European Parliament as 'probably the most independent central bank in the world' (1998). Since rules for changing EU Treaties were far harder than those for changing a national constitution, the creation of a central bank by Union Treaties paradoxically allowed for a hyper-constitutionalisation of the ECB.

Indeed, the ECB was unusually independent in comparison with other EU institutions, not just other central banks. As Kenneth Dyson (2000: 11) has remarked, '[t]he ECB has the potential to play an active role as a supranational executive body that exceeds the autonomy of action available to the European Commission' (Hodson 2011). Consider how Union institutions are normally constrained. First, powers are often distributed across several institutions. Most matters – and not just legislation – need to be more or less co-decided by several institutions under rules that require high levels of agreement within and across those institutions. Second, the Union, in any case, rarely enjoys its own exclusive competence in which it is free to decide what it wants without regard for what national and sub-national authorities are attempting to do in the same policy field. Sure, the Union claims that its laws take priority over any national measures that conflict with them. But that only leads on to the third constraint. The Union may claim primacy for its laws, but its decisions have to be implemented by national or sub-national authorities, over which the Union only has limited coercive resources.

In contrast, these constraints are weak in the case of the ECB. It acts in one of the few areas where the Union does have exclusive competence. Within the Eurozone it has monopoly control over monetary policy. Moreover, it decides monetary policy on its own initiative and without having to concern itself with any other veto holders among the other Union institutions. Finally, the ECB's implementing agents are not national governments, but national central banks, which themselves are part of the epistemic community of independent central banking of those already subscribed to its empirical and normative assumptions. Moreover, as seen, national central bankers are themselves the dominant part of the ECB's governing Council.

Yet the extent of the ECB's powers and its independence can only be understood in conjunction with the narrowness and simplicity of its mandate. Sure, the ECB is an unusually powerful central bank. Sure, the ECB is unusually powerful in comparison with other Union executive institutions. Sure, the ECB has monopoly control of monetary policy. Yet it is only mandated to use those powers for one, single purpose: to ensure 'price stability'. Also recall that money is assumed to be 'neutral'. Even the one single thing the ECB is mandated to do – to ensure price stability – is assumed to involve no long-run trade-offs with other values or objectives.

Moreover, the chances of the ECB not being distracted from its mandate would be increased precisely by it not needing to make monetary policy for one system of democratic politics. Even strongly independent central banks may be shy of making sensitive changes to monetary policies close to elections. The

ECB, however, is not constrained in that way given that it is the central bank of 20 political systems (19 member states and the EU itself) with different electoral cycles. Even if central bankers from member states approaching elections wanted to avoid monetary policy changes they would probably be outvoted. If, then, the unity of the ECB's legal order supports its independence, so, maybe, does the polycentricity of its political order of many democracies.

Thus, we can now see the full force of the expectation that the ECB would be able to approximate decisions based on knowledge and legality, not value preferences, not political partisanship, not discretionary powers. Any value preferences would not matter in the long run. Any electoral cycle would be unlikely to dominate. Any powers would be just those needed to achieve the single purpose set out in its mandate without the bank having any discretion to weigh that purpose against others. The ECB, then, would have limited agency. As Fritz Scharpf has put it, the ECB was supposed to be a 'government of law based on the legitimacy of legality' and not 'of men' (Scharpf 2015: 392, see also Joerges 2014).

Responsibility. The idea that the ECB could largely base its decisions on its knowledge and mandate alone, nonetheless, left many puzzles unanswered: how to make the ECB independent enough to base its decisions on knowledge alone and yet be sure that it would use its expertise for no other purpose than delivering their mandate; how to hold the ECB to its mandate without circumscribing the independence it needed to deliver its mandate; and how, indeed, without compromising the ECB's independence, to preserve the ultimate rights publics must have in a democracy to control, recall or redesign the power of any public body?

The simplicity of the ECB's mandate could itself be expected to facilitate political and legal responsibility (Issing 1999: 508–509). Any member state – or any one citizen – has a legal right to bring a case questioning whether the ECB is acting within its mandate. Still, whether they believe arguments for independent central banking, whether they believe that a central bank's mandate is well defined, and whether they believe central banks have acted well within a mandate are all for publics to judge. Moreover, any one of a central bank's decisions must presumably be open to being used in an overall evaluation of its performance, again as the public or its representatives to see it. This, in turn, argues for continuous appraisal, or at least some agreed procedure of public evaluation that can be used at any one time. Assuming that the unelected must at some point justify themselves to the elected, theories of independent central banking need theories of representation, not just democratic theory.

Indeed, it is, arguably, a defect in the ECB's institutional design that representatives could have a larger role in defining the bank's own mandate without that compromising the bank's independence. What is crucial here is the distinction between goal independence where central banks can define their own objectives, and operational independence where they can only decide how to achieve goals delegated to them by a democratic process (Rogoff 1985b). The ECB has near complete goal independence, and not just operational independence. The Treaty merely stipulates that the ECB shall achieve price stability. Otherwise it leaves all important questions in the specification of that goal to the ECB itself: notably, the level of inflation to be targeted, as well as the foregoing questions of whether over-shooting and under-shooting are equally undesirable, and of how quickly the euro area should return to the target in the event of deviations from it.

But, even accepting things could be better, how is the public represented in arrangements for evaluating the ECB's mandate and its delivery; and with what implications for how the ECB's use of its knowledge is justified to publics and their representatives? One way of reconciling independence with some element of control is to delegate powers to a public body and then spread out surveillance of that body between several other institutions and actors in such a way that 'no one controls the agency and yet the agency is controlled' (Moe 1990: 143). In the case of the ECB multiple practical dependencies and reporting obligations could conceivably require it to justify itself and maintain the active co-operation of individual governments, the Commission, the Council of Ministers, the EP and national parliaments, and even the Court, without any one of these bodies being in a position to compromise the independence of the bank.

Two relationships within that overall structure of responsibility are of special importance. Jane Mansbridge (2009) distinguishes sanction and selection theories of representation. There are limits to how far elected representatives can sanction a central bank without that compromising its independence. But central bankers can be selected for their known motivation and expertise. Maybe the selection of the ECB's president and Executive Council by heads of government represented in the European Council deserves more attention. The alternative option – of central bankers choosing their president from their own number – was explicitly rejected. For sure, 'packing' is constrained by continuous turn-over of central bankers. Yet it is important to the kind of central banking that the Eurozone gets that the European Council chooses the ECB president. Had Axel Weber (president of the Bundesbank 2004–2012) and not Mario Draghi been appointed ECB president, the Eurozone would probably have had a different monetary policy since 2012.

However, in practice, the EP has become the main forum in which the ECB's delivery of its mandate is evaluated. Several points are important here. First, the ECB has itself sought a strong relationship with the EP (Amtenbrink and Van Duin 2009: 570). While the ECB has many reasons for wanting to maintain the confidence and active co-operation of many different actors within the Union's dispersed institutional order, it has, in practice, privileged the EP as the forum in which it justifies its decisions in public to representatives of the public. Although the Treaty only requires an annual hearing, the ECB's founding president, Wim Duisenberg, agreed to hearings every third month with the EP.

Indeed, the Bank has repeatedly acknowledged that expert bodies themselves need to seek relationships with representative institutions if they are to have the legitimacy, credibility, visibility or even the knowledge needed to function as epistocracies. It is wholly unsurprising that the ECB should find it difficult to justify itself as an epistocracy without also making plausible claims of its own for how its decisions are justifiable to processes of public parliamentary representation. Independent central banks need to turn both away and towards elected governments and parliaments: to form some relationships with them while avoiding others. Independent central banks need, as it were, to be exempted from democratic politics as a form of political competition, not from democracy as a structure of justification. Problems – such as 'time inconsistency' that make it hard to optimise policy over all time periods – only require the decoupling of monetary policy from electoral cycles. They hardly justify freeing central banks from the normal obligations in a democracy to justify decisions to publics. To the contrary, a public body that is not regularly re-authorised and controlled by a competition for the people's vote is all the more obliged to justify its decisions to the public, a point that the ECB has, again, repeatedly emphasised. However many other audiences they address, it would also seem important that independent central banks justify themselves to parliaments. Only parliaments are formally elected on a basis of universal and equal suffrage.

Second, the structure of the EU's political system allowed the ECB to form a relationship with the European Parliament of a kind an independent central bank would find hard to develop with most national parliaments. Precisely because there is no governing majority in the EP, the ECB can have what is termed a 'monetary dialogue' with the EP without coming under pressure orchestrated by a governing majority. For sure, ECB presidents have also appeared before committees of national parliaments. However, the ECB is mandated to deliver price stability for the Eurozone as a whole. Hence, the EP – rather than national parliaments – remains the representative body most likely to evaluate justifications for ECB decisions in ways compatible with its mandate. As the ECB (2017) has put it,

> Our monetary policy is for the eurozone as a whole […] A single monetary policy requires single accountability […] This ensures that everyone in Europe has the same opportunity to hold us to account through the same bodies, namely the EP as complemented by judicial review by the Court of Justice of the European Union.

Third the ECB has not simply adjusted to the EU's political order and representative institutions. The EP has also adjusted to the demands of holding a central bank to account. Using the EP as a forum for the public justification of ECB decisions depended also, of course, on the EP. As Fabian Amtenbrink (2002: 158) has put it, the value of a central bank justifying its decisions to a representative body depends on the quality of the 'questions asked' and not just the 'answers' given. Policy decisions cannot be made more authoritative by surviving 'trial by debate' (Manin 1995) where parliaments are not themselves critical, informed and representative of diverse opinions.

Perhaps in a hope of motivating effective internal participation and debate in its monetary dialogue with the ECB, the EP sought from the start of the ECB's work in 1998 to embed the latter in an ambitious interpretation of the Parliament's treaty rights. The EP billed its right to be consulted on the appointment of the executive board of the ECB as full 'confirmation proceedings'. Each nominee was required to fill in a written questionnaire and appear in person before the Economic and Monetary Affairs Committee of the Parliament (EMAC). A mechanism for requesting the withdrawal of nominees was also written into the EP's own rules of procedure. Beginning with the 'confirmation proceedings' the EP sought to press the ECB into ever closer specification of its targets, forecasts and policy rules. MEPs would then use the ECB's own previous statements as benchmarks to judge the ECB in each subsequent hearing. It was thus hoped that the ECB's relationship with the EP could be turned into a form of self-appraisal on the part of the Bank, made all the more devastating by the impossibility of dismissing it as a political interference, whose assumptions derived from anywhere else than the ECB's own independent central bankers themselves. It was finally made clear that grave or persistent failure to live up to the standards that the ECB had set itself would be grounds for the EP to use its treaty rights to request an unscheduled meeting with the EP. Such a move, the EP believed, would be publicly perceived as a 'summons' (European Parliament 1998; Lord 2003).

Yet there are problems in adjusting the EP to the work of the ECB as well as vice versa. To oversee the ECB, the EP has itself had to develop some knowledge of independent central banking in order to sustain a 'monetary dialogue' on equal terms with the ECB. This has been helped by the EP's general character of a 'working parliament' (Kurunmäki 2014; Tingsten 1938). In other words, the EP often responds to the challenge of holding complex modern epistocracies and bureaucracies to account by seeking to share in the knowledge and work of those bodies. David Beetham (1985) has summarised that 'Weberian' (Weber 1917 [1994]: 176–177) concept of parliamentary oversight as follows: 'Since knowledge forms the major source of bureaucratic power' the opportunity to share that knowledge 'is necessary' if parliaments are to control public 'decisions effectively.' Hence the EP has appointed a monetary expert panel and commissioned research from outside experts (Amtenbrink and Van Duin 2009). A possible danger, though, is that overcoming asymmetries of information that favour the ECB may require the EP to acquire a knowledge of central banking that makes it more of an expert body than a representative body (Lord 2018) in its monetary dialogue with the ECB. The monetary dialogue with the ECB may itself depend on a specialised division of labour within the parliament that means ECB decisions are rarely debated by all representatives representing all points of view.

A further problem is that justification of ECB decisions to the EP may be insufficient for parliamentary control without some means of sanctioning inadequate justifications. That said, there is no reason why the need for a central bank to justify itself to representative bodies should not be an important ingredient of what we know central banks care about most, namely, their credibility.

Bodies that depend on the credibility of their reputation are deeply constrained to maintain that reputation (Carpenter 2010), including, one supposes, by providing credible public justifications for their decisions to representative bodies.

In sum, then, assumptions about democracy, constitutionalism and representation were all important to the empowerment of the ECB. Perhaps the most optimistic, even Panglossian, interpretation might run as follows. The powers of the ECB would constitutionalise – within the hard-to-change treaties of the EU – a guarantee of the democratic process against political manipulation of monetary policy. The powers of the ECB would, then, themselves be constitutionally limited by the treaties to a narrowly defined responsibility for price stability. Indeed, the economic case for independent central banking implied the ECB would be an unusually innocent form of economic constitutionalism. The normal objection that economic constitutionalism removes value choices from the democratic political process would not apply. Since inexpert or electorally motivated monetary policy would change nothing in the real economy in the long run, publics would not give up value choices in delegating independent central banks. They would simply end up with less of a 'bad', namely, inflation.

Nor would a second objection to economic constitutionalism apply, namely, that it involves a kind of 'rule by ancestors' that locks subsequent cohorts of voters into economic institutions and policy choices that are hard to change. The ECB's mandate would, in a sense, be timeless: subsequent generations, and not just the present one, could be assumed to prefer an arrangement that simply promised lower inflation, given any one level of growth and employment that would, in any case, be determined exogenously to central banking. The ECB would, in turn, be required to justify its decisions to elected representatives whose only practical sanction would be to cast doubt on the credibility of assumptions whose credibility the ECB would, in any case, want to test in reasoned debate. So, what went wrong?

The elusiveness of purely epistemic central banking

When the ECB started work in 1998, the economist Charles Goodhart advised the European Parliament that, even if money is neutral in the long run, it did not strictly follow that decisions of a central bank could avoid all value preferences or discretionary judgements. A central bank would still need to ask the following questions: is it better to respond to unexpected inflation with a short sharp tightening of policy, or in a gentler but drawn-out way? Is the risk of inflation falling below its target as undesirable as the risk of it exceeding its target? Should a central bank alter monetary policy in response to particular prices that can affect the stability of entire financial systems – notably asset price-bubbles – even where there is no danger of inflation overall? It is not hard to see how these are matters of normative judgement and social preference that require more than expertise. However, provided the foregoing inconveniencies were marginal and temporary, money could still be managed without making long-term trade-offs of value. The idea that decisions could be based on knowledge of how to achieve an inflation target – and not on contestable preferences – would be intact.

The crisis, however, drastically undermined the idea that the ECB needs to exercise little power that goes beyond the use of its knowledge to achieve an inflation target that anyway entails no long-run trade-off with other values. Financial crises require central banks to be discretionary power-holders that are comfortable enough in that role to be credible in it. The crisis, arguably, only became a crisis because the ECB had to wrestle with assuming powers to backstop public debt for which it had neither clear mandate nor inclination. As Paul de Grauwe (2013: 164–165) has put it, 'probably the worst decision was made by the ECB early on in the crisis when it decided not to take on the responsibility of systematically providing liquidity to the government bond markets.' The crisis only stopped being a crisis when a new ECB president made the ultimate discretionary commitment to do 'whatever it takes' to save the euro. If a central bank can only guarantee a currency against self-fulfilling market panics where it is known to have unlimited ability to act as the lender of last resort to (solvent) banks and buy key financial assets such as government bonds, then it will unavoidably have to make discretionary decisions. To be a firefighter, it has to follow the fire and not just its mandate.

Indeed, the financial crisis forced the ECB into power-holding roles that went well beyond the use of its knowledge to deliver a mandate strictly confined to price stability. The ECB ended up making decisions that involved exercising the most fundamental of political powers: powers over who should be in government; powers over which member state democracies won out where they disagreed on reform of the Eurozone; powers over who should remain in the Eurozone, and on whose terms; and powers over property rights, the solvency of states, and the distribution of massive financial losses between citizens and financial institutions. These powers grew as the ECB had to decide whether it was going to give or withhold liquidity from particular banks in particular member states; and as the ECB became a 'guarantor of public debt' (de Grauwe 2016: 154) once it was conceded that it should buy bonds in the secondary market.

The Irish, Italian, Greek and Spanish cases all illustrate just how far the crisis drew the ECB into drastic exercises of political power. By forcing Ireland to bail out its banks in 2009, rather than restructure them, the ECB determined that Irish taxpayers, rather than banks, would carry losses (Sandbu 2015). By cutting off liquidity to Greece in 2015, the ECB resolved the stand-off between Greece and creditor member states in favour of the latter. Then, of course, there were the famous letters from ECB President Jean-Claude Trichet to the prime ministers of Italy (Berlusconi) and Spain (Zapatero). As Agustín Menéndez (2012: 59) puts it, the letters made 'explicit the kind of reforms the ECB regarded as necessary within days of it expanding its securities market programme to Spanish and Italian debt'. Yet, leaving aside whether the ECB arbitrarily dominated member states in any of these cases, it is questionable whether it can avoid any need to make tough calls in a crisis. The ECB has a duty to publics to avoid losses on financial assets. It also needs to support the financial system without encouraging irresponsible risks by making it safer to take those risks (moral hazard).

The crisis also revealed a latent power-game between the ECB in its role as monetary policymaker and the collective of Eurozone governments in their role as fiscal policymakers. Any system of independent central banking divides responsibility for monetary and fiscal policy. That creates a continuum of possibilities between monetary policy dominated by fiscal policy and fiscal policy dominated by monetary policy (Sargent and Wallace 1981). Where a currency area lies on the continuum is not only a matter of its institutional design but also of strategic choices and interactions between monetary and fiscal/political authorities, which can try to push one another into unwanted policy outcomes (Henning 2016). The euro crisis was, arguably, deepened in its early stages, by a stand-off in which eurozone governments tried to force the ECB into monetary accommodation and buying government debt, while the ECB tried to force Eurozone governments into fiscal consolidation and structural reforms (Henning 2016).

However, as well as exercising powers over whole national democracies and allocating huge losses between member states, and as well as slipping into a monetary/fiscal power-game with all member states, the ECB also ended up exercising significant powers over the life-chances of individual citizens (Höegenauer and Howarth 2016). For example, the Zapatero letter indicated the ECB would support 'Spanish banks if and only if' (Stiglitz 2016: 155) changes were made to labour market legislation. Yet if in backstopping the financial system it can also influence matters such as labour regulation, it follows that the ECB has some power over what John Rawls (2003: 5–8) terms the overall structure of laws, public policies and opportunities under which people live their lives, not to mention how 'fairly' that overall structure then 'hangs together' as an overall 'scheme of social co-operation' (ibid).

Is there any way back to an ECB that just uses its knowledge to deliver a mandate given by others? Overly optimistic assumptions about the neutrality of money – and therefore the innocence of independent central banking – are often thought to be associated with overly optimistic assumptions about economic knowledge and behaviour in general. If not blessed of perfect rationality and foresight, market participants are largely assumed to make the best use of the knowledge available to them. Hence efficient market hypothesis (EMH) predicts that, on average, better informed economic actors and behaviours win out, until the economy performs much as it would have done with perfect knowledge. As it happens, many of those influential in the creation of the euro identified what was wrong with EMH and why the markets would therefore fail to do such useful things as aligning member states' fiscal policy with the ECB's monetary policy. Alexandre Lamfalussy told the Delors Committee, 'It would not be wise to rely on the free functioning of financial markets to iron out the differences in fiscal behaviour between member states. The interest premium to be paid by a high deficit member country would be unlikely to be very large, since market participants would act on the assumption that EMU solidarity would prevent the bankruptcy of the deficit country' (quoted in James 2012: 249).

Yet the limitations of EMH do tell us why any European Central Bank would probably have to exercise vastly more power than any required in just using expertise to meet a simple mandate to control inflation. EMH implied, first, that fiscal indiscipline would be priced into the borrowing costs of individual governments responsible for any laxity, and, second, that central banks only need to be known to have a credible commitment to keeping 'inflation low' (de Grauwe 2013: 157) for markets to have all the information they needed to ensure the stability of the overall financial system. The first implied the ECB would not need to use monetary policy to discipline governments, the second that it would not need to supervise financial markets. The ECB could, to repeat, just get on with delivering its tightly circumscribed and politically given mandate to keep inflation low. However, one piece of information the markets might price all too efficiently was, as partially suggested by the Lamfalussy quotation, the probability that neither governments which issued too much debt nor banks which bought too much debt would be allowed to go bankrupt. Hence markets would not necessarily discipline governments into an optimum (or even a sustainable) mix between monetary and fiscal policy. As for hopes that the ECB would be able to avoid a role in supervising financial systems, it is endemic to financial systems that they will – in the absence, inter alia, of central bank supervision – end up producing 'booms and busts culminating in banking crises' (de Grauwe 2013). This is simply because the overall level of systemic risk is unknowable to any market participant. Indeed, Paul Tucker (2018) has argued that central banks are necessarily a part of what he calls the fiscal state and the emergency state. They cannot avoid contributing to the financial sustainability of states or to backstopping financial systems in emergencies.

Nor can the problem of the 'policy-mix' – between the ECB's monetary decisions and the aggregate of the fiscal policies of Eurozone governments (Enderlein 2006; Foresti 2015: 533) – be solved if the ECB concentrates only on delivering its own mandate without making more discretionary political judgements required for co-ordination with other authorities. Wim Buiter (2006: 2–3) explains the difficulty: 'Where communication, co-operation and co-ordination between the central bank' and budgetary authorities 'are seriously impaired, central bank independence can do more harm than good. The costs of non-co-operation are apt to be especially serious if the dominant macro-economic problem is unwanted deflation'. Moreover, the crisis deflated the ECB's knowledge claims at the same time as demonstrating that it may need to exercise powers that go well beyond use of technical knowledge to deliver a simple and restricted mandate. Many decisions taken during the crisis divided the bank's Governing Council. Before the crisis, the Governing Council took many decisions without voting at all (Issing 2008b: 153). Since the crisis it has been unable to make several decisions without taking votes, including votes that famously outvoted the Bundesbank (Plickert and Steltzner 2018). That, of course, is a clear indicator that central banking is not based on knowledge that is so unproblematic that any two central bankers will mostly use it in the same way. To the contrary, monetary policy is likely to involve allocating values, employing judgements, exercising discretion and making mistakes, and not only in emergency roles but also in interacting with fiscal authorities to determine policy-mixes. ECB has never been – and could never be – a pure form of 'rule of the knowers' (Estlund 2008: 7).

Conclusion

I began by arguing that understanding of where knowledge and democracy may require one another would benefit from studies of attempts to combine the two in actual processes of institutional design and evolution. What has the case of the ECB, in very brief summary, told us?

I start with lessons for where democracy may require knowledge. Time-inconsistency problems identified by arguments for independent central banking broaden our understanding of why democracies may not be able to make some choices at all unless they delegate some decisions away from forms of democratic politics whose operation over particular time periods – such as specific electoral cycles – makes it unlikely that an outcome can be achieved over another period.

It seems to me that is an insight of foremost importance. But why limit it to central banking. It is not hard to imagine other predicaments in democratic politics where there might be time-inconsistency problems (Blinder 1997). Surely there are conflicts between short- and long-term incentives in a whole number of common resource problems where democratic majorities of today can deplete some finite resource to the great cost of democratic majorities of tomorrow? Such predicaments afflict many aspects of the public finances and any instance where one generation can over-exploit finite opportunities to create debt to saddle future generations with financial burdens. Maybe, indeed, climate change raises at least as many time-inconsistency problems as independent central banking. So, should democracies generalise delegation to those with some knowledge of trade-offs between the present and the future to more cases of time-inconsistency problems? If, on the other hand, we are shy of making that a general practice in our democracies, what is to justify only doing it in the case of central banking?

Perhaps something of an answer lies in what I have called epistemic-democratic-monetary constitutionalism. Democracies may want to delegate monetary policy away from standard processes of political competition that depend on electoral cycles so that governments cannot abuse monetary policy to improve their own chances of re-election. If, however, democracies choose to constitutionalise central bank independence, it would be odd not also to constitutionalise some specification of how central banks are to use their knowledge. Democracies can presumably only justify delegations to knowers where they themselves are clear on what it is about knowledge and the use of knowledge that can justify that delegation. If some constitutionalisation of monetary policy is ever required to prevent abuse of the democratic process itself, it is presumably also a requirement of any delegation that it should not itself be open to abuse of the democratic process. It should not go beyond the independent use of knowledge to achieve just those goals that publics believe justify the independent use of knowledge.

As seen, it was thought sufficient to meet that requirement that the ECB should be established under a simple mandate to control inflation in a world in which decisions about money are neutral – and therefore without value trade-offs – in the long run. That assumption may itself be contestable. It is also insufficient where the ECB has to unavoidably exercise many other powers – to ensure overall stability of the financial system and an acceptable 'policy-mix' between its monetary policies and fiscal policies of governments – that go well beyond a simple mandate to control inflation. That, however, need not invalidate arguments for independent central banking. Independence might be amply justified by time-inconsistency problems and by a need to constrain governments from abusing monetary policy to influence their own re-election even if 'perfectionist' assumptions about the neutrality of money are implausible.

However, this is what does follow: if central banking is unavoidably a matter of power and value preferences, then its democratic control is also unavoidable. Citizens in democracies must obviously have some way of controlling as equals all powers that are exercised over them if they are to count as ruling themselves. It is not even clear that giving up rights of democratic control can itself be democratically legitimate (Eriksen 2019). So, yes, independent central banks must, in democracies, be democratically justified epistocracies and not purely technical ones (Holst 2011: 6–7).

Independent central banking cannot be a justified exception to democratic politics. Arguments for independent central banking can only restrict what forms democratic politics and control can take. Both time-inconsistency and democratic-monetary–constitutionalism arguments require monetary policy to be made independently of any electoral cycle. For sure, that excludes a lot. It excludes monetary policy from the main organising principle of mass democracy, namely, a competition for the people's vote (Schattsneider 1960; Schumpeter 1942).

However, as seen, exempting central banks from normal processes of political competition cannot be an argument for exempting them from normal standards of public justification in a democracy. Independent central banking needs to be embedded in overall democratic politics of public justification. That is, in turn, part an institutional challenge and part an epistemic one. What institutions can secure public justification of knowledge used in central banking? And how can we know when our institutions have delivered those justifications? I suspect that academic and public debates are only beginning to identify what all this might require. Now that we know how illusory is a search for a form of central banking that avoids fundamental exercises of political powers, how should we organise a form of democratic policies and debate that gives central banks some ex ante guidance and ex post critique of its use of those powers (Lord 2019)? How should we secure some sort of sanction – perhaps, through loss of reputation or credibility – that is itself compatible with justifications for central banking and does not undermine them? How, to recall the arguments from Mill, Habermas and Talisse with which the chapter opened, should we ensure that different arguments for different monetary policies are tested against one another, and that all points of view have equal access to that deliberation?

References

Amtenbrink, F. (2002) 'On the Legitimacy and Democratic Accountability of the European Central Bank: Legal Arrangements and Practical Experiences', in A. Arnull and D. Wincott (eds.) *Accountability and Legitimacy in the European Union* (pp. 147–163). Oxford: Oxford University Press.

Amtenbrink, F. and van Duin, K. (2009) 'The European Central Bank before the European Parliament: Theory and Practice after Ten Years of Monetary Dialogue', *European Law Review*, 34(4): 561–583.

Barro, R. and Gordon, D. (1983) 'Rules, Discretion and Reputation in a Model of Monetary Policy', *Journal of Monetary Economics*, 12(1): 101–121.

Beetham, D. (1985) *Max Weber and the Theory of Modern Politics*. Cambridge: Polity Press.

Beetham, D. (2013) *The Legitimation of Power*. Basingstoke: Palgrave.

Bickerton, C. and Accetti, C.I. (2017) 'Populism and technocracy: Opposites or complements?' *Critical Review of International and Social Philosophy*, 20(2): 186–206.

Blinder, A. (1997 November/December) 'Is Government too Political?' *Foreign Affairs*, 76: 115.

Bohman, J. (2007) *Democracy across Borders from Demos to Demoi*. Cambridge: MIT Press.

Buiter, W. (2006) 'The Sense and Nonsense of Maastricht Revisited: What Have We Learned about Stabilization in Monetary Union?' *Journal of Common Market Studies*, 44(3): 687–710.

Carpenter, D. (2010) *Reputation and Power: Organizational Image and Pharmaceutical Regulation at the FDA*. Princeton, NJ: Princeton University Press.

Dyson, K. (2000) *The Politics of the Euro-Zone, Stability or Breakdown?* Oxford: Oxford University Press.

Dyson, K. and Featherstone, K. (1999) *The Road to Maastricht*. Oxford: Oxford University Press.

Enderlein, H. (2006) 'The Euro and Political Union: Do Economic Spillovers from Monetary Integration Affect the Legitimacy of EMU?' *Journal of European Public Policy*, 13(7): 1133–1146.

Eriksen, E.O. (2019) *Contesting Political Differentiation: European Division and the Problem of Dominance*. London: Palgrave Macmillan.

Estlund, D. (2008) *Democratic Authority, a Philosophical Framework*. Princeton, NJ: Princeton University Press.

European Central Bank (2017, March 30) 'Central Bank Independence Revisited', Keynote address by Y. Mersch, member of the Executive Board at the Symposium on Building the Financial System of the Twenty-first century, Frankfurt Am Main. Available at: https://www.ecb.europa.eu/press/key/date/2017/html/sp170330.en.html.

European Parliament (1998) *Resolution on Democratic Accountability in the Third Phase of EMU* (The Randzio-Plath report). Brussels: European Parliament.

Ferguson, N. (2008) *The Ascent of Money*. Harmondsworth: Penguin.

Frattiani, M. and Von Hagen, J. (1991) *The European Monetary System and European Monetary Union*. San Francisco, CA: Westview Press.

Foresti, P. (2015) 'Monetary and Debt-concerned Fiscal Policies Interactions in Monetary Unions', *Journal of International Economics and Economic Policy*, 12(3): 541–552.

Gaus, G. (2011) 'On Seeking the Truth (Whatever That Is) through Democracy: Estlund's Case for the Qualified Epistemic Claim', *Ethics*, 121(2): 270–300.

Grauwe de, P. (2013) 'The Political Economy of the Euro', *Annual Review of Political Science*, 16(1): 153–170.

Grauwe de, P. (2016) 'The Legacy of the Eurozone Crisis and How to Overcome It', *Journal of Empirical Finance*, 39: 147–155.

Gros, D. and Thygesen, N. (1998) *European Monetary Integration*. Harlow: Addison, Wesley, Longman.

Habermas, J. (2003) *Truth and Justification*. Cambridge: Polity.

Habermas, J. (2015) *The Lure of Technocracy*. Cambridge: Polity.

Harris, S. (1930) *The Assignats*. Cambridge, MA: Harvard University Press.

Henning, R.C. (2016) 'The ECB as a Strategic Actor: Central Banking in a Politically Fragmented Monetary Union', in J. Caporoso and M. Rhodes (eds.) *The Political and Economic Dynamics of the Eurozone Crisis* (pp. 167–199). Oxford: Oxford University Press.

Hodson, D. (2011) *Governing the Euro Area in Good Times and Bad*. Oxford: Oxford University Press.

Högenauer, A.L. and Howarth, D. (2016) Unconventional Monetary Policies and the European Central Bank's Problematic Democratic Legitimacy, *Journal of Public Law*, 17(2): 1–24.

Holst, C. (2011, October 20–22) 'Epistocracy, Conceptual Clarifications'. Paper Presented to Workshop on 'Epistemic Democracy in Practice', Yale University.

Howarth, D. and Loedl, P. (2005) *The European Central Bank, the New European Leviathan*. Basingstoke: Palgrave.

Issing, O. (1999) 'The Eurosystem: Transparent and Accountable or "Willem in Euroland"', *Journal of Common Market Studies*, 37(3): 503–519.

Issing, O. (2008a) 'The Euro: Does a Currency Need a State?' *International Finance*, 11(3): 297–310.

Issing, O. (2008b) *The Birth of the Euro*. Cambridge: Cambridge University Press.

James, H. (2012) *Making the European Monetary Union*. Harvard, MA: Belknap Press.

Joerges, C. (2014) 'Brother, Can You Paradigm?' *International Journal of Constitutional Law*, 12(3): 769–785.

Kurunmäki, J. (2014) 'Rhetoric against Rhetoric: Swedish Parliamentarianism and the Interwar Crisis of Democracy', in K. Palonen, J.M. Rosales and T. Turkka (eds.) *The Parliamentary Politics of Dissensus: Parliament in Debate* (pp. 171–199). Santander: Cantabria University Press and McGraw Hill Interamericana de Espána.

Kydland, F. and Prescott, E. (1977) 'Rules Rather than Discretion: The Inconsistency of Optimal Plans', *Journal of Political Economy*, 85(3): 473–492.

Locke, J. (1924 [1690]) *Two Treatises of Government*. London: Everyman.

Lord, C. (2003) 'The European Parliament in the Economic Governance of the EU', *Journal of Common Market Studies*, 41(2): 249–267.

Lord, C. (2017) 'Exploring the Connection between Knowledge and Democracy', In M. Gora, C. Holst and M. Warat (eds.) *Expertisation and Democracy in Europe* (pp. 17–32). Abingdon: Routledge.

Lord, C. (2018) 'The European Parliament: A Working Parliament without a Public?' *Journal of Legislative Studies*, 24(1): 34–50.

Lord, C. (2019) 'No Epistocracy without Representation. The Case of the European Central Bank', *European Politics and Society*, 20(1): 1–15.

Lucas, R. (1972) 'Expectations and the Neutrality of Money', *Journal of Economic Theory*, 4(1): 103–124.

Manin, B. (1995) *Principes du Gouvernement Représentatif* [Principles of Representative Government]. Paris: Calman-Lévy.

Mansbridge, J. (2009) 'A "Selection Model" of Political Representation', *Journal of Political Philosophy*, 17(4): 369–398.

May, S.C. (2011) 'Book Review of Talisse's Democracy and Moral Conflict', *Ethics*, 121: 685–690.

Menéndez, A. (2012, May 15) 'European Crisis'. Paper Presented to ARENA Seminar. Oslo: ARENA Centre for European Studies.

Mill, J.S. (1972 [1861]) *Utilitarianism, On Liberty and Considerations on Representative Government*, London: Dent.

Moe, T. (1990) 'Political Institutions: The Neglected Side of the Story', *Journal of Law, Economics and Organisation*, 6(special issue): 213–253.

Moravcsik, A. (1998) *The Choice for Europe: Social Purpose and State Power from Messina to Maastricht*. Ithaca, NY: Cornell University Press.

Müller, J.W. (2017) *What Is Populism?* London: Penguin.

Padoa-Schioppa, T. (1987) *Efficiency, Stability and Equity: A Strategy for the Evolution of the Economic System of the European Community*. Oxford: Oxford University Press.

Plato (c. 360 B.C. [1955]) *The Republic*. Harmondsworth: Penguin.

Plickert, P. and Steltzner, H. (2018, January 17) Das Anleihekaufprogramm soll 2018 auslaufen, *Frankfurter Allgemeine Wirtschaft*. Available at: https://www.faz.net/aktuell/wirtschaft/bundesbank-chef-jens-weidmann-im-gespraech-15401992.html. (accessed 16 December 2019).

Rawls, J. (2003) *Justice as Fairness: A Restatement*. Cambridge, MA: Harvard University Press.

Richardson, H. (2003) *Democratic Autonomy*. Oxford: Oxford University Press.

Rodrik, D. (2011) *The Globalization Paradox: Democracy and the Future of the World Economy*. New York: WW Norton.

Rogoff, K. (1985a) 'Can Exchange Rate Stability Be Achieved without Monetary Convergence? Evidence from the EMS', *European Economic Review*, 28(1–2): 93–115.

Rogoff, K. (1985b) 'The Optimal Degree of Commitment to an Intermediate Monetary Target', *Quarterly Journal of Economics*, 100(4): 1169–1189.

Ruggie, J. (1982) 'International Regimes, Transactions and Change: Embedded Liberalism in the Postwar Economic Order', *International Organization*, 36(2): 379–415.

Sandbu, M. (2015) *Europe's Orphan, the Future of the Euro and the Politics of Debt*. Princeton, NJ: Princeton University Press.

Sargent, T. and Wallace, N. (1981) 'Some Unpleasant Monetarist Arithmetic', *Federal Reserve Bank of Minneapolis Quarterly Review*, 5(3): 1–18.

Scharpf, F. (2015) 'After the Crash. A Perspective on European Multi-Level Democracy', *European Law Journal*, 21(3): 384–405.

Schattsneider, E. (1960) *The Semi-Sovereign People: A Realist's View of Democracy in America*. New York: Holt.

Schumpeter, J. (1942) *Capitalism, Socialism and Democracy*. New York: Harper.

Sen. A. (2002) *Rationality and Freedom*. Cambridge, MA: Belknap Press of Harvard University Press.

Stiglitz, J. (2016) *The Euro and Its Threat to the Future of Europe*. London: Allen Lane.

Stiglitz, J. and Weiss, A. (1981) 'Credit Rationing in Markets with Imperfect Information', *American Economic Review*, 71(3): 393–410.

Talisse, R. (2009) *Democracy and Moral Conflict*. Cambridge: Cambridge University Press.

Tingsten, H. (1938) 'Nordisk Demokrati', *Nordens kalender*, 9: 41–50.
Tucker, P. (2018) *Unelected Power: The Quest for Legitimacy in Central Banking and the Regulatory State*. Princeton, NJ: Princeton University Press.
Verdun, A. (1999) 'The Role of the Delors Committee in the Creation of EMU: An Epistemic Community?' *Journal of European Public Policy*, 6(2): 308–328.
Weale, A. (2018) *The Will of the People: A Modern Myth*. Cambridge: Polity Press.
Weber, M. (1917[1994]) 'Parliament and Government in Germany under a New Political Order', in P. Lassman and R. Speirs (eds.) *Weber: Political writings* (pp. 130–271). Cambridge: Cambridge University Press.
Weiler, J. (1997) 'Legitimacy and Democracy of EU Governance', in G. Edwards and A. Pijpers (eds.) *The Politics of European Union Treaty Reform* (pp. 249–287). London: Pinter.
Wray, L.R. (2019) *From the State Theory of Money to Modern Money*. Oxford: Oxford University Press.

5

REPUTATIONAL THREATS AND DEMOCRATIC RESPONSIVENESS OF REGULATORY AGENCIES

Tobias Bach, Marlene Jugl, Dustin Köhler and Kai Wegrich

Introduction[1]

This chapter studies decision-making behaviour of independent regulatory agencies. Theoretical accounts of delegation to regulatory agencies emphasise that potential losses of political accountability of regulators are traded off against potential gains in regulatory efficiency. The theory of credible commitment suggests that independent (non-majoritarian) regulatory agencies are more effective in regulating markets than organisations under direct political control because of their long-term orientation (as opposed to short-term, myopic decisions by office-seeking politicians) and because of their expertise and professionalism (Gilardi 2008; Majone 1997). The independent regulatory agency model hence builds on the idea of output-legitimacy, as opposed to the conventional model of input-legitimacy in which bureaucratic organisations are located at the end of a chain of delegation from the electorate to legislators and governments (Strøm 2000).

The institutional architecture of the regulatory state has fuelled debates about the problems of democratic accountability of regulators and about alternative modes of accountability (Bach and Wegrich 2016; Scott 2000). The bottom line is that regulatory agencies operate in a political context and are subject to multiple accountability relations. Although political institutions may be constrained in directly controlling regulatory agencies, the latter operate in a political context and need to demonstrate their benefit to a diverse set of stakeholders, including elected politicians. The relationship between public organisations and multiple stakeholders is at the core of bureaucratic reputation theory (Carpenter and Krause 2012; Maor 2015). This theory suggests that audiences hold distinct views about public organisations, and that reputation-sensitive organisations try to cultivate favourable reputations among relevant audiences. Those reputations among relevant stakeholders are essential because they are a source of power vis-à-vis other actors and ultimately ensure organisational survival.

The chapter draws on bureaucratic reputation theory to conceptualise the relationship of regulators with their broader context. More specifically, it builds on the idea that regulatory agencies use accountability relationships to cultivate distinct reputations among multiple actors holding those agencies to account (Busuioc and Lodge 2017). In line with a growing body of research, we use regulatory agencies' communicative behaviour to study reputation management (Bach et al. 2019; Bach et al. 2021; Busuioc and Rimkutė 2019; Carpenter 2010a; Maor et al. 2013; Moschella and Pinto 2019). In empirical terms, the chapter assesses whether independent regulatory agencies respond through communicative action to negative public judgements ('threats') which are reported in the news media. The main assumption is that regulatory agencies are well aware of their dependency on a supportive environment. They are therefore more likely to react to negative public judgements targeting fundamental aspects of their institutional identity, rather than those aspects that are of marginal importance to their distinct reputational profile. Moreover, we argue that despite being independent from direct political control, regulatory agencies are well aware of the political context in which they are operating. We therefore suggest that regulatory agencies will try to accommodate political actors' criticism and are more likely to respond to political actors' negative judgements relative to other actors' negative judgements.

The chapter uses data from a systematic media analysis covering the financial regulatory agency and the utility regulator in Germany in a period from 1998 until 2016. These are prominent examples of regulatory agencies with multiple responsibilities and with high levels of autonomy (Ruffing 2015). We coded all articles in *Frankfurter Allgemeine Zeitung*, a major broadsheet newspaper with extensive coverage of business affairs, which included a positive or a negative judgement on these two regulators. We also coded the source of the judgement, as well as which reputational dimension was targeted, and whether the regulatory agency responded to the threat (as reported in the same article). This allows us to assess regulators' reputational profiles and whether their response patterns vary systematically with the reputational dimension and the type of actors from which reputational threats originate.

The next section outlines our theoretical argument. Then we present the motives for our case selection and describe our data collection and methodology. After that, we provide an empirical analysis of regulatory agencies' communicative responses to reputational threats, followed by a discussion and conclusion.

Analytical framework: accountability, reputational threats, and communicative responses of regulatory agencies

This section develops a theoretical argument about the reputation-seeking behaviour of regulatory agencies from the distinct perspective of public accountability.

The model of independent regulatory agencies has become a hallmark of the regulatory state (Gilardi 2008). The main argument for making regulatory agencies independent from direct political control has its foundations in economic theory. From this perspective, independent regulators are a technology of credible commitment for politicians to a given set of policy objectives. In order to ensure the trust of market actors in regulatory decisions, politicians delegate powers to regulators, which operate independently of the political election cycle. Hence, this model has an inbuilt scepticism against the ability of democratically elected politicians to effectively regulate market activities (Roberts 2010). The political independence of regulatory agencies thus ensures that regulatory policies are stable over time, which according to the theory of credible commitment would not be the case if regulatory decisions were in the hands of politicians, who are assumed to have time-inconsistent policy preferences (Majone 1997).

The problem of politically independent regulators is that conventional models of democratic accountability, which are based on the parliamentary chain of delegation and control, consider independent agencies as being potentially out of (democratic) control. A main endeavour of political science studies of regulatory agencies has therefore been to understand 'accountability in the regulatory state' (Scott 2000). Here, we can only briefly sketch some of the challenges of accountability in the regulatory state (see Bach and Wegrich 2016 for a summary). A first characteristic is 'the problem of many hands', which denotes that there are multiple actors involved in providing public services, making it more difficult to clearly identify responsibilities and to hold actors to account (relative to the provision of public services under the auspices of the government). A second characteristic is a multitude of account-holders (forums) which can demand information from another actor (account-giver) and may pass a significant judgement on the latter (Bovens 2007). This situation has been labelled 'the problem of many eyes'. A main implication is that regulators are accountable to multiple actors using distinct criteria of accountability (legal, financial, procedural etc.) and hence are under control, even though no single actor effectively controls the regulator (Scott 2000).

The literature has identified multiple challenges to ensuring accountability in the regulatory state. First, a major challenge for regulatory regimes is to strike a balance between accountability overload on the one hand, where regulatory agencies are confronted with multiple and potentially conflicting external demands, and accountability deficits on the other, where distinct aspects of regulatory agencies' activities fall between the cracks of different account-holders' distinct focus (Bach and Wegrich 2016). A related argument suggests accountability relations suffer from problems of 'drifting principals' who do not take their roles vis-à-vis regulatory agencies seriously (Schillemans and Busuioc 2015). This turns the conventional perspective on political control upside down, which highlights that regulatory agencies (and bureaucratic organisations more generally) have a tendency to develop into 'runaway bureaucracies' that undermine the policy preferences of their political principals (or, when looking at accountability relations, will try to avoid being held accountable) (McCubbins et al. 1987). Second, independent regulatory agencies (and other non-majoritarian institutions) have been accused of producing technocratic decisions that fail to account for the legitimate interests of affected stakeholders (Roberts 2010). Third, complex regulatory regimes pose particular challenges in terms of pinning down responsibility for policy failures, as they diffuse blame for such failures among multiple actors and open up possibilities of mutual blame attribution among politicians, regulators, and regulatees (Bach and Wegrich 2019).

This chapter makes an empirical contribution towards understanding how independent regulatory agencies account for their activities when faced with public judgements. In terms of understanding the relationship between (independent) regulatory agencies and relevant stakeholders (or audiences), we are confronted with a 'paradox of autonomy' (Bach 2015). This paradox suggests that autonomisation increases, rather than decreases public organisations' accountability load. The higher the formal autonomy of public organisations, the higher and the more complex the demands of accountability (i.e. explaining behaviour towards relevant account-holders) they face. In other words, regulatory agencies' independence from direct political control increases, rather than decreases, the importance of paying attention to relevant audiences and of being accountable, that is, explaining behaviour.

This chapter uses bureaucratic reputation theory to analyse how independent regulatory agencies respond to complex demands of public accountability. Bureaucratic reputation theory conceives of public agencies as political actors in their own right. In this perspective, the power of public agencies does not result from the delegation of formal powers by politicians, but from the agencies' own cultivation of favourable reputations among relevant audiences (Carpenter 2010b). This theory points to the importance of understanding bureaucratic behaviour as emerging from a relationship with a broad set of audiences, rather than focussing on the relationship with the political principal. A basic assumption of bureaucratic reputation theory is that reputation is multi-dimensional (Busuioc and Lodge 2017; Busuioc and Rimkutė 2019; Carpenter and Krause 2012). The theory suggests that organisations develop a distinct reputational profile, highlighting some reputational dimensions rather than others. In terms of public accountability, this means that account-giving will be biased in the sense that regulatory agencies are more likely to render account in areas that are the core of their reputation relative to non-core areas of reputation. From a reputational perspective, the rendering of public accountability is an opportunity for public agencies to cultivate favourable reputations (Busuioc and Lodge 2017). Accordingly, organisations will 'respond with higher degrees of attention toward their audiences' signals' (Busuioc and Lodge 2017: 95) if the latter target the core reputational profile of the organisation.

Public organisations may cultivate a distinct reputation in multiple ways. Among others, scholars have uncovered reputation-seeking behaviour through the use of public participation in decision-making (Moffitt 2010); the speed of decision-making (Carpenter 2002); changes in organisational outputs and policy instruments (Hinterleitner and Sager 2019; Maor and Sulitzeanu-Kenan 2016); changes in regulatory enforcement activities (Carpenter 2010a); the prioritisation among multiple tasks (Gilad 2015); and priority-setting in leadership decisions (Bækkeskov 2017). This chapter follows a body of scholarship that focusses on agencies' communicative behaviour as a means of reputation-seeking.

Public organisations can use communicative behaviour to cultivate a favourable reputation in different ways. For instance, they may change the kind of activities or qualities they emphasise in their proactive communication such as top leadership speeches (Carpenter 2010a; Moschella and Pinto 2019) or regular reporting (Busuioc and Rimkutė 2019). Another type of regulatory agencies' communicative behaviour consists of reactions ('talk') or non-reactions ('silence') to negative public judgements. Maor et al. (2013) address this type of behaviour explicitly and show how a financial regulator is more likely to react to public judgements targeting functional areas for which it enjoys a comparatively weak reputation, whereas it tends to remain silent on functional areas where it enjoys a strong reputation. In a study of a financial regulator, Bach et al. (2021) demonstrate that regulatory agencies display differential responses to public judgements depending on the reputational dimension that is targeted. Gilad et al. (2015) study the substance of communicative responses to public judgements, showing how a regulator responds differently to judgements on overregulation as opposed to lenient regulation. Bach et al. (2019) study communicative responses to public judgements by financial regulators before, during, and after the financial crisis. They find that financial regulators are primarily exposed to performative threats and show different response patterns to such threats across countries. This chapter follows the approach by Maor et al. (2013), Bach et al. (2019), and Bach et al. (2021) by distinguishing between communicative responses and non-responses to reputational threats. Hence, whether a regulatory agency responds to a reputational threat (understood as a negative public judgement) or not will be used as an indicator of reputation-seeking behaviour.

The basic theoretical expectation is that regulatory agencies will exhibit differential response patterns to public judgements. This chapter focusses on negative public judgements or reputational threats, building on the main analytical focus of bureaucratic reputation theory: 'look at the audience, and look at the threats' (Carpenter 2010a: 832, italics in original). We therefore expect that regulators will exhibit distinct regulatory profiles and differential reactions to threats depending on the reputational dimension that is being targeted. The key reputational dimensions include an organisation's ability to achieve the organisation's core mission (performative reputation); its compliance to existing rules of decision-making and due process (procedural reputation); its status as a guardian of important societal values (moral reputation); and its technical expertise and organisational capacity (technical reputation) (Busuioc and Rimkutė 2019; Carpenter and Krause 2012). A fifth dimension concerns the organisation's internal management, such as the efficient use of resources (processual reputation) (Boon et al. 2019).

As outlined above, a core argument for delegating decision-making powers to regulatory agencies was their expertise. Therefore, we expect technical reputation to be a key component of regulatory agencies' reputational profile (Busuioc and Rimkutė 2019). Moreover, following the logic of output-based legitimacy, we expect regulatory agencies to cultivate their performative reputation. Finally, the independent regulatory agency model also implies the unbiased implementation of regulatory policies towards regulatees. For instance, this is particularly relevant for the regulation of infrastructure sectors with incumbent regulators (former state monopolists). Hence, we would also expect regulators to cultivate a reputational profile in terms of procedural reputation. That said, we cannot know beforehand which of these dimensions are at the core of a single regulatory agency's reputational profile (Bach et al. 2021) and we therefore have to formulate general expectations about differential agency responses to threats targeting different dimensions. We expect regulatory agencies to react differently to public accountability demands depending on whether those demands are central to the agencies' reputational profile, and whether the agency has a weak or a favourable reputation concerning a given reputational dimension (Bach et al. 2021; Busuioc and Lodge, 2017; Maor et al. 2013). We suggest the following *reputational profile hypothesis*.

> H1: Independent regulatory agencies are (1) more likely to react to negative public judgements targeting reputational dimensions which are central to their mission and for which they enjoy a weak reputation and (2) less likely to respond to negative public judgements targeting reputational dimensions that are peripheral to their mission.

Another basic assumption is that organisational reputation is located among multiple audiences, and that some audiences are more relevant for the organisation than others are. Accordingly, we suggest that regulators' responses to threats originating from different kinds of actors are a valid indicator of their internal calculus about these actors' relative importance. In terms of democratic responsiveness – the overarching theme of this volume – such an analysis also allows us to gauge whether regulatory agencies respond differently to threats originating from political actors relative to other types of actors. Agencies' differential responsiveness to various types of actors is well documented in the literature. For instance, Carpenter (2002) shows that the time-to-approval of medical drugs by the US regulator FDA is a function of public attention and the number and wealth of disease-specific interest organisations. Focussing on reputation-seeking through communicative behaviour, Maor et al. (2013) and Bach et al. (2021) show that a regulator's inclination to respond to public judgements is higher for politically powerful actors over which the regulator has little influence, compared to other types of actors. Hence, this body of scholarship suggests that regulatory agencies are relatively more inclined to respond to audiences that have a credible potential to undermine their reputation (and, in consequence, their autonomy).

We suggest that independent regulatory agencies are more likely to respond to negative public judgements by political actors relative to other actors. While being independent from direct political control, regulatory agencies have to be responsive to their environment in order to be able to attract continuous support (e.g. financial resources) to the agency. In this sense, political actors are powerful as they ultimately decide about regulatory agencies' tasks and budgets. The *democratic responsiveness hypothesis* reads as follows.

> H2: Independent regulatory agencies are more likely to react to negative public judgements originating from political actors in comparison to other audiences.

Case selection: regulatory agencies in Germany

The chapter focusses on two of the most prominent regulatory agencies in Germany. The financial regulator in Germany *(Bundesanstalt für Finanzdienstleistungsaufsicht, BaFin)* was created in 2002 following the merger of three separate regulators for banking, insurance, and securities. The reform also implied a change in the integrated regulator's formal autonomy. The predecessor organisations of BaFin were semi-autonomous agencies, whereas BaFin is a legally independent agency (Bach and Jann 2010). BaFin's formal autonomy is first and foremost related to managerial autonomy with regard to financial, personnel, and organisational matters. A key difference to the status quo ante is the agency's budget, which is fully funded via fees paid by the regulated industries, and which provides the agency with a greater leeway in financial decisions. However, BaFin is not legally protected from hierarchical control by its parent ministry (the Ministry of Finance) in policy implementation, including the handling of single cases. That said, empirical research indicates a high degree of actual autonomy of the BaFin vis-à-vis the ministry, due to limited oversight capacities and information asymmetries in favour of the regulator (Handke 2012). Although the ministry has tried to gain more control over BaFin by imposing formal reporting requirements, in particular with regard to the regulator's multiple EU level activities, the agency's involvement in supranational decision-making has been shown to further increase BaFin's actual autonomy from its parent ministry (Ruffing 2015).

The Federal Network Agency (BNetzA) was established in 2005 as a multifunctional regulator covering energy and postal services and, since 2006, also railways. Its main function is to ensure the liberalisation of former state monopoly markets. Its predecessor organisation *(Regulierungsbehörde für Telekommunikation und Post, RegTP)* was created in 1998 following a hiving-off process of ministry tasks and personnel to a self-standing organisation (Bach and Jann 2010). BNetzA is considered as being among the most formally autonomous agencies in the federal administration, and empirical research suggests that it also enjoys substantial de facto autonomy (Ruffing 2015). In terms of formal autonomy, there are clear limitations to political control by the ministry in charge, as all instructions by the ministry have to be published and explained, which is unusual in the German context and a clear indicator of formal protection from political control. In addition, major decisions of BNetzA are made by so-called ruling chambers, which are collegial bodies that follow a quasi-judicial procedure.

Thus, the two regulatory agencies studied in this chapter both enjoy substantial levels of de facto autonomy, despite having somewhat different degrees of formal autonomy. They are widely considered as typical examples of the regulatory agency model which is based on the idea of higher degrees of discretion in substantial decision-making compared to agencies with executive tasks (Bach 2018). Hence, while they do not comply with the strict definition of non-majoritarian institutions, as responsible ministers have the possibility to use hierarchical means of control over agency decisions, ministers are clearly restrained in the exercise of hierarchical control.

Data and methods

The following analysis builds on a database of media articles covering the federal network agency and its predecessor organisation, as well as the federal financial supervisory agency. In a first step, we collected all articles from the *Frankfurter Allgemeine Zeitung* that mention either BNetzA, RegTP or BaFin in the title or text of the article in the time between their respective founding (1998 for RegTP and 2002 for BaFin) and 2016; this resulted in a total of 7,158 articles. The *Frankfurter Allgemeine Zeitung* is one of Germany's leading quality newspapers and has a strong and dedicated focus on economic topics. In a second step, we read all articles and selected those 1,445 articles (about 20 per cent) which contain an opinion about the agency. We then coded those articles together with a research assistant and repeatedly evaluated the consistency of our coding. The unit of analysis in this research is single newspaper articles. In this chapter, we only analyse articles containing a negative opinion about one of the two agencies under scrutiny (N=923).

The outcome variable is a binary variable indicating whether an article contains a reaction put forward by the respective agency (coded as '1') or not (coded as '0'). We define a communicative reaction as a response that directly refers to a judgemental opinion within the article in question; this may be a statement by an agency representative (such as the agency head or a press spokesperson) or a decision by the agency that is explicitly described in the article. In the latter case, we assume that the agency has informed the public about the policy action, which is then reported by the press. The number of agency responses to reputational threats is N=202 or 21.9 per cent of all articles containing reputational threats.

The following analysis focusses on the effects of three main independent variables: the agency mentioned in the article, the reputational dimension(s), and the type of actor(s) who raised an opinion. We coded a variable for the agency affected as '1' if the article and opinion address the BaFin and as '0' if they address the BNetzA/RegTP. For the coding of reputational dimensions we follow the categorisation by Carpenter and Krause (2012) (performative, technical, moral, procedural reputation) and Boon et al. (2019) (processual reputation) and used a codebook developed by the latter authors. Based on those dimensions, we will be able to test the reputational profile hypothesis.

For the source of the opinion judgement, we coded dummy variables for 17 potential sources including governmental actors, private firms, NGOs, experts and international actors. Table 5.1 contains a detailed breakdown of those actors. In the analysis, we aggregate those actors to four categories: political actors, regulatees and stakeholders, judicial institutions and other regulators, and other kinds of actors. This categorisation allows us to test our theoretical argument about regulatory agencies' responsiveness to political actors (democratic responsiveness hypothesis).

We further employ two control variables. We control, first, for the media salience of the respective agency in a given period, for which we computed the number of all articles published about the agency in the respective month based on our larger database of 7,158 articles mentioning the respective agency including those with and without a judgemental opinion. Finally, we include the year in which the article was published to control for potential time effects. Table 5.1 reports descriptive statistics for all variables in the final dataset.

TABLE 5.1 Descriptive statistics for all articles with threats

Variable	Mean	Std. Dev.	Min	Max	N
Agency (1= BaFin, 0= BNetzA/RegTP)	.4972914	.5002637	0	1	923
Reaction	.2188516	.4136919	0	1	923
Salience	22.49079	11.49482	1	63	923
Dimension					
Performative	.6933911	.4613355	0	1	923
Technical	.084507	.2782975	0	1	923
Moral	.1451788	.352472	0	1	923
Procedural	.2166847	.4122093	0	1	923
Processual	.2058505	.4045409	0	1	923
Opinion source detailed					
Minister parent ministry (1)	.0065005	.080407	0	1	923
Parent department (1)	.0065005	.080407	0	1	923
Minister non-parent ministry (1)	.0097508	.0983169	0	1	923
Member of cabinet (1)	.0010834	.0329154	0	1	923
The government (1)	.0010834	.0329154	0	1	923
Government party (1)	.0216685	.1456775	0	1	923
Non-governmental party (1)	.0314193	.1745426	0	1	923
Political actor other level (1)	.0184182	.134531	0	1	923

(*Continued*)

90 Tobias Bach et al.

Variable	Mean	Std. Dev.	Min	Max	N
Interest group (2)	.1516793	.3589042	0	1	923
Private company (2)	.3618635	.4808001	0	1	923
Citizens (2)	.0184182	.134531	0	1	923
Media (2)	.0444204	.2061389	0	1	923
Expert (2)	.0628386	.2428039	0	1	923
Non-governmental public organisation (3)	.1180932	.3228934	0	1	923
International political actor (4)	.0541712	.2264779	0	1	923
Former or present employee (4)	.0021668	.0465242	0	1	923
Government organisation same level (4)	.0032503	.0569493	0	1	923
Governmental organisation other level (4)	.0162514	.1265092	0	1	923
Not explicit (4)	.227519	.4194576	0	1	923

For dimension and opinion source one article may fit several categories. The opinion sources are categorised as follows in the analysis: (1) political actors, (2) regulatees and stakeholders, (3) judicial institutions and other regulators, and (4) other.

Analysis

In a first step, before moving to the analysis of reputational threats, we look at all articles containing an opinion on the regulators, both positive and negative (N=1,279). This provides us with a 'reputational profile' of the two regulators as evidenced by newspaper reporting. In particular, this kind of analysis shows for which reputational dimensions the two regulators have a favourable reputation (Table 5.2). Overall, we see that negative opinions clearly outweigh positive opinions, which is hardly surprising given a widely diagnosed 'negativity bias' of the public (Hood 2011). In other words, media reports on regulatory agencies are much more likely to consider negative judgements, rather than positive judgements. In terms of single reputational dimensions, the most striking finding is that for both agencies, positive judgements on their technical reputation outweigh negative judgements. In view of H1, this suggests that we would expect the two agencies to have a lower propensity to react to negative judgements on this (core) dimension, relative to other dimensions. For both agencies, a reputation for being expert bodies and having appropriate capacities to perform their tasks stands out as the dimension in which the regulators have the most positive public standing.

For the other core dimensions of regulatory agencies' reputation (performative and procedural), negative opinions clearly overweigh positive ones. Moreover, in absolute terms, the performative dimension is the most targeted for both regulators.[2] Independent regulatory agencies' ability to fulfil their mission – such as ensuring banking stability or fair access to utility-based services – is at the core of public accountability, as reflected by newspaper reporting. In relative terms,

TABLE 5.2 Reputational profile: opinion by agency and dimension *(here: all articles with an opinion)*

		Agency			
		BaFin		BNetzA/RegTP	
		Positive	Negative	Positive	Negative
Dimension	Performative	22.6% (68)	72.1% (217)	26.3% (89)	63.1% (214)
	Technical	57.4% (31)	37.0% (20)	51.9% (14)	48.2% (13)
	Moral	26.7% (4)	73.33% (11)	11.8% (2)	88.2% (15)
	Procedural	31.9% (23)	65.3% (47)	33.3% (26)	62.8% (49)
	Processual	27.7% (18)	66.2% (43)	34.7% (17)	63.3% (31)
	Multiple	17.7% (36)	62.1% (126)	12.4% (28)	60.9% (137)
	Total	**25.4% (180)**	**65.4% (464)**	**24.0% (176)**	**62.5% (459)**

Cell entries are rounded row percentages per agency (frequencies in parentheses), percentage points missing to 100% (per dimension and per agency) are articles with mixed (positive and negative) opinions.

TABLE 5.3 Reputational dimension addressed in threats by agency *(threats only)*

		Agency		Total
		BaFin	BNetzA/RegTP	
Dimension	Performative	46.8% (217)	46.6% (214)	46.7% (431)
	Technical	4.3% (20)	2.8% (13)	3.6% (33)
	Moral	2.4% (11)	3.3% (15)	2.8% (26)
	Procedural	10.1% (47)	10.7% (49)	10.4% (96)
	Processual	9.3% (43)	6.8% (31)	8.0% (74)
	Multiple	27.2% (126)	29.9% (137)	28.5% (263)
	Total	100% (464)	100% (459)	100% (923)

$\chi^2(5) = 4.54$ *(insignificant).*
Cell entries are rounded column percentages (frequencies in parentheses).

both BaFin and BNetzA are most heavily criticised on the moral dimension, that is, whether they consider the consequences of their decisions for those who are adversely affected and show flexibility and compassion under such circumstances (Busuioc and Rimkutė 2019). That said, following our analytical framework, we consider the moral dimension as peripheral for regulatory agencies' reputational profile, together with processual reputation.

Table 5.3 contains a breakdown of negative opinions by agency and provides a further illustration of the relative importance of different reputational dimensions when it comes to threats. We note in particular (again) that the performative dimension is the main target of negative opinions, and using a χ^2 test we find no significant differences between the two regulators in terms of the content of reputational threats.

92 Tobias Bach et al.

We now move on to the statistical analysis of regulatory agencies' responses (or non-responses) to reputational threats. Table 5.4 reports the results of logistic regression models for all articles with negative judgements and including control variables. The above analysis of positive and negative opinions (Table 5.2) indicated similar reputational profiles for both agencies; yet we analyse the agencies' responses separately, rather than having one regression model including both

TABLE 5.4 Logistic regression of agencies' tendency to respond to threats

Variables	*BaFin*		*BNetzA/RegTP*	
	Coefficient	*OR*	*Coefficient*	*OR*
Dimension				
Performative	1.186★★★	3.274	0.559★	1.749
	(0.415)		(0.308)	
Technical	0.165	1.180	0.741	2.097
	(0.475)		(0.506)	
Moral	0.0226	1.023	0.724★★	2.063
	(0.390)		(0.314)	
Procedural	0.772★	2.164	0.0549	1.056
	(0.419)		(0.296)	
Processual	0.167	1.182	0.480	1.615
	(0.368)		(0.318)	
Opinion source				
Political actors	0.462	1.588	−0.303	0.739
	(0.545)		(0.514)	
Regulatees and stakeholders	0.496	1.642	0.649★	1.914
	(0.468)		(0.377)	
Judicial institutions and other regulators	1.389★★★	4.010	0.933★★	2.541
	(0.493)		(0.430)	
Other	0.0503	1.052	0.389	1.475
	(0.503)		(0.399)	
Salience	−0.00715	0.993	0.0207	1.021
	(0.0158)		(0.0244)	
Year-fixed effect	Yes		Yes	
Constant	−3.503★★★	0.0301	−1.735★★	0.176
	(1.068)		(0.754)	
Observations	464		459	
Log likelihood	−181.18		−247.83	
LR chi-square	$\chi^2(24) = 48.2$★★★		$\chi^2(28) = 45.8$★★	
Pseudo R-squared	0.117		0.085	

★★★ $p < 0.01$, ★★ $p < 0.05$, ★ $p < 0.1$

Entries are unstandardised logistic coefficient estimates with standard errors in parentheses; for each model odd ratios (OR) are reported in a second column. One article may fit several dimensions and source categories.

agencies. This approach takes into consideration that individual agencies may deploy different reputation management strategies. As one article may contain more than one dimension and opinion source, we include a dummy variable for every dimension and each opinion source, there are no baseline categories left out.

According to H1, we expect a higher propensity of reaction to negative public judgements targeting reputational dimensions which are central to the agency mission and for which an agency enjoys a weak reputation. Following the analysis of reputational profiles, this applies to the performative and the procedural dimension for both agencies. A corollary is that we do not expect a higher propensity of reactions to reputational threats targeting the technical dimension, which is central to the agencies' mission, but for which they enjoy a more favourable reputation. At the same time, we expect a lower propensity to respond to negative public judgements targeting reputational dimensions that are peripheral to the agency mission. For both agencies, this applies to the moral and processual dimensions.

Turning to the empirical results, we find that both agencies are more likely to respond to performative threats relative to other kinds of reputational threats, which corresponds to H1. BaFin also displays a higher propensity to react to procedural threats relative to other kinds of threats, and this effect is also substantially large (OR>2). In contrast, the likelihood of BNetzA responding to procedural threats is not statistically different from other kinds of reputational threats. When it comes to the technical dimension, neither of the regulatory agencies display a higher propensity to react, which is in line with our expectations. As to the peripheral dimensions, our theoretical expectations are fully confirmed for BaFin, but only partially confirmed for BNetzA. As can be gleaned from Table 5.4, BNetzA is more likely to respond to moral threats relative to other reputational dimensions, which is contradictory to our expectations, as we do not consider this dimension to be at the core of regulatory agencies' ideal typical reputational profile.

When it comes to regulators' response behaviour as to the opinion source (i.e. the kind of actor from which a reputational threat originates), the democratic responsiveness hypothesis suggests a higher propensity of responses to negative public judgements originating from political actors in comparison to other audiences. In contrast to this hypothesis, both regulators are not particularly likely to respond to threats originating from political actors, all else being equal. The democratic responsiveness hypothesis is thus not empirically supported. This does not mean that regulatory agencies are indifferent to the opinion source. We find that both regulatory agencies are more likely to respond to judicial institutions and other regulators' public judgements (e.g. in the case of BaFin, the central bank). For BaFin, this effect is substantially large (OR>4). For BNetzA (but not for BaFin), we find a significantly higher propensity of reactions to reputational threats originating from regulatees and stakeholders relative to other opinion sources.

Discussion and conclusion

This chapter has empirically tested two hypotheses concerning independent regulatory agencies' responsiveness to reputational threats. In view of the overall theme of this book, we focus on our (null) findings concerning the democratic responsiveness hypothesis. Our findings suggest that regulators are not more responsive to political actors than to others, which speaks to a broader conceptualisation of agencies' accountability to multiple actors in general and demands greater attention to the role of courts in particular in holding regulators accountable. Future research on agency accountability could assess the generalizability of this finding and disentangle whether it is due to drifting (weak) political principals or strong (and so far underestimated) courts, or whether the behaviour of these two types of account-holders is complementary. A related question is about appropriate levels of responsiveness to criticism – when exactly is a regulatory agency responsive enough? The descriptive analysis shows that in the majority of articles, regulatory agencies remain silent when facing reputational threats. On average, both agencies do not respond to approximately 78% of all reputational threats (Table 5.1). Those instances could be considered as unresponsive behaviour, but they could also be considered as instances of failed communication by the regulator.

Moreover, our unexpected findings could imply that press articles report only a biased selection of agencies' responsiveness. It might be fair to assume that responsiveness to political actors happens mostly behind closed doors and thus remains unnoticed by the media and the public. This challenges the assumptions underlying several earlier studies: is an agency's public responsiveness really representative of its overall account-giving? Do political actors such as ministers or government ministries use public criticism or negative judgement of agency behaviour regularly or as an exceptional tool in specific situations? And (even) if public judgements are a regular tool, how do we know that newspaper articles are an accurate operationalisation? It seems fair to assume that the media reports on agencies' criticism and responses in a selective way.

A related point is whether an agency directs its response at the criticising actor or account-holder or whether it uses this actor's criticism to defend or nurture its reputation in front of a broader or different audience. From a reputational perspective, criticising and responding may also be considered as 'myth and ceremony' rather than instrumental, goal-directed behaviour. When an agency responds publicly to a threat by a political actor, does it really aim at that actor or the public more broadly? Again, from a normative perspective, we need to ask whether it is desirable that account giving happens in public, or whether it is sufficient that account-giving to political actors happens behind closed doors. These are important questions hinting at an even more complex communicative behaviour of regulators and their account-holders; future research along these lines can help to refine and update the assumptions of reputation theory.

This brings us to the unexpected findings regarding regulatory agencies' reactions to threats originating from political actors. A plausible interpretation is that a fair share of accountability (and reputation building) from agencies to political principals happens behind closed doors (Maor et al. 2013). In other words, our methodological approach has an obvious blind spot, as we are unable to see distinct types of reputation management. The literature shows that public organisations may cultivate reputations in multiple ways; and communicative behaviour (in the narrow sense of talking to the media or publishing press releases) is only one possible reaction among many others. A task of future research is to unpack different types of responses to public accountability, which may range from changes in the internal prioritisation of tasks with the aim of improving performance on a given reputational dimension to other types of communication, such as annual reporting (Busuioc and Rimkutė 2019).

A reputational approach to accountability also directs attention to the reputational stakes of account-holders (Busuioc and Lodge 2017). Similar to account-givers, account-holders, such as politicians, regulatees, or other stakeholders, can also be understood as driven by reputational concerns. A core implication is that unless holding regulatory agencies to account is a core function of an account-holder, the latter will have limited incentives to invest in this kind of activity. From such a perspective, ensuring the democratic responsiveness of independent regulatory agencies is only partially a story of, for example, mandating transparency rules, and instead a story of making account-holding a key reputational concern of democratic actors. A lesson from such a perspective is that regulators are responsive via other channels than simply the hierarchical chain of delegation, but that very much depends on other actors raising their voices and putting pressure on regulators. This is the well-known mechanism of 'fire alarms' which functions as a source of information about potentially problematic behaviour of bureaucratic agents for political principals (McCubbins and Schwartz 1984). The problem, then, is not one of regulators getting more autonomy, but one of ensuring that other actors have the resources and incentives to hold non-majoritarian organisations to account.

In terms of explaining the regulators' differential reactions to different types of reputational threats, the reputational profile hypothesis received some empirical support, whereas other empirical findings are puzzling in view of our theoretical expectations. We based our assessment of reputational profiles on a simple measure of whether praises or threats dominate among public judgements. However, when looking more closely at the regulators' reputational profiles (Table 5.2), we also find clear differences. For BaFin, we see that the performative reputation is more under threat (higher share of negative opinions) than for BNetzA. In the regression models, we also see a stronger effect size and clearer significance of the performative dimension when compared to BNetzA. A similar yet less clear-cut pattern emerges for procedural reputation. For BNetzA, we see that technical and moral reputation are clearly more under threat (i.e. the agency has a relatively weaker reputation on these dimensions) than for BaFin. In the regression analysis, we see a stronger effect size and statistical significance for the moral dimension, as well as a stronger effect size (but insignificant) for technical dimension when compared to BaFin. In sum, our findings resonate with a view that regulatory agencies will show a higher propensity to react to threats on those aspects of their reputation which are weakest (Maor et al. 2013).

The broader implication of agency-specific variation is whether it is defendable to develop general hypotheses on response behaviour for different types of regulatory agencies, or whether such an endeavour needs to consider the specifics of each organisation. After all, bureaucratic reputation theory emphasises that reputation management is about cultivating the unique contribution of an organisation to public governance (Carpenter 2010b). In view of the overarching question regarding the democratic responsiveness of non-majoritarian institutions, this raises interesting questions as to potential limitations of expecting similar patterns of accountability for organisations with very different kinds of tasks and stakeholders. From a normative point of view, independent agencies' selective response might as well be considered problematic. In this regard, we may end on a positive note. From the viewpoint of output-legitimacy, the agencies' higher likelihood of responses to performative threats is very much in line with normative expectations. That said, a favourable reputation may also serve as a kind of 'accountability buffer' for independent regulatory agencies. This suggests that a positive reputation may undermine democratic responsiveness as the agency does not feel the pressure to respond to public criticism.

Notes

1 We would like to thank the participants of the workshop 'Making Non-Majoritarian Institutions Safe for Democracy' (Oslo, 2019), in particular David Demortain, for their helpful comments on an earlier version of this chapter.
2 The 'multiple threats' category includes articles in which at least two reputational dimensions are being targeted. In the statistical analysis, we use the individual dimensions that are part of multiple threats.

References

Bach, T. (2015) 'Wie "tickt" die öffentliche Verwaltung? Autonomie, Reputation und Responsivität von Regulierungsbehörden am Beispiel des Bundesinstituts für Risikobewertung', in M. Döhler, J. Franzke, and K. Wegrich (eds.) *Der gut organisierte Staat. Festschrift für Werner Jann zum 65. Geburtstag* (pp. 161–179). Baden-Baden: Nomos, Edition Sigma.
Bach, T. (2018) 'Administrative Autonomy of Public Organisations', in A. Farazmand (ed.) *Global Encyclopedia of Public Administration, Public Policy, and Governance* (pp. 171–179). Cham: Springer International Publishing.
Bach, T., Boon, J., Boye, S., Salomonsen, H.H., Verhoest, K. and Wegrich, K. (2019) 'In the Line of Fire: European Financial Regulators before, during, and after the Crisis', *Der Moderne Staat*, 12(1): 5–29.
Bach, T. and Jann, W. (2010) 'Animals in the Administrative Zoo: Organisational Change and Agency Autonomy in Germany', *International Review of Administrative Sciences*, 76(3): 443–468.

Bach, T., Jugl, M., Köhler, D. and Wegrich, K. (2021) 'Regulatory Agencies, Reputational Threats, and Communicative Responses', manuscript.

Bach, T. and Wegrich, K. (2016) 'Regulatory Reform, Accountability and Blame in Public Service Delivery: The Public Transport Crisis in Berlin', in T. Christensen and P. Lægreid (eds.) *The Routledge Handbook to Accountability and Welfare State Reforms in Europe* (pp. 223–235). London: Routledge.

Bach, T. and Wegrich, K. (2019) 'The Politics of Blame Avoidance in Complex Delegation Structures: The Public Transport Crisis in Berlin', *European Political Science Review*, 11(4): 415–431.

Boon, J., Salomonsen, H.H., Verhoest, K. and Pedersen, M.Ø. (2019) 'Media and Bureaucratic Reputation: Exploring Media Biases in the Coverage of Public Agencies', in T. Bach and K. Wegrich (eds.) *The Blind Spots of Public Bureaucracy and the Politics of Non-Coordination* (pp. 171–192). Cham: Springer International Publishing.

Bovens, M. (2007) 'Analysing and Assessing Accountability: A Conceptual Framework', *European Law Journal*, 13(4): 447–468.

Busuioc, M. and Lodge, M. (2017) 'Reputation and Accountability Relationships: Managing Accountability Expectations through Reputation, *Public Administration Review*, 77(1): 91–100.

Busuioc, M. and Rimkutė, D. (2019) 'Meeting Expectations in the EU Regulatory State? Regulatory Communications Amid Conflicting Institutional Demands', *Journal of European Public Policy*, 27(4): 547–568.

Bækkeskov, E. (2017) 'Reputation-Seeking by a Government Agency in Europe: Direct Evidence from Responses to the 2009 H1N1 "Swine" Influenza Pandemic', *Administration & Society*, 49(2): 163–189.

Carpenter, D.P. (2002) 'Groups, the Media, Agency Waiting Costs, and FDA Drug Approval', *American Journal of Political Science*, 46(3): 490–505.

Carpenter, D.P. (2010a) 'Institutional Strangulation: Bureaucratic Politics and Financial Reform in the Obama Administration', *Perspectives on Politics*, 8(3): 825–846.

Carpenter, D.P. (2010b) *Reputation and Power: Organisational Image and Pharmaceutical Regulation at the FDA*. Princeton, NJ: Princeton University Press.

Carpenter, D.P. and Krause, G.A. (2012) 'Reputation and Public Administration', *Public Administration Review*, 72(1): 26–32.

Gilad, S. (2015) 'Political Pressures, Organisational Identity, and Attention to Tasks: Illustrations from Pre-crisis Financial Regulation', *Public Administration*, 93(3): 593–608.

Gilad, S., Maor, M. and Bloom, P.B.N. (2015) 'Organisational Reputation, the Content of Public Allegations, and Regulatory Communication', *Journal of Public Administration Research and Theory*, 25(2): 451–478.

Gilardi, F. (2008) *Delegation in the Regulatory State: Independent Regulatory Agencies in Western Europe*. Cheltenham: Edward Elgar.

Handke, S. (2012) 'A Problem of Chief and Indian: The Role of the Supervisory Authority BaFin and the Ministry of Finance in German Financial Market Policy', *Policy and Society*, 31(3): 237–247.

Hinterleitner, M. and Sager, F. (2019) 'Blame, Reputation, and Organisational Responses to a Politicized Climate', in T. Bach and K. Wegrich (eds.) *The Blind Spots of Public Bureaucracy and the Politics of Non-Coordination* (pp. 133–150). Basingstoke: Palgrave Macmillan.

Hood, C. (2011) *The Blame Game: Spin, Bureaucracy, and Self-Preservation in Government*. Princeton, NJ: Princeton University Press.

Majone, G. (1997) 'From the Positive to the Regulatory State: Causes and Consequences of Changes in the Mode of Governance', *Journal of Public Policy*, 17(2): 139–167.

Maor, M. (2015) 'Theorizing Bureaucratic Reputation', in A. Wæraas and M. Maor (eds.) *Organisational Reputation in the Public Sector* (pp. 17–36). New York: Routledge.

Maor, M., Gilad, S. and Bloom, P.B.N. (2013) 'Organisational Reputation, Regulatory Talk, and Strategic Silence', *Journal of Public Administration Research and Theory*, 23(3): 581–608.

Maor, M. and Sulitzeanu-Kenan, R. (2016) 'Responsive Change: Agency Output Response to Reputational Threats', *Journal of Public Administration Research and Theory*, 26(1): 31–44.

McCubbins, M.D., Noll, R.G. and Weingast, B.R. (1987) 'Administrative Procedures as Instruments of Political Control', *Journal of Law, Economics, & Organisation*, 3(2): 243–277.

McCubbins, M.D. and Schwartz, T. (1984) 'Congressional Oversight Overlooked: Police Patrols versus Fire Alarms', *American Journal of Political Science*, 28(1): 165–179.

Moffitt, S.L. (2010) 'Promoting Agency Reputation through Public Advice: Advisory Committee Use in the FDA', *The Journal of Politics*, 72(3): 880–893.

Moschella, M. and Pinto, L. (2019) 'Central Banks' Reputation Management and Communication Policy Reversals and the Federal Reserve Talk', *Public Administration*, 97(3): 513–529.

Roberts, A. (2010) 'The Rise and Fall of Discipline: Economic Globalization, Administrative Reform, and the Financial Crisis', *Public Administration Review*, 70(1): 56–63.

Ruffing, E. (2015) 'Agencies between Two Worlds: Information Asymmetry in Multilevel Policy-Making', *Journal of European Public Policy*, 22(8): 1109–1126.

Schillemans, T. and Busuioc, M. (2015) 'Predicting Public Sector Accountability: From Agency Drift to Forum Drift', *Journal of Public Administration Research and Theory*, 25(1): 191–215.

Scott, C. (2000) 'Accountability in the Regulatory State', *Journal of Law and Society*, 27(1): 38–60.

Strøm, K. (2000) 'Delegation and Accountability in Parliamentary Democracies', *European Journal of Political Research*, 37(3): 261–289.

6
ACCOUNTABILITY AND INTER-INSTITUTIONAL RESPECT

The case of independent regulatory agencies

Andreas Eriksen

Introduction[1]

As described in Chapter 1, political power is increasingly shifted to institutions that appeal to professional expertise rather than electoral responsiveness for their legitimacy. Independent regulatory agencies are a prime example in this regard. For example, there is currently much talk of the 'agencification' of the European Union. In areas of critical societal concern, such as financial stability or food safety, public authority has been handed to agencies formally designed to operate at arm's length from elected representatives. The standard legitimation strategy has been to claim that such independence from electoral accountability is democratically justifiable as long as there are alternative mechanisms of public accountability.

For example, in one of the most influential contributions to a normative framework for assessing the trend of agencification, Giandomenico Majone (1996: 300) suggests that the problem of regulatory legitimacy is solved as long as there is a functioning 'system of multiple controls'. Squaring legitimacy with independence from electoral politics is supposedly achieved by subjecting regulatory agencies to a decentralised regime of complementary forums and procedures rather than a fixed centre of political control. The framework is presented as a normative elaboration of the much-quoted phrase, '[n]o one controls [the agency], yet it is clearly under control' (Moe 1987: 291). In line with this, the legitimacy of independent agencies is typically framed in terms of their accountability to forums such as parliamentary committees, courts, and, especially, a growing range of auditors. The control mechanisms may be diverse in terms of how they target judgements and behaviour (Holst and Molander 2017: 242–243), but their accountability function is at core to make agencies explain and justify their behaviour to forums with a legitimate claim to demand an account (Bovens et al. 2014: 6). But how do we know that such control mechanisms promote public reason? That is, *how does accountability serve legitimacy?*

In the eyes of many analysts today, we should not take it for granted that accountability is an unconditional legitimacy enhancer. Some even claim the contrary: 'Yes, we are better off without accountability!' (Ossege 2012: 601). Analysts are increasingly arguing that accountability can just as easily skew agencies in undesirable directions. They are 'puzzled' by 'the unrivaled popularity of accountability, given an empirical track record that documents how supposedly accountability-enhancing measures lead to gaming, cheating and slacking, and a decline in moral responsibility and/or intrinsic motivation' (Busuioc and Lodge 2016: 248). In line with this, it is common to hear worries that agencies can become 'too accountable' (Kovacic and Hyman 2012: 6); there is a critical focus on the pathologies of 'multiple accountabilites disorder' (Koppell 2005) and 'accountability overkill' (see Bovens et al. 2008: 228–229 for a concise review).

Against this background, there is a growing sense that something completely different is needed, something other than a 'system of multiple controls'. Analysts hope that awareness of the pathologies that result from badly designed systems will 'signal the dawn of a new age' (Halachmi 2014: 570). Insofar as accountability is to serve legitimacy, the claim is that it must represent a real alternative to traditional institutional mechanisms. In this 'new age', it is expected that 'an evolving political culture, administrative ethos, and professionalism may replace the need for periodic reporting, auditing, and other modes of oversight' (Halachmi 2014: 570).

This chapter takes a fundamental departure from both the diagnosis and the medicine outlined above. First, the diagnosis is not 'accountability overload'. We cannot simply take official rhetoric at face value and assume that all kinds of control mechanisms deserve the accountability label (Eriksen 2020). Much of what goes into the 'accountability overload' basket may perhaps better be described as 'sludge', defined as 'excessive or unjustified frictions, such as paperwork burdens, that cost time or money; that may make life difficult to navigate' (Sunstein 2019: 3). In order to count as accountability practices, mechanisms must qualify as reasonable attempts to check fidelity to mandate. Regarding the medicine, we should not 'replace' generic modes of oversight with 'culture', 'ethos', and 'professionalism'. Rather, the task is to embed control mechanisms in the appropriate *mode of interaction*. The argument of this chapter is that the basic norms of accountability interaction cannot be unpacked without an attitudinal component: accountability practices require an appropriate form of *inter-institutional respect*.

In order to make this case, the chapter has a constructive part followed by a brief critical part. The constructive part begins with an explanation of why we should be concerned with the attitudes that govern accountability practices. In connecting the current approach to 'expressive' theories of law, it should be clear how evaluating institutions in terms of respectful interaction is both familiar in actual practice and fruitful in normative terms. In the case of independent regulatory agencies, the relevant form of respect takes the form of *recognition* of the regulatory domain. The recognition model is applied to the case of accountability for agency performance in order to vindicate its normative bite.

Having outlined the recognition model on its own terms, the critical part proceeds by explaining how the attitudes that govern two currently dominant models fail to serve legitimacy. The principal-agent approach sees accountability interaction as governed by a concern with *restraining* agencies. It paints an essentially antagonistic picture, as it is about maintaining control over a potentially drifting agent. This perspective is currently challenged by analysts who see accountability interaction as governed by *reputational* concerns. Although the reputation model's portrayal is more harmonious than the restraint model, it is still concerned with strategic self-interest, because it sees accountability interaction as mere self-presentation. While both of these models may arguably be helpful as explanatory and predictive theories, they overreach when they make prescriptive claims. And in failing to gain normative traction, they distort accountability as a legitimacy-enhancing concept.

Institutional respect

In this section, I will argue for an 'expressivist turn' in accountability studies. Even if readers of this chapter eventually disagree with my specific recognition model, they may still find the more general project of evaluating accountability practices in attitudinal terms useful. Here, I will make the relatively uncontroversial assumption that there is nothing metaphysically suspect about attributing attitudes to institutions[2] and instead focus on the normative point in doing so. My approach follows the expressive theory of action and law as developed by Elizabeth Anderson and Richard Pildes (2000). The main point of an expressivist framework is that we evaluate actions in terms of how well they express the required attitude. For example, we criticise people and institutions for being uncaring or disrespectful. In doing so, we are saying that their actions fail to be responsive to the value in question. The norms for expressing attitudes like care and respect regulate our responsiveness to values; they set standards for justifications of action.

Three features of the expressivist framework are especially useful for evaluating accountability practices. First, the framework makes accountability into a matter of *inter-institutional address* rather than simply the subjection of agencies to various types of control mechanisms. In doing this, it takes us beyond the standard focus on generic modes of oversight. The appropriateness of a control mechanism is seldom given in the abstract; it typically depends on the attitudes (form of address) that govern the use of the mechanism. For example, consider these remarks from a frustrated director of one of the European Union's independent agencies:

> It's very good to be accountable but if you have to explain each time to everyone what you are doing, what is your task, what will be your future,

> it's a bit tiring. The Parliament, the Commission, everyone, they want a lot of reports but what do they do with these reports? (Respondent #45) Or again,
>
> I never get any feedback. This is also a bit frustrating. No feedback whatsoever. I would also be pleased to have sometimes criticism why not, or congratulations on the work done, because it was not so easy (Respondent #45)
>
> Busuioc (2013: 133–134)

As these remarks indicate, reports and hearings do not serve accountability unless they are employed with some genuine engagement. Debates on which kinds of mechanisms are effective only make sense against the background assumption that they will be intelligently applied according to the mode of interaction that is appropriate to the inter-institutional relationship.

In this regard, it is useful to compare the agency case to Anderson and Pildes's (2000: 1556–1564) example of US federalist jurisprudence regarding constitutional constraints on national power in relation to the states as a lower tier of government. The states are distinct constitutional entities that can legitimately be influenced in many ways by what Congress decides, but the Supreme Court has highlighted that there are constraints on how Congress may address or seek to steer states. In particular, there is a prohibition on 'commandeering' in the sense of coercion, and this prohibition is grounded in the 'dignity of the states'.[3] The appropriate mode of interaction between these institutions requires Congress to address states in a mode sensitive to their sovereignty, and the Court criticises transgressions of these constraints for expressing 'disrespect for the constitutionally stipulated relations between the federal government and the States' (Anderson and Pildes 2000: 1559). What is particularly relevant here is how Congress is criticised for *how* it seeks to influence states, not for the generic act of influencing itself. Similarly, we should be concerned with how control mechanisms are employed in relation to agencies, not with generic modes of oversight independently of their attitudinal mode of employment.

Second, the expressivist framework enables us to identify the *kinds of justifications* that count for accountability practices. That is, it brings out the need for normative standards that demarcate accountability from other kinds of interaction. For example, a much-quoted definition in the accountability literature states that

> [a]ccountability is *a relationship between an actor and a forum, in which the actor has an obligation to explain and to justify his or her conduct, the forum can pose questions and pass judgement, and the actor may face consequences.*
>
> Bovens (2007: 450, italics in original)

On the one hand, this takes us in a normative direction, in the sense that 'justification' means explaining why an action is *acceptable*. On the other hand, there is a broad variety of potential modes of judging acceptability. As it stands, the standard definition is compatible with justifications that are accepted for all kinds of reasons; from sly calculation to indifferent acquiescence, from partisan motives to legal-procedural rigorism. That is, it is compatible with the employment of control mechanisms for reasons that do not serve legitimacy.

However, this permissiveness disappears if we see accountability practices as governed by attitudinal conditions. In other words, conceiving of accountability as a particular mode of interaction helps us identify the *form* of relevant justifications (i.e. the nature of the conditions of satisfaction). Hence, we need an attitudinal component to distinguish justificatory strategies that serve accountability from strategies that serve other purposes. The space of justificatory reasons remains indeterminate without a kind of inter-institutional respect that delineates acceptability.

Third, the expressivist framework alerts us to the way accountability practices embody *public meanings*. The meaning of an action can be public in the sense that it expresses an attitude regardless of the intentions of the agent. This is familiar from everyday interaction. For example, a joke that trades on cultural stereotypes may not be intended as derogatory or demeaning, but it may nevertheless express a conception with a public meaning that calls for an excuse. Similarly, control mechanisms may be designed without intending to convey distrust, but they may express this attitude nevertheless. By underscoring the public meaning of actions, the expressive framework provides a normative foundation for evaluating accountability practices in terms of their mode of address. In this regard, consider Onora O'Neill's (2002) protest against what she calls 'the new accountability':

> The pursuit of ever more perfect accountability provides citizens and consumers, patients and parents with more information, more comparisons, more complaints systems; but it also builds a culture of suspicion, low morale and may ultimately lead to professional cynicism, and then we would have grounds for public mistrust.

Naturally, distrust may be warranted in some cases. However, O'Neill's point is that control systems increasingly tend to convey distrust in indiscriminate ways, without the warrant of prior signals of untrustworthiness and that this perversely undermines the conditions of trust. Let us nevertheless assume that such control mechanisms are effective according to some narrow metric, such as client satisfaction or measurable output. With the help of the expressivist framework, we can see why it is incoherent to argue that control mechanisms serve legitimacy if their employment amounts to what Beryl Radin (2006, ch. 4) describes as 'demeaning professionals'. In order for accountability to serve legitimacy, it must be governed by an attitude concerned with the proper functioning of institutions according to the standards appropriate to their specific societal domain. As Jerry Mashaw (2006: 119) puts it, accountability is about preventing 'the (inappropriate) use of rules of behaviour that apply in one realm of human action in another'. The task, then, is to ground accountability interaction in a domain-sensitive attitude.

Insofar as accountability is a legitimacy-enhancing concept, it refers to practices that respect the institution's mandate, with all the interpretive complexity that entails. The expressivist objection in this regard does not rely on the subjective experience of professionals, as this could make any use of control mechanisms objectionable or acceptable depending on whether role holders are thin- or tough-skinned. Rather, the objection is that indiscriminate distrust can endow control mechanisms with a public meaning that can amount to a form of institutional disrespect, no matter how it is actually experienced by the addressee.

In the following, I will argue that the attitude of recognition is especially suited to ground accountability interaction. That is, the recognition model represents a substantive idea of what respect between independent agencies and their account holders require. As a matter of terminology, it might be useful to explain how my view of the relation between respect and recognition differs from two other philosophical accounts. Stephen Darwall (1977) has famously delineated 'recognition respect' as distinct from 'appraisal respect'. Recognition respect is owed to people simply in virtue of being persons, while appraisal respect is directed at specific characters or achievements. My account follows Darwall in seeing recognition as a *form* of respect, but my conception of recognition is more concerned with affirmation of social and institutional identity than with the dignity that attaches to personhood as such. In this regard, my account tilts more towards John Skorupski (2005: 341), who sees recognition as an attitude expressed 'within a determinate community and its historically evolved morality'. However, my account does not see respect and recognition as separate concepts in the way Skorupski does. Rather, recognition is a historically or institutionally *embedded* form of respect.

The recognition model

As a first step towards developing my expressive model, this section will explain how key features of recognition are relevant to our assessments of accountability practices. Following Axel Honneth's (2012: 80) proposal to demarcate recognition in a theoretically inclusive way, there are four features that are broadly agreed on: first, it concerns the affirmation of positive features in the individual or institution. Second, recognition manifests itself in attitudes or behaviour, not mere words. Third, acts of recognition have positive affirmation as an intentional goal in the sense that it is not merely a contingent by-product of interaction. Fourth, recognition is a genus concept of which there are many species. Love, rights-governed respect, and admiration are forms of recognition that belong to different spheres and modes of interaction. How are these four features of recognition relevant to accountability interaction?

Positive affirmation

Control mechanisms are clearly defective *qua* accountability practices if they do not function as potential conduits of affirmation by external institutions. Although they must sound alarms when transgressions are detected, they must also convey some kind of positive affirmation when agency mandates have been complied with. The point of accountability is distorted if the absence of sanctions is simply interpreted as insufficient grounds for external intervention or just part of some kind of inter-institutional coalition building. The positive outcome of an accountability procedure, such as passing a review or having the budget approved, contains more substantive expressive power.

Consider the international definition of 'performance auditing' as 'an independent, objective and reliable examination of whether government undertakings, systems, operations, programmes, activities or organisations are operating in accordance with the principles of economy, efficiency and effectiveness and whether there is room for improvement' (INTOSAI 2013: 2). When in good working order, this kind of accountability practice seems to have the potential to affirm an agency's activity as 'in accordance with the principles of economy, efficiency and effectiveness'. In other words, it conveys recognition of the agency's activities as adequately realising key dimensions of the mandate.

The centrality of this function is not really contested by empirical findings of mere strategic uses of performance standards. To the contrary, strategic use of performance standards is parasitic on the basic function of accountability practices to serve as conduits of normatively warranted affirmation. When performance mechanisms are used for political leverage or selective self-presentation, their function is to disguise private reasoning *as public currency*. This function presupposes that the disguise has some legitimacy-enhancing property. That is, it is in virtue of their function as institutional mediators of recognition that accountability practices offer possibilities of more strategic use.

Manifest expression

The second feature of recognition – that the attitude manifests itself in behaviour – calls for interpretive judgement regarding the public meaning of responses of account holders. As I see it, this feature can be given both a formal-procedural interpretation and a more informal interpretation that highlights trusting relationships. Examples of formally expressed recognition are approvals of budgets, increased responsibilities, or reinforced regulatory authority.

More informally, accountability practices can lead to the treatment of agencies as something akin to 'political actors in their own right' (Moe 1989: 282). Accountability practices can lead to this kind of recognition in the form of de facto authority to set the agenda and act on self-determined priorities. This kind of recognition is often described in terms of institutional autonomy:

'Tailored accountability arrangements are likely to positively affect the credibility of an agency, which may breed trust and increase actual autonomy' (Busuioc et al. 2011: 862). Here, 'actual autonomy' means the leeway that is provided through informal behaviour that develops alongside formal procedures (Groenleer 2014: 261).

Intentional goal

The intentionality feature says that affirmation must be a non-contingent part of the expressive repertoire of accountability practices. Naturally, this does not mean that account holders must have the attitude of recognition as a goal (as in 'we are going to promote the recognition of your work'). The point of the intentionality feature is that accountability practices must have the potential for the kind of affirmation that tracks the standards of agency work, as opposed to merely approval for some mandate-external reason. That is, the institutional goal is simply to confirm or disconfirm fidelity to mandate, but the expressive grammar of such confirmation takes the form of recognition. Evaluations of fidelity to mandate give public expression to the account holders' recognition of the agency.

Clearly, accountability practices can express other attitudes besides the kind of affirmation that counts as recognition. Accountability practices may lead to the disapproval and sanctioning of independent agencies. Being 'held accountable' is usually reserved for negative responses to some wrongdoing. But it is important to note that this is derivative of the more fundamental notion of being addressed as accountable, in the sense of being answerable for a distinct domain of institutional action. Recall that the definition of accountability is couched in terms of 'explaining and justifying' conduct. It is only insofar as agencies cannot justify themselves in the process of being addressed as accountable that they are appropriately held accountable in the derivative sense of having sanctions imposed.

The species of recognition

This brings us to the fourth feature, which concerns the species of recognition. What kind of recognition should accountability practices potentially mediate in order to serve legitimacy? This deserves a more extensive conceptual elaboration, because it regards the way accountability practices should track the function of independent agencies in the broader democratic system. Here, my claim is that the recognition that serves legitimacy must be sensitive to the distinct form of *professional integrity* that regulatory work requires.

In this regard, the basic idea is that recognition takes domain-sensitive forms. As Hegel described in his *Philosophy of Right* (1991 [1820]) and associated lectures, there are different forms of recognition appropriate for different societal spheres of interaction.[4] The kind of recognition expressed in family relations is substantially different from market relations constituted by contract. For current purposes, it is relevant to briefly consider Hegel's account of the recognition appropriate for the members of 'corporations', by which was meant, roughly, professional associations supervised by the state.[5]

His claim was that corporations enable a special form of recognition; they provide a social space where role holders are recognised for the contribution of their skills to society and afforded 'honour of estate' (*Standesehre*) or social standing (Hegel 1991[1820], § 253).[6] Members of corporations are not merely recognised by society for their talents as such, but for directing these talents towards purposes that serve the common good as opposed to mere private interest. Similarly, independent regulatory agencies are part of a division of political labour that is supposed to serve a publicly justifiable conception of the common good. Hence, a somewhat similar idea of 'honour of estate' may be attached to the case of independent agencies. That is, the kind of recognition mediated by accountability practices should take a form that is appropriate to their function in this system.

Analysts may disagree as to the precise nature of this systemic function, beyond the general function of providing expertise. However, a broad delineation is sufficient for the current discussion. As described in the tradition of science and technology studies (STS), regulatory work is 'an intermediary or in-between domain of scientific practice, apart from both research and policy-making' (Demortain 2017: 146). This description has the advantage of acknowledging the political dimension of regulatory work, which contrasts with official descriptions that tend to emphasise regulatory agencies as strictly technical. The notion of an 'intermediary domain' highlights how regulatory work is engaged with material from other domains, material that has to be intelligently applied to the particular questions that agencies face. In their entrusted task of advising on and realising political ends, agencies can neither be politically adversarial nor stick to the demanding standards of accuracy that characterise science.

Accountability for performance

In order to see how the recognition model works in practice, this section considers how the four features of recognition apply to accountability for performance. The point here is not to assess 'performance management' as a specific instrument of accountability, but rather to indicate how the recognition model delivers standards for thinking about accountability for performance more generally. Despite some performance management instruments being described as 'recognition and reward systems' (Clotfelter and Ladd 1996), they are often criticised precisely for failing to convey recognition of the real mission of public organisations. A notorious problem is calibrating indicators to the complexities of typical missions, with poorly designed systems leading to 'gaming', understood as the practice of 'hitting the target but missing the point' because 'what is measured is what matters' (Bevan and Hood 2006: see also Molander et al. 2012: 224).

Performance-oriented agency expectations are deeply entrenched in US systems for agency oversight, yet they remain fundamentally controversial.

Allegedly, they have led to a one-sided focus on quantifiable results that fails to capture procedural aspects of agency mandates, such as transparent and representative consultation practices (Piotrowski and Rosenbloom 2002). Similarly, the agencies of the European Union are subject to growing expectations concerning 'performance measurement, performance reporting, and demonstrating efficiency' (Busuioc and Rimkutė 2019: 19). For example, budget approval by the European Parliament increasingly requires agencies to show results according to key performance indicators. What, then, does it take for an accountability practice to mediate recognition for performance? This section will discuss this in light of the four features of recognition presented above.

Accountability through affirmation

First, recognition is an act of affirmation of positive qualities. On the face of it, this conflicts with the default orientation of account holders who want to prove themselves as vigilant guardians. As Robert Behn notes, '[i]f you are in the accountability-holding business, you need to hold someone accountable for something' (Behn 2001: 13). In line with this, analysts find that '[p]erformance scrutiny is usually designed in order to focus on results that deviate from what is expected' (Johansson and Montin 2014: 221).

The recognition model explains how the 'hold-someone-accountable-for-something' mentality can conflict with the basic rationale of legitimacy-enhancing accountability practices. In particular, it makes plain how 'catching' someone is not the primary goal of accountability interaction. Instead, the primary purpose is to provide a public explanation and justification of agency work. It is against this background that warranted acts of sanction express a *withdrawal* of recognition in response to the agency's failure to live up to the standards of the reason-giving relationship.[7] In order for there to be any recognition to withdraw, however, there must first have been a relationship constituted by something other than antagonism and suspicion. This way of framing accountability practices changes (if not reverses) the justificatory burden of account holders. Absent actual indications of bad practice, the problem is not how to defend a low level of 'catches' but rather to justify the interventions that are actually carried out.

This has consequences for how accountability for performance should be operationalised. Instead of merely tailoring performance indicators to make any deviation easy to spot, they should be equally geared to making agency compliance with the mission intelligible. This calls for evaluating accountability practices according to a standard of *deference* in cases of reasonable disagreement. It is only when agency performance cannot be interpreted as a competent, good faith attempt to comply with the mandate that sanctions are appropriate.

Manifest responses to trustworthiness

The second feature of recognition is that it manifests itself in behaviour, not mere words. A particularly relevant form of behaviour is the expression of *trust* that is earned through a track record of good performance. Although instruments of distrust can make an untrustworthy institution trustworthy, they can also make a trustworthy institution untrustworthy (cf. Grimen 2009: 105). That is, failure to recognise an agency as trustworthy may become a self-fulfilling prophecy, given the widespread evidence of how external monitoring and sanctioning 'crowd out' existing professional motivations that could warrant trust in institutions (Cook and Gerbasi 2009: 226). The sense of distrust that is expressed through demanding and often misguided performance indicators saps time and energy in a way that detracts from a sense of purpose (Radin 2006: 115–116).

By framing accountability interaction as mediating recognition of a distinct domain of reasoning, the model helps explain how instruments of distrust may fail to serve legitimacy. And in a more constructive vein, it frames accountability as legitimacy-enhancing when it imposes controls in trust-preserving ways. The recognition model emphasises that external performance management should be sensitive to the danger of crowding out existing mandate-promoting motivations. This sensitivity must develop dynamically through interaction that establishes grounds for trust.

In this way, the model overcomes the standard dilemma with regard to making motivational assumptions; should one assume role holders to be unwaveringly public-spirited or cunning cheaters, that is, 'knights or knaves' (Le Grand 2003), 'Rousseau or Hobbes' (Piotrowski and Rosenbloom 2002: 647)? The recognition model holds that neither assumption is warranted as a general and *a priori* strategy; trust systems must evolve through recognition of actual manifestations of professional integrity in mission execution. And in overcoming this traditional dichotomy, the model highlights why it is problematic to see trust as the 'antithesis of accountability' (Mulgan 2003: 213). A more nuanced approach sees accountability as requiring careful and intelligent allocation of trust.

Affirmation as intentional act

Acts of recognition have positive affirmation as an intentional goal in the sense that it is not merely a by-product of interaction. In virtue of this feature, the recognition model puts an important constraint on the kinds of support that matter for performance accountability. In particular, *qua* recognition, the affirmation must be grounded in the standards of the mandate as opposed to mere expression of a policy preference that is not grounded in the relevant expertise (such as partisan concern with market efficiency or redistributive concerns). In cases where the affirmation merely flows from externally grounded policy preference, the professional integrity of the agency becomes a contingent factor as opposed to the intentional content of evaluation.

Consider procedures of stakeholder engagement. They may contribute to accountability in the sense that they put an agency in a justificatory relationship with affected parties. What makes it into an accountability relationship is that the conditions of justification track the mandate. By contrast, other kinds of stakeholder acceptance or support for agency proposals may have little or nothing to do with accountability. In some contexts, 'stakeholder engagement can be seen as a political game in which an agency seeks out support for its agenda while industry lobbyists, nongovernmental organisations (NGOs) and other actors seek to influence that agenda' (Wood 2018: 406). While playing this 'political game' may be a legitimate part of agency work, it is not thereby an accountability practice. Only when stakeholder engagement switches from a game of strategic influence to a good faith attempt to evaluate fidelity to mandate does the practice become an accountability practice.

To some, this constraint on the intentional content of accountability practices may appear too strict. It seemingly excludes practices that seek to make agencies *indirectly* accountable through systems that have other primary goals, such as efficiency or responsiveness. For example, it has become common to see 'competition' as a form of accountability (Peters 2010: 214). One version of this makes the allocation of funds depend on the competitive results between agency programs (OECD 2018: 7). However, the argument here is not that such quasi-market models of governance cannot play a part in accountability practices. Rather, the point is that they only contribute to accountability if they are *embedded* within a system of justification with standards that enable recognition of professional integrity. In order to play this part, performance instruments that make funding contingent on competitive results cannot operate merely as a signal of 'customer satisfaction'. Nor can the sanction of reduced funding simply be imposed as an automatic consequence. Rather, funding decisions should be addressed to the agency in a way that enables reasoned response in terms of the demands of the mandate.

This feature of the recognition model connects agency accountability to a more general concept of accountability. In theories of law and morality, what differentiates holding someone accountable from merely coercing them is that the addresser appeals to reasons that respect the integrity of the addressee. This 'respect constraint' on accountability is not limited to reciprocal, horizontal relationships. As Stephen Darwall puts it, 'even the addresser of a demand that is presumed to be based in an unreciprocated, hierarchical authority must assume that the authority on which the demand is based is one the addressee can freely and rationally accept' (Darwall 2006: 258).[8] In other words, if agencies are allocated funds without appeal to reasons that are acceptable in terms of professional integrity, they are coerced rather than held accountable.

Accountability through recognition of a distinct sphere of action

This chapter has followed the Hegelian thought that recognition is a genus concept of which there are distinct species that belong in different societal domains. The argument has been that the recognition appropriate for the accountability of independent agencies should track professional integrity and thereby the mandate's function in the broader democratic system. When it comes to accountability for performance, it is important that mechanisms do not make agencies political in the wrong way. As noted above, regulatory work is an intermediary domain between science and ordinary politics. Agencies are bound to engage in some forms of political reasoning (e.g. in light of the precautionary principle), while they are prohibited from others (e.g. partisan ideology). In this regard, the recognition model can help explain what it means for performance expectations to track this intermediary domain.

In order to see how, let us return to Radin's book *Challenging the Performance Movement* (2006), devoted to what the title suggests. With the backing of a wide range of examples, she argues that performance measures often conflict with the standards of professional integrity appropriate for agencies: 'In the name of accountability, they seem to increase politicized stances that lose sight of the goals of programs and policies' (Radin 2006: 63–62). Particularly relevant here are her examples of how external accountability holders sometimes repurpose standards to make them into means of censoring scientific results to suit partisan interest (Radin 2006: 85) and how standards are transformed from context-sensitive practice recommendations to strict cost-control instruments (Radin 2006: 76). Such examples illustrate how control mechanisms can be governed by logics that do not track the mandate: 'performance standards do have a life of their own, and even when professionals are engaged in their development and definition, they may be used in unanticipated ways' (Radin 2006: 76).

For current purposes, what is important is the way Radin's criticism appeals to professionalism as requiring a domain-sensitive form of accountability interaction. The recognition model is especially suited to capture the normative grounds for this kind of criticism, because it frames accountability as serving legitimacy through interaction that aims to affirm and uphold the standards of the regulatory mandate. According to this model, performance instruments that are guided by mission-insensitive conceptions of efficiency are harmful precisely because they threaten to corrupt the legitimate sphere of agency action. By contrast, performance instruments that respect the complexity of agency goals and the need for professional discretion can enable recognition-based accountability interaction that serves legitimacy. Naturally, this may make accountability procedures much more demanding for account holders. However, the alternative is a mode of interaction in danger of doing more harm than good.

Two competing models

So far, this chapter has developed and defended the recognition model as a concrete way to operationalise an expressive framework for assessing accountability interaction. There are of course other options, and there is no need to construct competing models from scratch in this regard. Currently dominant accountability perspectives clearly convey assumptions about the appropriate attitudes for accountability interaction. In this section, I will briefly delineate two alternative models and argue that both rely on attitudinal assumptions that are inappropriate for accountability interaction.

The restraint model

The first model can be found in the principal-agent tradition, which sees restraint as the basic mode of accountability interaction. According to the restraint model, accountability is governed by an attitude on the part of the principal that is geared to limiting discretion in strategic ways: 'Procedural requirements affect the institutional environment in which agencies make decisions and thereby limit an agency's range of feasible policy actions' (McCubbins et al. 1987: 244). In line with this, it has become common to speak of principal-agent theory as a 'paradigm for analyzing public accountability' because of its ability to explain how variations in institutional arrangements relate to the 'potential for inducing desirable behaviour by agents' (Gailmard 2014: 90). This 'paradigm' rests on a strictly strategic conceptualisation of the relationship between account holders and agencies. Here, the accountability system is not primarily governed by 'concern for due process and such-like legal niceties, but rather out of desire to mitigate agency loss due to moral hazard problems in the bureaucracy' (Gailmard 2014: 97). In other words, the basic assumption is that account holders and account givers have potentially diverging interests and that the accountability system should reflect ways for principals to restrain the actions of agents. Hence, 'the question is whether the principal can induce the more expert agent to take those actions that the principal would take if the principal had the same information as the agent' (Miller 2005: 204).

Concerning serving the legitimacy of public authority in general, this model may be useful as long as we are thinking of hierarchical bureaucratic structures. In ideal-typical terms, such delegation is a matter of increasing efficient implementation of predetermined ends (instrumental rationality). However, problems emerge as soon as the focus is shifted to independent agencies that are justified in terms of their ability to provide non-partisan knowledge and regulate according to impartial standards at arm's length from ordinary politics. Once independent agencies are constituted as institutions that form a distinct knowledge-based branch of government, they are answerable to their public mandates and not brute political preference (Vibert 2007). Naturally, agency independence from politics is typically a matter of degree both formally and informally (Vos 2016), but the kind of interaction that is governed by the restraint model fails to express even a basic respect for independent expertise. It fails because in conceiving of accountability as a matter of restricting the account giver's range of policy options, it makes the account holder into a *shaper* of the standards of agency reasoning according to its own interests rather than *checker* of compliance with impartial standards of expert-based reasoning.

With regard to independent agencies, then, the restraint model should be read as, at best, a forward-looking theory of *delegation* rather than of accountability. The legitimacy of independent agencies flows from their fidelity to the mandate as expert bodies. Insofar as they are institutionally appropriate, subsequent acts of restraint should be interpreted as a redesign of the mandate rather than as a form of answering to the mandate. This assessment does not presuppose a revisionary or idiosyncratic conception of accountability. As others have argued, accountability is an essentially *backward-looking* concept that should be distinguished from the forward-looking constitutive acts that define the authority of an agency (e.g. Busuioc 2009: 605; Mulgan 2003: 19). The current point is that this conceptual delineation entails attitudinal conditions; control mechanisms that primarily convey an attitude of restraint to favour the interests of the account holder do not serve legitimacy.

Importantly, the addition of a *multitude* of forums with different perspectives and interests (courts, auditors, stakeholders, etc.) cannot save the restraint model. Although a multitude of control mechanisms may result in the agency being 'under control', there is no reason to assume that the result would be legitimacy-enhancing if it followed the logic of the restraint model. The problem lies with its attitudinal prescription; it is about delimiting the sphere of action according to the preferences of the external institution. Insofar as each forum is attempting to restrain the agency according to its own logic, the result will be a set of *incompatible* expectations. Hence, the model is a recipe for inducing 'multiple accountabilities disorder' in agencies (Koppell 2005). Let us therefore turn to a model that is explicitly devoted to tackle the problem of incompatible expectations.

The reputation model

In the influential paper that introduced the term 'multiple accountabilities disorder', Jonathan Koppell (2005: 99) suggested that a cure would be to focus on 'one dimension of accountability'. That is, instead of seeking accountability for all dimensions – such as effective performance, procedural inclusiveness, and technical accuracy – the agency should choose according to its strengths. A key example in the paper is a situation where a public-private partnership – the Internet Corporation for Assigned Names and Numbers (ICANN) – is having a board meeting and is confronted by critics from non-profit groups. The critics wanted more representation of non-commercial interests. The chairwoman responded bluntly, 'With all due respect, we are less interested in complaints about the process [and more interested in] doing real work and moving forward' (Koppell 2005: 103). On Koppell's interpretation, ICANN is ignoring the procedural dimension of accountability in order to be accountable along the performance dimension.

In the same vein, Madalina Busuioc and Martin Lodge have developed a distinct theoretical approach that focuses on the reputational logic of accountability. Given that agencies cannot please all accountability forums, they have reason to 'stress particular aspects of their competence to enhance audience perceptions of niche roles, uniqueness, and appropriateness' (Busuioc and Lodge 2017: 93). According to this model, accountability practices have a stage-setting function, in that they allow agencies to build a reputation that enables efficient management of expectations.

To some extent, this is a descriptive account of what institutions actually do. Nevertheless, it relies on a conceptual framework that repeatedly delivers prescriptive conclusions. In particular, the demands of self-presentation are seen as delivering an appropriate normative standard for dealing with expectations: 'Reputation focuses organizational attention and equips organizations with a rationale for prioritizing among multiple external accountability demands' (Busuioc and Lodge 2016: 255). In the end, this logic is even considered a sensible foundation for formal institutional design, as the suggestion is to 'attach concrete reputational incentives to accountability structures' (Busuioc and Lodge 2016: 260).

However, there is strong reason to doubt that interaction grounded in strategies of reputation management can serve legitimacy. While it is clear that accountability interaction should avoid paralysing agencies with a host of incompatible demands, it is equally clear that the authority of the distinct dimensions of accountability cannot legitimately be treated as contingent on their reputational effects. Although it may be true that accountability practices will inevitably give rise to reputational incentives, the idea of deliberately institutionalising such incentives comes across as a de facto endorsement of a strategically selective attitude to the mandate. That is, instead of seeing agencies as bound by a duty to execute good faith interpretation of the mandate as a whole, the suggestion is that accountability practices should be driven by reputational considerations as part of their design.

To return to the case of ICANN, this organisation might prove to be more autonomous and effective by ignoring procedural requirements of stakeholder inclusiveness. But it would be misguided to simply assume that the resulting effectiveness is desirable from a public perspective. The effectiveness that is relevant for accountability is part of an interlocking set of considerations, it cannot be treated as an isolated concern (Eriksen 2020). The reputation model falsely assumes that agencies can 'do real work and move forward' *in an accountability-relevant sense* without procedures of adequate representation. The non-profit groups in Koppell's case wanted to know what reasons supported ICANN's business-backed policy for cracking down on 'cybersquatting'.[9] This request appears to track ICANN's mandate. At the time, the effective bylaw stated that ICANN 'shall operate to the maximum extent feasible in an open and transparent manner and consistent with procedures designed to ensure fairness' (ICANN 1998). This places a substantive constraint on what it means for the organisation to move forward. 'Getting things done' is not sufficient; 'things' must be done for publicly accessible and democratically acceptable reasons.

The main difference between the reputation model and the recognition model is that the latter takes the overarching mandate of agencies seriously as providing standards that govern accountability interaction. While the reputation model sees both agencies and their account holders as legitimately adopting a pick-and-choose approach to their organisational image, the recognition model demands that regulatory work be respected as a distinct domain that requires interpretive judgement that unites different concerns in a responsible manner.

Conclusion

The adage 'no one controls the agency, but the agency is under control' encapsulates a long-standing formula to the puzzle of regulatory legitimacy. It invokes a system of multiple controls that is supposed to square independence with accountability. As this chapter has argued, the plausibility of that solution presupposes that the notion of 'control' is interpreted with care. A multi-pronged control approach does not serve legitimacy unless accountability instruments are embedded in an appropriate mode of interaction. By engaging with practices of performance control, the chapter has illustrated some of the merits of the recognition model.

This general model may be applied in various ways, which arguably points both to its broader relevance and to its limitations in terms of substantive guidance. Clearly, what counts as due recognition will often be contested. The mandates of independent regulatory agencies are multi-interpretable and there is reasonable disagreement concerning the relevant standards of efficient performance, reasonableness, and accuracy. Nevertheless, there is little point in having such debates without clarity on the basic currency of accountability. Any critical assessment of accountability practices requires a distinction between unsuccessful attempts to calibrate mission-sensitive instruments and successful use of instruments for a different purpose altogether. The former is a failure of precision while the latter is a failure of recognition. While perfectly calibrated instruments can perhaps only exist as a regulative idea, instruments embedded in a logic of recognition are a basic precondition for legitimacy-serving accountability relations.

Notes

1 This chapter has benefitted from talks with the REFLEX team at ARENA Centre for European Studies and discussion in the Professional Ethics group at Centre for the Study of Professions.
2 Defences can be found in the now rich literature on collective agency. See Roth (2017) for an introduction.
3 Anderson and Pildes (2020) refer to the language of Justice Kennedy's opinion in Alden v. Maine 119 S. Ct. 2240 (1999).
4 See Honneth (2000) for an especially illuminating account.
5 More specifically, 'Strictly speaking, for Hegel a "corporation" is any society officially recognized by the state that is not itself part of the political state' (Wood 1990: 282n6).
6 See Herzog (2013: 77–78) for further analysis and references to relevant Hegel lectures.
7 In this way, the current model extrapolates accounts of interpersonal morality that see blame a matter of 'withdrawal of recognition' (Skorupski 1999: 180). Similarly, T.M. Scanlon (2008, ch. 4) sees blame as a way of taking the actions of another to indicate an *impairment* of a relationship.
8 Although this argument has primarily been developed for addressing individuals, there is no reason to exclude inter-institutional relations given that institutions are reason-responsive entities (cf. Scanlon 2008: 162).
9 'Cybersquatting' is the practice of registering domain names that are trademarked purely to profit from the domain. See Clausing (2000) for an extended discussion of the ICANN case.

References

Anderson, E.S. and Pildes, R.H. (2000) 'Expressive Theories of Law: A General Restatement', *University of Pennsylvania Law Review*, 148(5): 1503–1575.

Behn, R.D. (2001) *Rethinking Democratic Accountability*. Washington, D.C.: Brookings Institution Press.

Bevan, G. and Hood, C. (2006) 'What's Measured is What Matters: Targets and Gaming in the English Public Health Care System', *Public Administration*, 84(3): 517–538.

Bovens, M. (2007) 'Analysing and Assessing Accountability: A Conceptual Framework', *European Law Journal*, 13(4): 447–468.

Bovens, M., Schillemans, T. and Goodin, R.E. (2014) 'Public Accountability', in M. Bovens, R.E. Goodin and T. Schillemans (eds.) *The Oxford Handbook Public Accountability*. (pp. 1–22), Oxford: Oxford University Press.

Bovens, M., Schillemans, T. and 't Hart, P. (2008) 'Does Public Accountability Work? An Assessment Tool', *Public Administration*, 86(1): 225–242.

Busuioc, M. (2009) 'Accountability, Control and Independence: The Case of European Agencies', *European Law Journal*, 15(5): 599–615.

Busuioc, M. (2013) *European Agencies: Law and Practices of Accountability*. Oxford: Oxford University Press.

Busuioc, M., Curtin, D. and Groenleer, M. (2011) 'Agency Growth between Autonomy and Accountability: The European Police Office as a "Living Institution"', *Journal of European Public Policy*, 18(6): 848–867.

Busuioc, M. and Lodge, M. (2016) 'The Reputational Basis of Public Accountability', *Governance*, 29(2): 247–263.

Busuioc, M. and Lodge, M. (2017) 'Reputation and Accountability Relationships: Managing Accountability Expectations through Reputation', *Public Administration Review*, 77(1): 91–100.

Busuioc, M. and Rimkutė, D. (2019) 'Meeting Expectations in the EU Regulatory State? Regulatory Communications amid Conflicting Institutional Demands', *Journal of European Public Policy*, 27(4): 547–568.

Clausing, J. (2000) A Leader in Cyberspace, It Seems, Is No Politician, *New York Times*, April 10. Available at: https://www.nytimes.com/2000/04/10/business/a-leader-in-cyberspace-it-seems-is-no-politician.html [accessed 16 December 2020].

Clotfelter, C.T. and Ladd, H.T. (1996) 'Recognizing and Rewarding Success in Public Schools', in H.F. Ladd (ed.) *Holding Schools Accountable: Performance-Based Reform in Education* (pp. 23–63). Washington, D.C.: The Brookings Institution.

Cook, K.S. and Gerbasi, A. (2009) 'Trust: Explanations of Social Action and Implications for Social Structure', in P. Hedström and P. Bearman (eds.) *The Oxford Handbook of Analytical Sociology* (pp. 218–241). Oxford: Oxford University Press.

Darwall, S.L. (1977) 'Two Kinds of Respect', *Ethics*, 88(1): 36–49.

Darwall, S.L. (2006) *The Second-person Standpoint: Morality, Respect, and Accountability*. Cambridge, MA: Harvard University Press.

Demortain, D. (2017) 'Expertise, Regulatory Science and the Evaluation of Technology and Risk: Introduction to the Special Issue', *Minerva*, 55(2): 139–159.

Eriksen, A. (2020) 'Accountability and the Multidimensional Mandate', *Political Research Quarterly* [online first]. Available at: https://journals.sagepub.com/doi/full/10.1177/1065912920906880 [accessed 16 December 2020].

Gailmard, S. (2014) 'Accountability and Principal-agent Theory', in M. Bovens, R. Goodin and T. Schillemans (eds.) *The Oxford Handbook Public Accountability* (pp. 90–105). Oxford: Oxford University Press.

Grimen, H. (2009) *Hva er Tillti?* Oslo: Universitetsforlaget.

Groenleer, M.L. (2014) 'Agency Autonomy Actually: Managerial Strategies, Legitimacy, and the Early Development of the European Union's Agencies for Drug and Food Safety Regulation', *International Public Management Journal*, 17(2): 255–292.

Halachmi, A. (2014) 'Accountability Overloads', in M. Bovens, R.E. Goodin and T. Schillemans (eds.) *The Oxford Handbook of Public Accountability* (pp. 560–573). Oxford: Oxford University Press.

Hegel, G.W.F. (1991[1820]) *Elements of the Philosophy of Right*, [ed. A.W. Wood] [trans. H.B. Nisbet]. Cambridge: Cambridge University Press.

Herzog, L. (2013) *Inventing the Market: Smith, Hegel, and Political Theory*. Oxford: Oxford University Press.

Holst, C. and Molander, A. (2017) 'Public Deliberation and the Fact of Expertise: Making Experts Accountable', *Social Epistemology*, 31(3): 235–250.

Honneth, A. (2000) *Suffering from Indeterminacy: An Attempt at a Reactualization of Hegel's Philosophy of Right: Two Lectures*. Assen: Uitgeverij Van Gorcum.

Honneth, A. (2012) *The I in We: Studies in the Theory of Recognition*. Cambridge: Polity Press.

ICANN (1998) *Bylaws for Internet Corporation for Assigned Names and Numbers*. Available at: https://www.icann.org/resources/unthemed-pages/bylaws-1998-11-06-en#VI [accessed 16 December 2020].

INTOSAI (2013) *ISSAI 300: Fundamental Principles of Performance Auditing*. Vienna: INTOSAI.

Johansson, V. and Montin, S. (2014) 'What If Performance Accountability Mechanisms Engender Distrust?' *Urban Research & Practice*, 7(2): 213–227.

Koppell, J.G. (2005) 'Pathologies of Accountability: ICANN and the Challenge of "multiple Accountabilities Disorder"', *Public Administration Review*, 65(1): 94–108.

Kovacic, W.E. and Hyman, D.A. (2012) 'Competition Agency Design: What's on the Menu?', *GW Law Faculty Publications & Other Works*, Paper 628, 1–14.

Le Grand, J. (2003) *Motivation, Agency, and Public Policy: Of Knights and Knaves, Pawns and Queens*. Oxford: Oxford University Press.

Majone, G. (1996) *Regulating Europe*. London: Routledge.

Mashaw, J. (2006) 'Accountability and Institutional Design: Some Thoughts on the Grammar of Governance', in M.W. Dowdle (ed.) *Public Accountability: Designs, Dilemmas and Experiences* (pp. 115–156). Cambridge: Cambridge University Press.

McCubbins, M.D., Noll, R.G. and Weingast, B.R. (1987) 'Administrative Procedures as Instruments of Political Control', *Journal of Law, Economics, & Organization*, 3(2): 243–277.

Miller, G.J. (2005) 'The Political Evolution of Principal-agent Models', *Annual Review of Political Science*, 8(1): 203–225.

Moe, T.M. (1987) 'Interests, Institutions, and Positive Theory: The Politics of the NLRB', *Studies in American Political Development*, 2: 236–299.

Moe, T.M. (1989) 'The Politics of Bureaucratic Structure', in J.E. Chubb and P.E. Peterson (eds.) *Can the Government Govern?* (pp. 267–329). Washington, D.C.: The Brookings Institution.

Molander, A., Grimen, H. and Eriksen, E.O. (2012) 'Professional Discretion and Accountability in the Welfare State', *Journal of Applied Philosophy*, 29(3): 214–230.

Mulgan, R. (2003) *Holding Power to Account: Accountability in Modern Democracies*. Basingstoke: Palgrave Macmillan.

OECD (2018) *Best Practices for Performance Budgeting*. GOV/PGC/SBO(2018)7, 23 November.

O'Neill, O. (2002) 'Called to Account', *Reith Lectures 2002*, Lecture 3. Available at: http://www.bbc.co.uk/radio4/reith2002/lecture3.shtml [accessed 16 December 2020].

Ossege, C. (2012) 'Accountability–Are We Better off Without It? An Empirical Study on the Effects of Accountability on Public Managers' Work Behaviour', *Public Management Review*, 14(5): 585–607.

Peters, B.G. (2010) 'Bureaucracy and Democracy', *Public Organization Review*, 10(3), 209–222.

Piotrowski, S.J. and Rosenbloom, D.H. (2002) 'Nonmission-based Values in Results-oriented Public Management: The Case of Freedom of Information', *Public Administration Review*, 62(6): 643–657.

Radin, B. (2006) *Challenging the Performance Movement: Accountability, Complexity, and Democratic Values*. Washington, D.C.: Georgetown University Press.

Roth, A.S. (2017) 'Shared Agency', in E.N. Zalta (ed.) *The Stanford Encyclopedia of Philosophy*. Available at: https://plato.stanford.edu/archives/sum2017/entries/shared-agency/ [accessed 16 December 2020].

Scanlon, T.M. (2008) *Moral Dimensions: Permissibility, Meaning, Blame*. Cambridge, MA: Harvard University Press.

Skorupski, J. (1999) *Ethical Explorations*. Oxford: Oxford University Press.

Skorupski, J. (2005) 'Blame, Respect and Recognition: A Reply to Theo van Willigenburg', *Utilitas*, 17(3): 333–347.

Sunstein, C.R. (2019) 'Sludge Audits', *Behavioural Public Policy* [online first]. Available at: https://www.cambridge.org/core/journals/behavioural-public-policy/article/sludge-audits/12A7E338984CE8807CC1E078EC4F13A7 [accessed 16 December 2020].

Vibert, F. (2007) *The Rise of the Unelected: Democracy and the New Separation of Powers*. Cambridge: Cambridge University Press.

Vos, E. (2016) EU 'Agencies and Independence', in D. Ritleng (ed.) *Independence and Legitimacy in the Institutional System of the European Union* (pp. 206–227). Oxford: Oxford University Press.

Wood, A.W. (1990) *Hegel's Ethical Thought*. Cambridge: Cambridge University Press.

Wood, M. (2018) 'Mapping EU Agencies as Political Entrepreneurs', *European Journal of Political Research*, 57(2): 404–426.

7

ACCOUNTABILITY BEYOND CONTROL

How can parliamentary hearings connect the elected and the unelected?

Andreas Eriksen and Alexander Katsaitis

Introduction

Independent agencies wield public authority at arm's length from elected representatives and partisan politics. The principles of democratic legitimacy, however, require that public authority is politically accountable to elected representatives. How can a parliament employ hearings to ensure that the ends pursued by agencies have a democratic foundation?

On the standard view, accountability presupposes a certain division of labour. Political bodies, like parliaments, choose the ends of policy; the role of independent agencies is to provide expertise regarding empirical consequences and to implement the adopted policy (Richardson 2002; Vibert 2007). Accountability can then be conceptualised in terms of a principal-agent relationship, where safeguards are institutionalised ex ante and performance control is exercised ex post. On this account, independent agency expertise cannot be used to frame the political mandate itself; it is rather restricted to identifying empirical constraints: 'expertise acts as a kind of external filter on the deliberations of other parts of the division of labour such as politicians and ordinary citizens' (Christiano 2012: 42). In line with this, traditional principal-agent frameworks expect mechanisms such as written questions directed to agencies, agencies' annual parliamentary reports, and budgetary control to be used by the political actors as a source of technical information or reports on performance (Bach and Fleischer 2012; van Rijsbergen and Foster 2017). In a slogan, it is about the means of policy, not its ends.

In this chapter, we aim to contest the common conceptualisation that ties accountability to a strict division of political labour. We will focus on *hearings* as a mechanism that can serve accountability interests through what we call 'mutual attunement'. In order for there to be a coherent mandate for independent agencies to comply with, there has to a shared space of understanding. *Ex post* control measures cannot truly serve accountability unless the performance indicators are grounded in a sufficiently substantive justificatory relationship, which will be described in terms of an 'authority of connection'.

Insofar as hearings are governed by the aim of mutual attunement, we expect to observe three conditions. First, instead of a hierarchy where the principal sets ends and the agent reasons about the means, there will be reciprocal reasoning about ends. Second, there will an active interaction between actors where they constructively engage with questions and comments raised during the deliberation, rather than a passive statement of positions. Third, we expect to see a forward-looking outlook on policy that discusses potential future regulatory spaces, rather than a backward-looking account of the agency's actions.

We assess our conceptual argument through a case study. We conduct a content analysis of parliamentary hearings organised by the European Parliament's Committee on Economic and Monetary Affairs (ECON) and its interaction with participants from the European Securities and Markets Authority (ESMA), illustrating a different mode of engaging with independent agencies. We conduct the first systematic study assessing the deliberation that takes place within committee hearings between the members of the European Parliament (MEPs) and an agency. In doing so, we provide novel conceptual tools and material for further research into the relationship between agencies and elected representatives, and for normative assessments of its role in governance.

The EU context is an especially interesting test case, seeing as the literature has identified growing fears over weak accountability mechanisms and agency drift (Busuioc 2013; Dawson et al. 2015; Groenleer 2014; Levi-Faur 2011; Majone 2009). Our argument is not that such fears are unwarranted, but rather that the standards of assessment should track a feasible and normatively attractive model of accountability relationships. Most scholars agree that EU agencies are not making purely technical decisions (Busuioc 2013; Egeberg and Trondal 2017). Arguably, efficient agencies are impossible with the doctrine's prohibitive view on delegation (Everson et al. 2014). Our argument brings out why the political nature of agency reasoning about political ends is not, in and of itself, a threat to accountability. What matters is that agencies pursue ends in ways that are appropriately attuned to the reason-giving processes of politically representative bodies, such as parliamentary committees.

Two kinds of authority

In this section, we want to clarify the accountability question by unpacking two distinct modes of engagement. Drawing on Anthony Simon Laden's differentiation between the authority of command and the authority of connection (2012, Ch. 2), we explain how the traditional principal-agent approaches misses a key feature of accountability.

The authority of command is the most familiar kind of authority. It is about having the unilateral standing to change the normative environment. Addressees of this kind of authority are subordinates liable to receive instructions or sanctions. For our purposes, it is worth highlighting how this is the default mode of authority of the principal-agent approach, which focusses on the unidirectional ability to impose incentives on the agent. The basic premise of principal-agent models, as used in economics and political science, is that there is an information asymmetry between principals and agents. Seeing as the interests of the agent may diverge from the principal's, the authority of the principal manifests itself in incentives designed to align the agent's interests with the mandate (Miller 2005).

With regard to independent agencies, this leads to a control-oriented conception of accountability (Hammond and Knott 1996; McCubbins et al. 1987). The problem is couched in terms of how elected politicians can secure compliance without having the information to determine what specific outcome serves the interests of their constituents. The solution is framed in terms of administrative procedures that automatically steer the agency in the right direction – such as notice-and-comment requirements and evidentiary standards. What is particularly relevant here is that accountability is conceived as checking fidelity to pre-determined political ends. The main question is said to be 'how—or, indeed whether—elected politicians can reasonably effectively assure that their policy intentions will be carried out' (McCubbins et al. 1987: 243). In other words, the principal-agent framework's command structure rests on a strict division of political labour.

By contrast, the authority of connection leads to a conception of accountability that does not presuppose that political intentions are settled. The authority of connection concerns an essentially mutual answerability, where both parties shape a shared normative environment. In terms of standards of political interaction, this has much in common with the ideas of reciprocity and reasonableness associated with deliberative democracy (Gutmann and Thompson 1996; Rawls 2005). What Laden brings out, however, is that there is a form of authority involved in relations of reciprocity. It is the authority to confront others with considerations that must be responded to in terms of reasons rather than mere volition or decisional fiat (Laden 2012: 66–67). While one cannot command any specific action, one has the standing to demand that proposals be heard and given a reasoned response.

On the face of it, independent agencies do not have the political standing that the authority of connection requires. Formally speaking, they are executive or technical bodies, and as such they are considered end-takers rather end-shapers when it comes to political questions. However, this picture is misleadingly coarse-grained, and in the end it may obscure the conditions of a feasible and normatively attractive model of accountability. That is because the picture does not capture parliaments as potential addressees of political considerations articulated by independent agencies. In what sense are they addressees?

They are addressees in the sense that ignoring political reasons presented by independent agencies may detract from the legitimacy of the decision-making process. Independent agencies are institutionally committed to pursue public interest in a way that is guided by non-partisan considerations and ongoing consultation with relevant stakeholders (Mashaw 2018; Pettit 2004). Many administrative procedures are designed to promote impartial and inclusive reasoning; as opposed to mere compliance with settled political intentions of the elected politicians. Regarding the authority of connection, the important point is that both representatives of independent agencies and MEPs are bound by a commitment to the common good rather than partisan strategy or non-public interests (cf. Lord 2011: 916).

Arguably, this joins the two bodies in a way that enables the authority of connection. Naturally, they have different areas of expertise and are bound by distinct standards of argument, but independent agencies may have a legitimate standing to reason with the parliament about what ought to be done (ends), not simply what can be done (means). We call this process mutual attunement.

The argument pursued in this chapter is not that the accountability of independent agencies should be conceptualised in terms of one kind of authority rather than the other. Instead, both the authority of command and the authority of connection are necessary features of the accountability relationship to parliaments. The point is that command without connection with independent agencies does not serve accountability. Insofar as accountability is supposed to be a virtue of institutions, mere authority of command may be morally reckless given the access independent agencies have to relevant public reasons. Moreover, mere command without connection will also be ineffective. Independent agencies may prefer sanctions or irritating principals to the alternative of compromising their principles and professional judgement (Pollack 2007: 7; Waterton and Wynne 2004: 101–102).

Parliamentary hearings and measuring modes of authority

Hearings in most congresses and parliaments allow for the exchange of views between members of the parliament and various other actors over policy issues. Hearings offer the grounds for interactions between elected representatives within specialised committees and agencies that fall under their political responsibility (i.e. where they have agency oversight). Significantly, because of their deliberative nature, hearings may provide a venue for mutual attunement. However, without systematic analysing these interactions we limit our conceptual understanding of accountability to a static macro-form where aggregate institutional needs shade all interactions.

Therefore, if we are to observe an authority of connection rather than an authority of command between agency and parliament, we should observe a communication where specific conditions are met in their exchanges. Drawing on work on social reasoning (Laden 2012) and deliberative approaches to policymaking (Cohen and Sabel 2005; Eriksen and Fossum 2012), we identify three main criteria that can be used to assess whether we are observing an authority of connection or an authority of command in place, which we assess in this chapter. These criteria respond inversely under different modes of authority. The criteria are (i) relationship, (ii) interaction, and (iii) orientation. We discuss these measures below, and present them concisely in Table 7.1.

Relationship: hierarchy vs. reciprocity

The PA understanding of accountability assumes a distinct hierarchy under an authority of command, where the political principal dictates to the agent the limits and scope of its powers. In the context of deliberation, participants can appeal to their position (rank) to resolve disagreements, and/or force perspectives. Therefore, the participants are unequal in terms of formal authority, which spills over to their discussion in an observable manner.

By contrast, the authority of connection is grounded in reciprocal answerability. Each participant must appeal to reasons rather than mere expressions of will. As we will understand it here, the form of reciprocity required for connection can manifest itself against a background of institutional hierarchy. In our analysis, the relevant sign is how parties back their opinions and specifically disagreements; are they appealing to mutually shared standards as opposed to mere decisional fiat? Do political representatives attempt to force their perspective onto the discussion?

As Laden nicely puts it, 'particular instances of the authority of connection are not wielded like a sword, but jointly constructed like a bridge' (Laden 2012: 72). Hence, based on this view, refusing a suggestion is more like a dismissal than disobedience. In our analysis, we are concerned with how disagreements are dealt with; are they couched in terms of compliance or acknowledgment? If there is an authority of command structure in place, we expect to observe disagreements to be solved with final decisions made by the committee members.

Interaction: active vs. passive

Under a traditional system of agency oversight, due to the separation of ends and means, we expect principal and agent to exchange views on a broader theme without necessarily engaging in debate. Therefore, each institutional actor engages with a different aspect of the discussion's theme but not with the points raised by its counterpart. That is to say, under an authority of command, the communication between agency and the committee should resemble a series of monologues rather than a discussion.

Under authority of connection, there is a joint shaping of the normative environment. This requires that participants have the capacity to seek common ground by appeal to mutually acceptable reasons. It is a capacity to issue and respond to proposals, invitations, and questions, rather than merely assertions, instructions and answers. This capacity must be exercised on both sides of the relationship; speech-acts like proposals, invitations, and question are unsuccessful without appropriate uptake and response.

Therefore, we consider how policy ends are shaped; is there genuine engagement or is one part merely subservient? We expect that under an authority of connection, elected representatives and agency representatives interact through discussion rather than passive speech reading that serves a theatrical management of expectations. They discuss and mutually attempt to shape means and ends together. Conversely, if there is an authority of command we expect a passive interaction between representatives and agency.

Orientation: forward-looking vs. backward-looking

Having the standing (or de jure authority) to change the normative situation can be treated either as that settled in the past or as that depending on the ongoing interpretation of the relationship. The command perspective takes a backward-looking perspective; actors have been given prerogatives for unilateral use, and

TABLE 7.1 Expected measurement outcomes depending on the authority mode in place between parliament and agency communication

Relationship
Authority of connection
Reciprocity. Statements do not reflect a clear hierarchy between agent and principal but an open discussion. Points of disagreement are open-ended, that is, they are not resolved through direct order by the committee members.
Authority of command
Statements reflect a clear hierarchy between principal and agent.
Points of disagreement are close-ended, that is, they are resolved by direct order by the principal.

Interaction
Authority of connection
Interaction reflects active engagements. Statements reflect an exchange of views based on questions asked during the hearing time. Agency *and* parliament reflect on ends *and* means.
Authority of command
Passive Engagement. Statements comprise primarily read statements that reflect the discussions theme but do not engage with speakers' statements. Agency discusses *only* policy means. Parliament discusses *only* policy ends.

Orientation
Authority of connection
Forward-looking. Discussions address future policy actions such as potential future policy proposals.
Authority of command
Backward-looking. Discussions address past policy actions such as agency activity.

their authority is independent of the agreement of the addressee. In the connection perspective on authority, by contrast, the credentials are dependent on the interaction between participants. That is, the normative credentials of speech-acts depend on their ability to engage with the others in a way that is taken seriously and that enables mutual attunement. The authority of a proposal or invitation is, to some extent, acceptance-dependent.

Under an authority of connection we expect that agency and representatives engage in discussions primarily over future policy actions in an attempt to reach common ground over forthcoming expectations, rather than assess actions in the past. Conversely, under an authority of command model we expect that agency addresses past actions, which it reports to its political principals.

Why expect authority of connection

Having clarified the two modes of interaction and the associated measures, why should we expect to see one rather than the other? Some work on the EP's role in the accountability relationship with agencies has focussed on the role of the budgetary committees, where a principal-agent relationship of ex post control has been identified (Bach and Fleischer 2012: 161–162). Do we have reason to suppose things will be different in the specialised ECON Committee?

Based on a recent overview of the accountability practices ESMA is subjected to, one would suspect not. It suggests that political accountability involves the EP's and ECON's ability to 'interrogate the actor and to question the adequacy of the information or the legitimacy of the conduct' (van Rijsbergen and Foster 2017: 68). Practices of interrogation are much closer to authority of command than authority of connection. Nevertheless, there are reasons for the EP and ESMA to seek mutual attunement under the authority of connection. In this section, we explain three reasons for expecting of authority of connection, where each consideration highlights general aspects of relationships between elected politicians and agencies.

The first is *uncertainty*. As they attempt to regulate in the face of unknown unknowns, neither the agency nor the elected representatives can be sure about the line between means and ends. Moreover, key regulatory terms like reasonable precaution and proportionality tie professional considerations up with political values in complex ways. Thus, to address the constantly evolving regulatory demands of any domain, the responsible institutional players need to work out a shared space of reasons.

The second is *mutual dependence*. Often, the public image of an institution is connected to another institution's performance. An agency's reputation is linked to the public acceptability of the ends it pursues, which means it has an interest in engaging in evaluative matters regarding legislation (Carpenter 2010). Conversely, the parliament's reputation is linked to its capacity to enable efficient promotion of the public interest. For instance, limited support of an agency may turn it impotent, which, in turn, affects the parliament's public standing.

The third, which is particularly relevant in governance settings beyond the state, is the *dynamic* nature of institutional relationships. For example, it has been argued that the EU should be seen as a form of 'deliberative polyarchy', where, at the limit, principal-agent accountability gives way to peer-review (Cohen and Sabel 1997, 2004). Moreover, legal scholars doubt that a strong separation of powers between the legislative and executive branch along functional lines is either feasible or normatively attractive given the institutional realities (Carolan and Curtin 2018).

We are not suggesting that these expectations are equally warranted in all specialised parliamentary oversight committees. As a counterweight, here are three scope conditions on the authority of connection. First, when interacting with an agency with a comparatively *non-technical mandate*, politicians are less epistemically dependent and may have less incentive to attune themselves to agency judgement. Second, if an agency has a *bad or controversial public reputation*, committees may have an interest in appearing firm and critical in the authority of command mode. Third, partisan interests of committee members may *diverge* from the agency's mandate, making the interaction more strategic or confrontational. We do not think these scope conditions are particularly salient in the case of ECON and ESMA. The agency is fairly technical and recent, and it was created in response to a broadly recognised problem.

Research design: selecting a case study

To assess our expectations, we require information on the discussions held between a parliament and an agency during committee hearings. We focus on the EU's context for two reasons. First, the explosion of EU agencies has led to a rich literature examining accountability relations (Wonka and Rittberger 2010). Whereas the EP is identified as the 'locus of political accountability' vis-à-vis EU agencies (Busuioc 2013) researchers employ traditional approaches to assess its powers, such as MEPs' written questions, agency parliamentary reports, and budgetary controls.

While there is no doubt that EU agencies are held accountable by the EP under an authority of command, we argue that it is only a mode of authority in place within a broader system, where different modes of authority co-exist. Therefore, the EU provides fertile ground to test complementary accountability frameworks.

Second, following the financial crisis the EP, and specifically ECON, gained substantive policymaking powers due to the Europeanisation of financial regulation (Coen and Katsaitis 2019, 2021; Schoeller and Heritier 2019). Part of this move included the creation of the European Supervisory Framework, and the creation of ESMA (along with the EBA, and the EIOPA the form the ESA). We chose to focus on ESMA because it is an important example of a recent move towards delegating additional authority to agencies in the EU such as direct intervention and supervisory powers (Moloney 2011).

Indicatively, the agency was the centre of attention in a much-debated case that the United Kingdom brought before the Court of Justice of the European Union, where precisely the mandated political discretion of the agency was a core matter of contention (C-270/12). ESMA is therefore already a salient agency when it comes to conceptualising the political judgement exercised in supranational regulatory practice.

The agency mentions on its website that it is 'an independent EU Authority that contributes to safeguarding the stability of the European Union's financial system by enhancing the protection of investors and promoting stable and orderly financial markets'. Nevertheless, ESMA continues, 'Whilst ESMA is independent, there is full accountability towards the European Parliament where it appears before the Economic and Monetary Affairs Committee (ECON), at their request for formal hearings'.[1]

Therefore, from the EP's perspective, we decided to focus on ECON to which ESMA is directly accountable. The Committee is responsible for policy linked to the economic and monetary union. Moreover, it is responsible for the regulation of financial services, the free movement of capital and payments, taxation and competition policies, and policy linked to the international financial system.

The EP's committee hearings are recorded and available to the broader public through the EP's online archive. To assess the type of authority in place during ECON's hearings, we used the available search engine and located all ECON hearings where ESMA was a participant. We found seven hearings between 2011 and 2017 where ESMA was included; the relevant hearings were transcribed using f4transkript software, aided by a research assistant.

We conducted a content analysis taking into consideration our expectations and the outlined measures. Content analysis is a systematic examination and interpretation of a body of material in an effort to identify patterns and variation (see Berg 2009). There are different types of content analysis which depend on the degree of inductive reasoning applied (see Hsieh and Shannon 2005). In this chapter, we conducted a two-layered analysis. We first conducted a directed content analysis of the speakers' statements, which involves creating coding categories that have been derived from existing theories; in this case we developed measures drawing from deliberative theory and social reasoning (see Table 7.1).

We would like to highlight that our analysis assessed first the manifest meaning of the statements, and following that also examined the potential latent meanings within each theme if we deemed there was one. We are particularly interested in latent meanings because we are assessing the themes within each speaker's statement, but also the potential reaction to the themes by the other side. As such, our analysis contains a second layer of summative content analysis that explores potential latent meanings in the discussion.

To improve the validity of our analysis, each author and a research assistant involved in the hearing's transcription conducted a content analysis of the hearings. Each conducted an independent assessment of the relationship observed between MEPs and agency representatives, taking into consideration the literature on agency oversight, and the proposed conceptual frameworks. Whereas there was some minor variation between the three coders, all three identified a limited mode of authority of command, and identified a mode of authority of connection associated with the proposed measures.

Whereas automated text analysis provides an alternative methodology to our approach, we identified two key factors that led us to conduct a content analysis. To begin with, considering that even in automated text analysis ultimately the research must make some qualitative decisions (Benoit et al. 2009), and bearing in mind the need to identify manifest meaning across themes rather than specific words in the text, making predictive text reading difficult, employing an automated text analysis would limit our analysis's scope.

Moreover, to the best of our knowledge this is the first study assessing the actual content of the discussion that takes place within an EP committee hearing between its MEPs and an agency. As such, there is no other point of reference in the literature from which to draw pre-assigned values or principles of behaviour, which we can, in turn, correlate with specific strings of words. The undertaking of such an enterprise is a research project in itself. Being the first to assess the content of the discussion between MEPs and agencies this chapter aims to act as a point of reference for future work, outlining their structure, some behavioural principles, and guidelines for future research in this area, whether through automated text analysis or content analysis. In this spirit, the transcripts of the hearings are available to researchers through Harvard Dataverse.

Analysis

We begin our analysis with an overview of the hearings' structure. Overall, we identified a protocol of interaction in committee hearings that can be broken down into the following seven steps.

1 The committee chair makes a brief opening speech regarding the overall aim of the hearing.
2 The rapporteur makes an opening speech linked to the specific objective of the hearing, for example, the policy proposal's focus and general questions.
3 The participants make a speech discussing the hearing's point of discussion from their perspective; this speech is often pre-distributed to the MEPs beforehand.
4 The chair opens the discussion, where a set of MEPs' questions are directed to the panel. Most likely, the responsible shadow-rapporteurs or political group representatives responsible for the issue will ask the questions. Usually each political group will ask 1–2 questions per hearing, and each question can be directed to more than one panellist.
5 The panellists respond to the sets of questions.
6 The chair asks the rapporteur to draw conclusions.
7 The chair closes the hearing with a brief speech.

Considering this pattern, we identified variation in the hearings' purpose which influences their protocol of interaction, their participants, and to what degree they are forward- or backward-looking. Specifically, we identified two central types of hearings: (i) expertise-seeking hearings and (ii) oversight-seeking hearings (see Table 7.2). Out of the seven hearings assessed, two fall under the oversight category where the European supervisory authorities were invited to discuss their activity so far and future perspectives (ESMA, EBA, EIOPA). On the other hand five hearings out of seven reflected a discussion-panel type of hearing with a variety of actors invited.

In the first case, hearings seeking expertise consist of a diverse panel of participants involving a mix of representatives from EU agencies, think tanks, civil society, and national agencies and institutions, among others. The overall aim here is to conduct a debate/discussion where different perspectives over a particular issue are presented, for example hearing on FinTech or the MiFID II review. This hearing-type addresses either a space where a policy proposal has entered/soon will enter the legislative process (e.g. MiFID II) or discusses the potential needs for future regulation (e.g. FinTech). For the purpose of analysis, we call hearings that are primarily a deliberative forum *Type I*.

In this case, the hearing has all the steps mentioned above, but it is primed to be more forward-looking, and the discussion format is evidently more open. The MEPs ask questions the agency's opinion over distinct political issues, which we cannot be interpret as a form of control. Moreover, as the interaction between MEPs and agency is about reasoned engagement, the relationship shows reciprocity.

Example:

> I would like to thank … the panellists in the name of the ALDE group … And finally … What is your view on the Council's position and rapporteurs' position on the provisions …?
>
> Michale Theurer (13 June 2016 02:14:00)

In the second case, hearings that seek oversight involve the MEPs and an agency (or agencies) representative. In these hearings there is no rapporteur (i.e. step 2 is absent, while the chair conducts steps 6 and 7). These types of hearings are closer to an authority of command. Thus, they are relatively more backward-looking but not exclusively; the agencies discuss primarily their activity so far but also make future projections. For the purpose of analysis, we call hearings that have act as an oversight forum *Type II*.

Taking into consideration our analytic measures, it becomes apparent that there is a different mode of authority within the hearings. During steps 1–3, hearings take place under an authority of command where there is a distinct hierarchy, and the interaction is primarily passive as speakers essentially read written statements, which have been provided to the committee members before the hearing takes place. Moreover, speakers are more interested in making broader statements that contain a mix of forward- and backward-looking statements.

TABLE 7.2 Hearing type (I, II), title, date

Type	Title	Date
I	MiFID Review: Objectives for MiFID/MiFIR 2	5 December 2011
II	Hearing with ESA Chairs	19 September 2012
I	Market Abuse Directive	24 January 2012
II	Hearing with ESA Chairs	30 September 2013
I	Securitisation	13 June 2016
I	FinTech	29 November 2016
I	Recovery and Resolutions of CCPs	22 March 2017

This result partially explains why committee hearings tend to be lumped with other static forms of accountability such as written questions: their format makes it plausible that one type of authority permeates the procedure. However, as we show below this ignores the actual discourse that takes place during the discussion/debate (Zittoun 2009). While the hearing's general frame somewhat affects its structure, and specifically its outward/backward-looking component. Assessing the speakers' themes, we did not find a clear mode authority of command in steps 4–7. Focussing on the discussion component across hearings, we noted that our measures corresponded to an authority of connection. Below we provide an overview of our analysis vis-à-vis each measure, and some examples from the themes analysed to highlight our point.

Interaction

Assessing the themes content per speaker it became apparent that MEPs and agency representatives did not strictly divide their labour into a political jurisdiction of ends and an agency jurisdiction of means. Rather, both speaker categories employed a mix of means and ends in their speech, often under a broader theme. The general pattern observed was one where the speaker opens up with a broader comment that is linked to the political aspects of a policy/action in question, and follows up with a question linked to the agency's technical means. Significantly, this active engagement took place across hearings, including those that had an oversight objective. For example,

> … We're always very happy to have you [ESAs] and we hold in very high regard the work that you do … What do you think of the future of the credit rating …?
>
> *Sylvie Goulard (30 September 2013 00:43:44)*

> … And of course, here in Europe we want to have our share of the global economy pie … What do you think is the top priority … in the financial sector?
>
> *Cora van Nieuwenhuizen (29 November 2016)*

> ... I think the crisis is being exploited to put a European and international banking system in place ... But what about the real economy?
>
> Marco Valli (13 June 2016 02:21:16)

Moreover, we noted a deliberation in place where speakers engaged with the other side's points, that is, the agency representative took up the comments and questions raised by the MEPs in a constructive fashion. Similarly, MEPs considered points raised by the agency and posed relevant questions. We highlight that this engagement took place under an amicable environment where both sides provided positive framing devices over the procedure, their invitation to attend the hearing, and the agency's presence at the hearing. For example,

> Thanks for this response, but on ... I raised a specific issue ... which effort can ESMA make to ensure all over the common market that fees are limited and that they are fair and not burdening unfairly investors and their return?
>
> Sven Giegold (30 September 2013 00:58:12)

Relationship

Considering the relationship between MEPs and agency representatives during the discussion phase, we noted reciprocal reason-giving. To begin with, the extent of disagreement between committee members and agency was rather limited. Overall, MEPs or ESMA requested points of clarification or underscored key issues and/or objectives. Moreover, the response to these questions emphasised common reasoning and policymaking objectives. Furthermore, across all MEPs' statements we did not note an opinion pressed on to the discussion, or resolution of disagreement based on their authority forced onto the agency. The MEPs highlighted the agency's role in providing expertise necessary for the EP to progress with its policymaking responsibilities, while ESMA highlighted the EP's important role as a policymaker. As such, the relationship presented does not reflect one of principal and agent, but rather policymakers addressing different aspects of the policy domain's needs.

To the extent that a hierarchy was observed, this was noted in some specific instances where the MEPs and the agency highlighted the committee's role in shaping the agency. Nevertheless, these comments contained direct mentions by MEPs to expand the agencies powers Thus, further highlighting an organisational fuzziness where national vs. European perspectives were underscored, rather than legislature vs. agency. This lends support to our argument regarding the interconnectedness of institutional legitimacy, and the collective policymaking that takes place, while adding a Europeanisation dimension to it.

> ... The EPP will support you all [ESAs] when it comes to the budget, we believe your agencies need additional resources ... So our objective is your

objective, we want your agencies to fulfil your remit to the full and we want you to have the resources that you need. And the last thing we want is for you to be scapegoats when things go wrong.

Jean-Paul Gauzes (19 September 2012 01:52:53)

… Could you help us a bit more clearly [with] what you want? So which rights? Which rules? Which structures?

Sven Giegold (19 September 2012 02:15:18)

… what is that drives innovation, and what do we in the parliament have to do to ensure that we don't just simply put stumbling blocks in your way? How can we give room for innovation and competition to work its magic?

Beatrix von Storch (00:40:17)

… So, what kind of governance model for the colleges would you actually suggest? And then, on top of all this, is Brexit … can you comment on what you think the EU27 should do?

Perveche Beres (22 March 2017 00:41:16)

Orientation

As we mentioned above, the forward-looking or backward-looking focus of the participants has a correlation with the hearing's purpose. Hearings seeking oversight tend to address more ex post issues. Nevertheless, even within these hearings a substantial component discussed future projections of the agency's activities and the necessary budgeting it would need to achieve said activities. In this case, the committee requested from the agency's representative an assessment of the budget it would require (political means), which the committee was eager to support and even surpass.

Moreover, this forward-looking perspective is closely linked with an open-ended understanding of the hearings. Therefore, in a number of statements the agency opted to carefully assess a point raised by the MEPs and provide a response at a later time. As such, the hearings do not provide a closed set for the assignment of responsibilities but rather serve as learning enterprise that guides the policymaking process, and which can be re-visited as a point of reference by the EP and the agency in the future.

… What process do you envisage we're actually going to be following? How are we going to be treated as co-legislators in dialogue rather than as any other stakeholder …?

Kay Swinbrune (19 September 2012 01:57:44-2)

… On the longer-term funding of the ESAs, and that of ESMA specifically, I think the overall model where typically, the day-to-day supervision will be conducted at the national level … strong argument to do it at the EU level ….

Steven Maijoor, ESMA director (30 September 2013 01:28:14)

I think it's worth considering, but I don't have the answer today on that.
Verena Ross, ESMA executive director (13 June 2016 02:28:47)

Implications

In this chapter, we attempted to assess to what degree we observe an authority of connection or an authority of command in the discourse of committee hearings focussing on the exchanges between elected committee members and agency representatives. Based on our analytic measures, our content analysis provides a nuanced understanding of agency oversight in the context of committee hearings. While committee hearings' protocol of communication contains aspects reminiscent of an authority of command, the actual discourse that is part of the discussion section holds characteristics closer to an authority of connection.

The discourse highlights a reciprocity, where either side engages actively with points raised by the other addressing reasoned opinions not decisional fiat. Moreover, means and ends of regulation are discussed by both elected representatives and agency under a forward-looking attitude towards policy. We note that across all hearings the entire discussion is held in highly amicable environment. These results bring about some important implications.

First, the results paint an image that does not resemble the predominant understanding of accountability between political principals and technical agents. As both committee and agency deliberate and discuss the means and ends of future regulation, the relationship becomes intertwined. This lends support to scholars arguing in favour of accountability models moving beyond PA theory and closer to the fast-evolving reality on the ground (e.g. Cohen and Sabel 2005; Eriksen and Fossum 2012).

Furthermore, hearings contain value in terms of substantive engagement. We observe an interaction that attempts to address potential future regulatory needs both on a political and a technical level through meaningful discussion. The interaction observed suggests that claims of technocrats having won or that politicians have lost some general power struggle are misconceived. First, they misunderstand the overall legitimacy framework under which both institutions operate. The institutions are not isolated, but complementary; failures on one side reflect on the other. Thus, we observe a mutual interest in achieving fundamentally good policy. Attempting to create a common space of understanding and expectations through reasoned opinions is far from a power struggle. In addition, such claims employ an ideal setting that divides technical and political across the board, which, by default, are more merged in modern governance settings – particularly in day-to-day policymaking, as the analysis demonstrates.

However, we do not wish to overstate the implications of the findings. The mutual attunement we observe in the hearings assessed is part of a broader picture. The analysis indicates that a complex accountability universe exists. From a conceptual perspective, this chapter takes up authority of connection as an opposite pole ideal to the authority of command. It proposes criteria and measures to assess which pole a particular accountability mechanism lies in. Thus, future discussions on agency accountability should consider to what mode of authority a particular type of accountability tool corresponds.

The EP through ECON actively supports the further Europeanisation of financial policy; it has supported its creation, and would like to see its expansion. In doing so, the analysis points to a dimension little addressed in the literature, which is the mutual support between elected representatives and independent agency in further empowering European regulatory authority. Thus, one fails to capture the interaction with a perspective that sees the committee as geared exclusively to constraining, controlling or steering.

Conclusions

New governance confronts us with the issue of how to understand new modes of authority and accountability in dynamic settings. In this chapter, we have attempted to understand whether the political accountability of independent agencies can be understood outside a mode of authority of command with strict division of political of labour. Drawing on work on deliberative theory and social reasoning, we have argued that there is an authority of connection, where agency and parliament engage in a mutual attunement of expectations. Agency and parliament deliberate and develop a shared space of expectations. This is likelier to be revealed in forums that allow discussion and deliberation in real time, such as parliamentary hearings.

We examined our argument and provided theory-informed criteria that act as analytic measures testing the mode of authority in hearings' discourse. These criteria are (i) relationship, (ii) interaction and (iii) orientation. We tested our argument in the EU's context; specifically we focussed on the European Securities and Markets Authority and the committee it is accountable to, the EP's Committee on Economic and Monetary Affairs. We transcribed the entire population of hearings where ESMA was present since its creation (2011) until the first half of the 8th legislature (2017).

Our results reveal a discourse with little hierarchy; neither actor is limited to either means or ends, actors engage in an attempt to create a common space of expectations based on reasoning not fiat, and they are forward-looking in terms of policy. Significantly, the premise of division of labour where legislature defines normative ends that agencies aim to achieve, while agencies specify the terms of technical solutions, does not apply across the board. Rather, there are mechanisms where the labour is merged, and both agency and legislature attempt to contribute under a collective policymaking logic. While this is generalizable vis-à-vis EMSA, the proposed criteria should be tested on different hearings (other agencies) or on different accountability mechanisms.

Note

1 https://www.esma.europa.eu/about-esma/who-we-are [accessed 25 October 2019].

References

Bach, T. and Fleischer, J. (2012) 'The Parliamentary Accountability of European Union and National Agencies', in M. Busuioc, M. Groenleer and J. Trondal (eds.) *The Agency Phenomenon in the European Union: Emergence, Institutionalization and Everyday Decision-making* (pp. 152–171). Manchester: Manchester University Press.

Benoit, K., Laver, M. and Mikhaylov, S. (2009) 'Treating Words as Data with Error: Uncertainty in Text Statements of Policy Positions', *American Journal of Political Science*, 53(2): 495–513.

Berg, B.L. (2009) *Qualitative Research Methods*. Boston, MA: Pearson.

Busuioc, M. (2013) *European Agencies: Law and Practices of Accountability*. Oxford: Oxford University Press.

Carolan, E. and Curtin, D. (2018) 'In Search of a New Model of Checks and Balances for the EU: Beyond Separation of Powers', in J. Mendes and I. Venzke (eds.) *Allocating Authority: Who Should Do What in European and International Law?* (pp. 53–76). London: Bloomsbury Publishing.

Carpenter, D. (2010) *Reputation and Power*. Princeton, NJ: Princeton University Press.

Christiano, T. (2012) 'Rational Deliberation among Experts and Citizens', 27–51, in J. Parkinson and J. Mansbridge (eds.) *Deliberative Systems: Deliberative Democracy at the Large Scale*. Cambridge: Cambridge University Press.

Coen, D. and Katsaitis, A. (2019). A. Between cheap talk and epistocracy: The logic of interest group access in the European Parliament's committee hearings. *Public Admin*, 2019; 97: 754–769.

Coen, D. and Katsaitis, A. (2021) Governance, Accountability, and Political Legitimacy: Who Participates in the European Parliament?s Committee Hearings (ECON 2004-2014), *Journal of European Integration* (forthcoming)

Cohen, J. and Sabel, C. (1997) 'Directly-deliberative Polyarchy', *European Law Journal*, 3(4): 313–342.

Cohen, J. and Sabel, C. (2005) 'Global Democracy', *New York University Journal of International Law & Politics*, 37(4): 763–797.

Dawson, M., Enderlein, H. and Joerges, C. (eds.) (2015) *Beyond the Crisis: The Governance of Europe's Economic, Political, and Legal Transformation*. Oxford: Oxford University Press.

Egeberg, M. and Trondal, J. (2017) 'Researching European Union Agencies: What Have We Learnt (and Where Do We Go from Here)?' *Journal of Common Market Studies*, 55(4): 675–690.

Eriksen, E.O. and Fossum, J.E. (2012) 'Representation through Deliberation: The European Case', *Constellations*, 19(2): 235–339.

Everson, M., Monda, C. and Vos, E. (2014) 'What Is the Future of European Agencies?', in M. Everson, C. Monda and E. Vos (eds.) *European Agencies in between Institutions and Member States* (pp. 231–234). Alphen aan Den Rijn: Wolters Kluwer.

Groenleer, M.L.P. (2014) 'Agency Autonomy Actually: Managerial Strategies, Legitimacy, and the Early Development of the European Union's Agencies for Drug and Food Safety Regulation', *International Public Management Journal*, 17(2): 255–292.

Gutmann, A. and Thompson, D. (1996) *Democracy and Disagreement*. Cambridge, MA: Harvard University Press.

Hammond, T.H. and Knott, J.H. (1996) 'Who Controls the Bureaucracy? Presidential Power, Congressional dominance, Legal Constraints, and Bureaucratic Autonomy in a Model of Multi-institutional Policy-making', *The Journal of Law, Economics, and Organization*, 12(1): 119–166.

Hsieh, H.F. and Shannon, S. (2005) 'Three Approaches to Qualitative Content Analysis', *Qualitative Health Research*, 15(9): 1277–1288.

Laden, A.S. (2012) *Reasoning. A Social Picture*. Oxford: Oxford University Press.

Leyden, K.M. (1995) 'Interest Group Resources and Testimony at Congressional Hearings', *Legislative Studies Quarterly*, 20(3): 431–439.

Levi-Faur, D. (2011) 'Regulatory Networks and Regulatory Agencification: Towards a Single European Regulatory Space', *Journal of European Public Policy*, 18(11): 810–829.

Lord, C. (2011) 'The European Parliament and the Legitimation of Agencification', *Journal of European Public Policy*, 18(6): 909–925.

Majone, G. (2009) *Dilemmas of European Integration: The Ambiguities and Pitfalls of Integration by Stealth*. Oxford: Oxford University Press

Mashaw, J. (2018) *Reasoned Administration and Democratic Legitimacy*. Cambridge: Cambridge University Press.

Moloney, N. (2011) 'Reform or Revolution? The Financial Crisis, EU Financial Markets Law, and the European Securities and Markets Authority', *International and Comparative Law Quarterly*, 60(2): 521–533.

McCubbins, M.D., Noll, R.G. and Weingast, B.R. (1987) 'Administrative Procedures as Instruments of Political Control', *Journal of Law, Economics, & Organization*, 3(2): 243–277.

Miller, G.J. (2005) 'The Political Evolution of Principal-Agent Models', *Annual Review of Political Science*, 8(1): 203–225.

Pettit, P. (2004) 'Depoliticizing Democracy', *Ratio Juris*, 17(1): 52–65.

Pollack, M.A. (2007) 'Principal-agent Analysis and International Delegation: Red Herrings, Theoretical Clarifications and Empirical Disputes', *Bruges Political Research Paper*, No. 2. Bruges: College of Europe.

Rawls, J. (2005) *Political Liberalism. Expanded Edition*. New York: Columbia University Press.

Richardson, H.S. (2002) *Democratic Autonomy*. Oxford: Oxford University Press.

van Rijsbergen, M. and Foster, J. (2017) 'Rating ESMA's Accountability: "AAA" Status', in M. Scholten and M. Luchtman (eds.) *Law Enforcement by EU Authorities* (pp. 53–81). Cheltenham: Edward Elgar Publishing.

Schoeller, M.G. and Héritier, A. (2019) 'Driving Informal Institutional Change: The European Parliament and the Reform of the Economic and Monetary Union', *Journal of European Integration*, 41(3): 277–292.

Vibert, F. (2007) *The Rise of the Unelected*. Cambridge: Cambridge University Press.

Waterton, C. and Wynne, B. (2004) 'Knowledge and Political Order in the European Environment Agency', in S. Jasanoff (ed.) *States of Knowledge: The Co-production of Science and Social Order* (pp. 87–108). London: Routledge.

Wonka, A. and Rittberger, B. (2010) 'Credibility, Complexity and Uncertainty: Explaining the Institutional Independence of 29 EU Agencies', *West European Politics*, 33(4): 730–752.

Zittoun, P. (2009) 'Understanding Policy Change as a Discursive Problem', *Journal of Comparative Policy Analysis: Research and Practice*, 11(1): 65–82.

8

EXPERTISE AND THE GENERAL WILL IN DEMOCRATIC REPUBLICANISM

Kjartan Koch Mikalsen

Introduction[1]

Modern democracy depends on expert knowledge, yet at times democracy and expertise seem to be on odd terms. For some, establishing expert arrangements that diminish the direct or indirect influence of the people over political decision-making processes is a recommendable way of improving the quality of policymaking (Pettit 2004). For others, policy-relevant expertise is a potential threat to the equality of citizens, and might, if cut 'loose from effective control by the demos', lead to 'a kind of quasi guardianship' (Dahl 1989: 335). Still others see an outright contradiction between dependence on expertise and the egalitarian ideal of democracy as government by discussion (Turner 2003: 5).

Whether one takes an affirmative or a critical stance towards political expert arrangements,[2] the common problem underlying these evaluations concerns a perceived conflict between inclusion and exclusion. Whereas democratic government requires egalitarian and inclusive law-making procedures, expert deliberation is in important respects exclusive. The expert is someone who knows things known only to a few, and for this reason is the more reliable judge with respect to some subject matter.[3] Even if the reasoning behind expert judgements are potentially public, deliberation among experts will often remain relatively esoteric from the perspective of non-experts because of time constraints and the need for a division of labour (Moore 2014: 52–53). Accordingly, political expert arrangements have an air of Platonic guardianship about them. They appear to translate the epistemic superiority of the few into a form of political authority disharmonious with democratic ideals of equality and inclusion.

In this chapter, I take issue with the assumption that epistemic asymmetry between experts and laypersons is inimical to political equality. I argue that dependence on political expert arrangements stands in no fundamental conflict with the ideal of democratic government. Although expert arrangements come along with tensions and real concerns, none of them are fatal for the egalitarian idea of citizens giving laws to themselves. Contrary to Philip Pettit (2004), I see no reason to revise our fundamental ideas of what democratic government entails in order to better accommodate the need for expert knowledge in good government. The conventional understanding of democracy as a system of political self-legislation provides enough conceptual resources to justify delegation of political power to expert bodies. Contrary to Stephen Turner (2003), I see no need to make a trade-off between our equality as political reasoners and our reliance on expert knowledge in political matters. Our standing as political equals does not depend on epistemic parity in public discussion, so the mere existence of political expert arrangements does not subvert democratic self-legislation.

My starting point, in section I, is a critical exposition of Pettit's neo-republican case for a depoliticised democracy with institutions of unelected experts and stakeholder representatives authorised to propose policies in areas where electoral interests might trump considerations of the common good. Assuming that the common understanding of democracy as the empowerment of the people is incompatible with political expert arrangements, Pettit seeks to accommodate depoliticised institutions to democracy by reinterpreting the latter as empowerment of the right valuations. In section II, I argue that Pettit's revisionist move is superfluous. Based on Rousseau and Kant's democratic republicanism, I contend that delegation of authority to experts is not only compatible with popular sovereignty but also essential for empowering citizens in their common practice of self-legislation. In section III, I consider how recognition as an expert within a policy-relevant domain comes with opportunities for exerting undue political influence. Here, I also point out how public critique and institutionalised accountability mechanisms are important for mitigating this problem and for establishing conditions for rational expert agency in line with democratic norms. Finally, in section IV, I take issue with Turner's claim that epistemic asymmetry between experts and non-experts undermine the requisite equality of democratic deliberation. I argue that this claim rests on a flawed analysis, which not only overstates the link between epistemic and political dependence but also presupposes a too demanding ideal of public deliberation.

Neo-republicanism's revisionist ideal of democracy

'Democrats should worry when philosophers begin to speak the language of "republicanism"', warns John McCormick (2013: 89) in a critique of Pettit's neo-republican theory of freedom and government. Reading Pettit's (2004) case for depoliticising democracy through the formation of deliberative bodies of unelected experts and stakeholder representatives, this seems like a pertinent warning. Pettit's argument addresses various ways in which electoral interests might influence political decision-making to the detriment of the common good. Yet, as McCormick (2013: 105) aptly points out, Pettit's main worry is not 'that elected elites will *depart* from the will of the people', but 'that elected elites will be *too* responsive to popular majorities when the latter desire policies that supposedly undermine the common good or threaten the interests of minorities'. Pettit (2004: 54–58) highlights how 'popular passion', 'aspirational morality', and 'sectional interest' may thwart rational deliberation as to what best serves society as a whole by referring to policy issues such as criminal sentencing and prostitution legislation, as well as the problem of lobbying by well-organised minority interests. His concern is that the interest in being re-elected might induce representatives to make irresponsible decisions resonating with emotional and unreflective popular judgement instead of decisions based on a concern with the common good and considerations regarding overall consequences of choosing one way or the other.

As a remedy against the danger that the poor judgement of the people might stand in the way of good policymaking, Pettit proposes appointment of depoliticised commissions and forums that diminish the direct power of elected representatives over especially contentious and sensitive issues. Such depoliticised institutions should be composed of a mix of relevant expertise and representatives capable of speaking in the best interest of the people. Their tasks would include formulating guidelines, as well as monitoring and evaluating changes in existing practice. They should work 'at arm's length from parliament' so as to 'give a boost to the rule of deliberative democracy in public life' (ibid.: 56–57). Presumably, removing certain decisions from the direct control of elected representatives will increase the likelihood that the most adequate considerations guide political decision-making.

The problem with this proposal is not the idea of establishing deliberative expert bodies working relatively independent of parliament, but its justification, which reflects the oligarchic and aristocratic heritage of Pettit's neo-republicanism (Urbinati 2012). For one thing, it is less than clear why we should suppose unelected persons to be more capable than the population at large in freeing themselves from prejudice, short-sightedness and selfish desires. Not only is this to exaggerate the virtues of the unelected, but it is also a failure to acknowledge the ability of most people to make sound judgements. Moreover, even if one grants that there are policy areas where irrational popular opinion threatens the common good, the problem of specifying what particular areas should be depoliticised remains. Pettit does not tell where we should draw the line, and one might fear that potentially all policy issues are candidates for delegation to unelected bodies (McCormick 2013: 107).

Certainly, Pettit insists that his proposal is not adverse to the ideal of democratic government, at least under his own revisionist interpretation of this ideal as 'the empowerment of public valuation' (Pettit 2004: 60). In his view, the role of democracy is to prevent the state from becoming a dominator exercising arbitrary power over its citizens. Hemmed in by constitutional constraints, a combination of electoral and contestatory institutions is supposed to compel government to exercise its power 'in a way that tracks […] the welfare and world-view of the public' (Pettit 1997: 56). Constitutional constraints, such as rule of law-principles and separation of powers, serve this purpose by making the exercise of political power more complicated than it would be in their absence. Setting up institutional checks obstructs the will of the powerful, and thus guards against abuse of political power (ibid.: 173). Electoral and contestatory institutions for their part guard against false negatives and false positives with respect to the common good. The former type of institution, referring primarily to regular elections, increases the chances that all candidates for policies reflecting the common good will be given a hearing. The latter type of institution, which comprises bicameralism, independent judiciaries, tribunals, public hearings and more, makes it possible to 'scrutinise' and 'weed out' policies that do not answer to common interests by channelling disapproval and protests against laws and decisions not justifiable to all citizens (Pettit 2001: 159).

Conceived in this way, democratic politics can easily accommodate unelected bodies of experts and stakeholder representatives. Constitutional constraints rely on the existence of public institutions operating independent of elected bodies, and effective contestation requires an institutional basis distinct from the political bodies that issue laws and decrees. If democracy is 'a system for empowering the public reasons recognized among people' (Pettit 2004: 60), then delegating authority to unelected experts and elites is not opposed to democratic ideals, even if it creates greater distance between electorate and political decision-makers. Insofar as they counter electoral interests, the proposed measures serve to empower the right valuations – that is, those valuations held in common by the electorate.

By contrast, if one conceives democracy as a system for empowering the collective will of the people, then, claims Pettit, 'the depoliticization required by deliberation must be seen as inimical to the democratic ideal' (ibid.: 59). On Pettit's interpretation, democracy conceived as self-legislation by the people primarily requires institutional means that enable the people collectively to assert itself. Among such means, referendums and regular elections are the most important. Given this interpretation, it might seem quite natural to assume a conflict between democratic and deliberative demands. If democracy is conceived as popular control, then facilitating public deliberation through depoliticised institutions does seem to compromise democracy.

However, this analysis rests on a too narrow and formalistic interpretation of the conventional and non-revisionist democratic ideal. Rather than excluding delegation of political authority to unelected expert bodies, political autonomy or self-legislation by the people is a capacious ideal that provides conceptual space for a robust egalitarian justification of political expert arrangements. Where Pettit contrasts deliberative expert bodies and popular power, I argue in the next section that such bodies are indispensable means for establishing a system of government that empower the people as the ultimate source of valid laws. Accordingly, there is no need for a revisionist interpretation of the democratic ideal in order to reconcile it with deliberative demands.

Expert bodies in democratic republicanism

Pettit does not explicitly say so, but it is reasonable to assume that the conception of democracy as empowerment of the collective will of the people is also supposed to cover what he elsewhere calls a 'Franco-German tradition of republicanism' that originates in the political thinking of Rousseau and Kant (Pettit 2013: 169). In this tradition, we find commitment to an idea of freedom akin to the republican ideal of non-domination, as well as to the republican idea that non-dominating relations between persons can only obtain in a suitable system of public laws and institutions.[4] At the same time, Pettit accuses the founders of Franco-German republicanism for having 'totally betrayed' the older Italian-Atlantic tradition of republican thinking that he favours by 'espousing the idea of popular sovereignty' (ibid.: 187).

While Rousseau and Kant renounce 'democracy in the strict sense of the word' as a despotic form of government 'not suited for men' (Rousseau 2011: 200; Kant 1996a: 324), they both see self-legislation by the people as a key feature of the true republic. Ancient Greek democracy – democracy in the strict sense – could not satisfy republican ideals because it did not involve the separation of legislative and executive powers. Since the same body of citizens took on the roles of legislator, executor, and judge, ancient democracy was a form of arbitrary rule, where shifting majorities dominated shifting minorities. Like monarchy and aristocracy, democracy – conceived as rule of the many or majority rule – still meant someone's rule (*kratia*) over another. 'Ruling and being ruled in turn' was essential to democratic liberty (Aristotle 1981: 362), and there would always be one part of political society ruling over another part. By contrast, popular sovereignty is the principle of subjection to nothing but self-imposed laws. Republican government, as Rousseau and Kant conceive it, requires legislation by *one, undivided demos*, where the *demos* is 'the totality of those who are subject to the law' (Brunkhorst 2005: 71). Such identity of author and subject of law depends on the separation of powers. Republicanism aims at the abolishment of domination by reconciling political hierarchy with the fundamental equality of citizens. This ideal can be approximated only if a polity keeps the branches of government separate and gives primacy to the legislative branch.

An important reason Pettit considers Rousseau and Kant's vindication of popular sovereignty a betrayal is the implied rejection of a balanced or 'mixed' constitution that distributes power to separate agents so that power can be a check to power.[5] Instead of a system of checks and balances, Rousseau and Kant propose an asymmetrical institutional structure characterised by strict functional separation of powers, undivided sovereignty, and subordination of executive to legislative power. In their view, the executive branch should take no part in the legislative function of the state, and instead serve as an '*agent* of the state' charged with the administration and enforcement of law (Kant 1996a: 460; Rousseau 2011: 192–193). The legislative branch is for its part disconnected from executive and adjudicative functions. Its power is limited to issuing general laws equally binding on all subjects of law, whereas application and execution of the law belong to its subordinate organs: the judiciary and the executive.

We can think of this structure as an institutional 'veil of ignorance' that prevents legislation or redefinition of the law with a view to a particular case (Maus 2011: 50). It is a constitutional setup that serves the dual function of preventing self-authorisation by the executive and facilitating self-legislation by the people conceived as a united whole. On the one hand, binding executive and adjudicative functions to enacted laws enables persons holding public offices to 'exercise public authority rather than private power' (Weinrib 2016: 53). Since their authority does not stem from themselves, they do not subject us to arbitrary power when they apply and enforce the law. If they act within their mandate, they act as representatives of a public will rather than private actors guided by their own private purposes. On the other hand, limiting the authority of the legislative branch to law-making enables legislators to perform as a 'general united will' representing all and no one in particular (Kant 1996a: 457). Confined to issuing general laws, legislators can act as the concurring will of all citizens rather than a particular majority exercising unilateral power over someone else.

This emphasis on the unity of the self-legislating people does not make the Franco-German tradition of republican thinking inherently hostile to the idea of integrating expert bodies in the system of government. As an ideal of just government, popular sovereignty means that the people – either directly or via representatives – should be the source of all laws. This is fully compatible with delegating authority to unelected bodies as long as the latter remain under parliament's 'ultimate control', which is a condition Pettit carefully builds into his own proposal (Pettit 2004: 55, 57). Sovereignty entails the authority to reform public institutions, so popular sovereignty does not rule out delegation under the provision that the people retains the final say in law-making. To the contrary, the republican ideal of political self-legislation allows us to make a strong case in favour of political expert arrangements.

Arguably, delegating authority to expert bodies is not only compatible with, but also essential for approximating republican ideals. A general prohibition against political expert arrangements would be impermissible because it would be inconsistent with a republican system of self-legislation. To see why this is the case, it is important to note that the general united will of the people cannot be reduced to the contingent aggregate preferences of an actual assembly of persons. As the source of valid laws, the general will does not concur with just any majority decision, because valid laws are restricted to such that a people as a united whole can possibly agree to. The possible agreement of a people means consistency with each citizen's equal freedom under public laws, where freedom refers to a person's independence in relation to others. To be possible expressions of the general united will of the people, laws must be compatible with the independence of all subjects of law vis-à-vis every other person with which they interact.

The requirement that valid laws must be compatible with the independence of all subjects of law reflects a deontic norm of 'reciprocal independence' (Zylberman

2016: 295–296), which is integral to the political practice of self-legislation by the people. Reciprocal independence obtain when all interacting persons are free to pursue ends of their own choice independently of the choice of others. Independence in this sense does not require that we are unaffected by what others do. Surely, the actions of other people often frustrate our pursuance of ends, but this is compatible with reciprocal independence as long as our interaction does not involve subordination to another person's arbitrary choice. 'Liberty', Rousseau writes, 'consists less in doing one's will than in not being subject to someone else's' (Rousseau 2001: 260).

Since it involves a prohibition against subordination, reciprocal independence is comparable to the neo-republican ideal of non-domination: 'the condition under which you live in the presence of other people but are at the mercy of none' (Pettit 1997: 80). Yet, unlike the prevailing interpretation of non-domination as an overarching consequentialist good that political institutions should promote, reciprocal independence, as a *deontic* norm, serves as a restraint on the way purposes – good or bad – are pursued. Whatever a person does in a private or public capacity, her deeds are subject to the restraint implied in reciprocal independence. Only those things are permitted that conforms to the universal right to be one's own master, understood relationally as having no one else as one's master (cf. Kant 1996a: 387, 393–394). Reciprocal independence does not entail detailed prescriptions regarding what laws should be enacted, but the norm rules out laws and arrangements that make someone the master of others. Laws that turn persons into passive subjects 'would place a people, taken as a collective whole, in practical contradiction with itself' (Peterson 2008: 238). Such laws are contradictory in a practical sense, because in sacrificing someone's independence the people dissolves itself as a united whole.

Reciprocal independence is a moral standard of which republican institutions are partly constitutive. In contrast to dominant liberal and neo-republican approaches, Franco-German republicanism does not justify political and legal institutions instrumentally as means for realising moral results that are (at least in principle) specifiable independently of public institutions. As a moral ideal, reciprocal independence is indeterminate and impossible to realise in a world without public institutions that make, apply, and enforce laws (Maus 1994: 153; Ripstein 2009: 145–181). Absent such institutions, interacting persons would unavoidably subject each other to arbitrary choice because any enactment, adjudication, or enforcement of laws would be the act of a particular party to the interaction. Accordingly, political and legal institutions relate to reciprocal independence as enabling conditions, and not as more or less useful means for producing a morally desirable result.

This approach to political and legal institutions is consequential for how we understand the role of expert arrangements within systems of republican self-legislation. As a moral standard internal to republican institutions, reciprocal independence obliges states to act with a view to their own maintenance and improvement as freedom-enabling institutional structures. In order to bring themselves into conformity with their own justification, states should continually approximate the ideal of a self-legislating legal community where citizens collectively author the laws that bind them, and where binding laws are limited to laws required for harmonising the freedom of each person with the freedom of all others (Weinrib 2016: 58–60). The arrangements and measures needed for approximating this ideal depend on a wide array of expertise. For one thing, establishing a system of public justice requires both competent bureaucrats and people trained in the law. Moreover, to ensure that citizens do not become the dependents of particular others and to secure their own material foundations, states are responsible for the provision of essential public services: infrastructure, education, public health, social welfare, national defence, environmental protection, and much more. Effective and sustainable provision of such services requires expertise in the form of skilled and educated public servants.

More generally, government in accordance with republican ideals requires public discussion and policymaking informed by expert judgements. If the institutional structure of the state is to be brought closer to its own moral standard, then the general will of the people must proceed from public deliberation enlightened by state-of-the-art knowledge. To determine whether specific laws and policies are favourable to collective self-legislation and the reciprocal independence of citizens, one must consider competent judgements about probable causes of current predicaments and the likely consequences of laws and policies under consideration. Given the complexity of modern societies, responsible decision-making depends on consultation with the most reliable sources of knowledge of relevant empirical restraints. Elected or unelected officials who refuse to do so fail to act in conformity with the duties that come along with the offices they hold. While they might still act within their mandate, their exercise of public power is necessarily defective because they attend insufficiently to the conditions for realising a system of public laws and institutions that reconciles public power with the equal freedom of citizens.

This explains why there can be no general prohibition against political expert arrangements in a democratic republic. Since knowledge of how laws are likely to affect the life and freedom of those bound by them depends on expert knowledge, a general prohibition seems incompatible with a political community where the government represents the united will of the people. Such a constraint would not only rule out essential means for improving the public institutions that enable citizens to interact on terms of reciprocal independence but also undermine the people as a united public will authorising its own government. As a united whole, the people can only agree to laws and institutional arrangements that preserve the equal freedom of all citizens. A government that does not rely on truth-tracking expert arrangements does not seem capable of ensuring that this requirement is met. Absent expert arrangements, a political system is, at best, democratic in name only. Even where citizens have a right to vote and officials are constrained by constitutional laws, disregard of expert knowledge in policymaking means that political representatives can exercise power according to their own fickle and idiosyncratic ideas about how the world works. Under such conditions, voting first and foremost seems to serve as a mechanism for choosing a master that can exercise arbitrary power for a certain period. Rather than establishing a system of self-legislation by the people, this would turn citizens into the passive subjects of time-limited rule.

The argument in favour of political expert arrangements implies that there is an epistemic dimension to democracy. However, it does not involve commitment to an epistemic theory of democracy, where the latter implies 'that there exists some procedure-independent fact of the matter as to what the best or right outcome is' (List and Goodin 2001: 280). Democratic legislation must be 'truth sensitive' (Christiano 2012), but not because there are extra-legal truths that serve as separate sources of legitimacy. The purpose of political expert arrangements is not to help us pursue valuable ends that matter apart from political society. Instead, they serve as necessary means for approximating a system of law and government that conforms to its own immanent purpose:

> Find a form of association that defends and protects with all common forces the person and goods of each associate, and, by means of which, each one, while uniting with all, nevertheless obeys only himself and remains as free as before.
>
> *Rousseau (2011: 164)*

From this perspective, expert arrangements provide knowledge indispensable for approximating a system of public and self-imposed laws that to the fullest extent realises equal freedom for all. Rather than tracking moral truths beyond democratic procedures, they enable truth-tracking policymaking internally related to popular sovereignty. Accordingly, political expert arrangements need not be conceived as devices adverse to the idea of an autonomous people giving laws to itself. Their main function is to empower citizens in their common practice of self-legislation, not to depoliticise democracy. If philosophers stick to the Franco-German variant, there is no reason democrats should worry about the language of 'republicanism'.

Tensions between political expertise and democratic self-legislation

In the former section, I emphasised how expert knowledge is essential in democratic law-making. Against this, one might object that I have played down how political expert arrangements involve relations of rank and hierarchy that might hollow out democratic procedures. Does not giving experts a special place in the system of government unjustifiably increase their power to the detriment of others? Holding a position in the system of government certainly increases the power of the office holder. Inasmuch as political and legal institutions are constitutive of reciprocal independence there can be nothing intrinsically wrong with giving someone such a position. At the same time, uniting political expert arrangements with democratic law-making is not frictionless and unproblematic. Even if expert knowledge is essential for responsible decision-making, recognition as expert within a policy-relevant domain also comes along with opportunities for exerting undue political influence.

The opportunity to exert undue political influence is most obviously linked to an expert's formal role as a holder of public office. In this connection, the worry is that political problem solving becomes reduced to technocratic management. Proceeding from presumably incontrovertible normative premises, officials might conceive problem solving primarily in terms of finding the most effective means for goal attainment. As a result, both the horizon of relevant concerns and the involvement of citizens might be unjustifiably restricted with respect to political decision-making. The role of expert officials is not confined to cost-effective implementation of predetermined and unquestionable policy goals. In formulating policy advice or interpreting the legal mandate constituting their role as officials, experts necessarily make judgements that extend beyond the bounds of their own fields of expertise. To the extent that expert officials see themselves as value neutral instruments in the hands of policymakers,[6] the worry is that one constrains the space for public discussion about policy-relevant issues in problematic ways.

The power to problematically constrain the space for public discussion need not be directly linked to an expert's formal role as public official. A recognised standing as expert within a policy-relevant domain can have some of the same effect. Like everyone else, experts perceive the world from a limited perspective determined by a range of contingent factors, such as experience, training in particular professions or scientific disciplines, methodological ideals, or subjective expectations. Since their perspectives differ, different experts will typically approach political issues in diverging ways. What problems experts see and how they perceive them will be coloured by the terms and methods of their various fields of specialisation, as will assessments of possible remedies. Accordingly, the recognition as policy-relevant expert comes with the power to define both the terms in which a problem should be understood and the range of realistic ways of dealing with problems. Again, the risk is that experts curtail the space for public debate and policymaking, and, consequently, that one overlooks relevant perspectives. Whether an expert works as public official or takes the role as public intellectual, she can define and frame problems in ways that, consciously or unconsciously, marginalise the perspectives of both non-experts and experts within other domains.

A related problem concerns expert disagreement, which leads to the questions of who the relevant experts are and on what grounds we can trust them. The problem can be conceived as an epistemological question concerning warranted beliefs (Goldman 2001), but it also has obvious significance for democratic deliberation. Like the problem of framing and marginalisation, expert disagreement requires us to consider whose arguments and points of view should prevail in political decision-making. How do we make it so that relevant concerns guide political decision-making?

Discussing how we can square pervasive dependency on experts and expert arrangements with democracy, Cathrine Holst and Anders Molander has proposed three sets of institutional mechanisms for holding experts to account (Holst and Molander 2017: 242–243). First, in order to make experts comply with basic epistemic norms, they propose laws and guidelines that specify investigation procedures in some detail, procedures for reviewing expert performance, and for excluding experts with a bad record of accomplishment. Second, in order to review expert judgements, they propose checks in the form of fora comprising peers, experts in other fields, bureaucrats and stakeholders, legislators, or the public sphere. Third, in order to assure that expert groups work under good conditions for enquiry and judgement, they propose organising the work of such groups in a way that fosters cognitive diversity.

Holst and Molander view these accountability mechanisms as remedies or countermeasures to the misbehaviour of experts whose judgements are biased or influenced by private interests. The measures address unreasonable disagreement rooted in experts' over-confidence or partiality, as opposed to reasonable disagreement rooted in 'burdens of judgement' (Rawls 1993: 54). By targeting objectionable conduct and reasoning, they reduce the risk of fallacies and the 'intrusion of non-epistemic interests and preferences' (Holst and Molander 2017: 242).

To my mind, this is a too misanthropic grounding of the proposed institutional mechanisms. While they certainly might help increase the trustworthiness of experts, we should not confine their importance to reducing the impact of biases and partisan interests. Even trustworthy experts are not omniscient, but finite beings representing limited perspectives. However impartial and conscious of the limited reach of their own knowledge, they do not know what the world looks like from all other perspectives. Nor are they in position to decide what concerns are relevant and how they should be weighted in public inquiries and decision-making processes. Accordingly, we do not have to suspect anyone of poor performance or pursuance of self-serving interests in order to see the significance of formulating public guidelines, subjecting expert judgements to review, and organising diverse expert groups. Instead, these measures should be conceived as part of an institutionalised system of public scrutiny and criticism that is important no matter how ideal the expert. Public guidelines might provide expert bodies with a relatively clear mandate. Subjection to review can uncover significant objections to expert proposals. Diversity brings in more perspectives and possibly better input to expert deliberations.

Creating an institutionalised system of public scrutiny and criticism is aligned with the idea that making use of one's own reason involves reasoning together with others. Essential to rational agency is 'an attitude of suspicion towards one's own judgements' corresponding to 'a certain attitude of respect towards the opinions of other rational beings' (Neuhouser 2008: 207, 209). Recognising herself as one among other rational agents, the rational person considers the judgements of others an external touchstone of her own judgement. Only the 'logical egoist' who wants 'to appear as a rare human being' considers it superfluous to test her own opinion against that of another (Kant 2007: 240–241). In this perspective, we might think of the mechanisms and measures proposed by Holst and Molander as a way of institutionalising conditions of rational expert agency.

At the same time, we should not expect institutional measures to solve all problems. Accountability mechanisms may be constitutive of epistemically and politically robust expert performance, but there are no institutional guarantees for good practice. Nor can we expect institutions to do away with expert disagreement – disagreement that political parties and interest groups in turn may use strategically to further their own agendas.[7] In addition, there is the worry that political control regimes could do more harm than good by compromising the independence of expert bodies (Moore 2014: 51). Discretion and institutional independence contribute to expert performance, and so accountability could come at the price of diminished output quality, which would impair the purpose of political expert arrangements.[8]

With respect to making democratic and epistemic concerns pull in the same direction, expert arrangements that include lay participation seem ambiguous. On the one hand, bringing in the voices of non-experts in addition to other expert voices in some cases could prevent political expert arrangements from becoming vehicles of technocratic politics. On the other hand, the result could as well be 'undue and disproportional consideration of arguments that are irrelevant, obviously invalid or fleshed out more precisely in expert contributions' (Holst and Molander 2017: 244). One can also question to what extent lay participation is a democratising measure. It is by no means obvious that the few lay participants included in some expert body represents the people rather than the views and interests of a particular segment of a state's citizens.[9]

However important formal procedures for scrutinising the performance of experts might be, institutional design alone does not ensure that all relevant voices and arguments influence political decision-making. There might always be unheard voices and there is always the risk that the wrong voices win through. This is a general problem of all forms of government, and it does not apply exclusively to political expert arrangements. In the last resort, the problem points towards the public sphere and the *freedom of the pen* as 'the sole palladium of the people's rights' (Kant 1996a: 302). Free political speech allows citizens to bring attention to problems and aspects of the social world overlooked by experts and political representatives. As an open and anarchic space reproduced by communicatively interacting citizens, the public sphere can work 'as a sounding board' that 'amplif[ies] the pressure of problems [...] and dramatise[s] them in such a way that they are taken up and dealt with by parliamentary complexes' (Habermas 1996: 359). In addition to defects in laws and policies, public criticism can address defects in public institutions, including political expert arrangements. Through public criticism, citizens might not only bring blind spots into focus but also contribute to institutional reforms that makes the governmental system more congruent with the principle of popular sovereignty. Given the privileged position from which many experts speak, it may be difficult effectively to contest expert opinion, but lay citizens can also redefine a situation or a problem through persistent voicing of dissent and discontent.

Does epistemic asymmetry undermine democratic equality?

Because of the opportunity to exert undue influence, political expert arrangements involve a persistent challenge for democratic law-making. Still, we should not accept the more radical claim, voiced by Stephen Turner, that epistemic asymmetry between experts and the general public necessarily undermines our equality as citizens of a democratic republic.

According to Turner, political dependence on expertise implies a lack of reciprocity that 'is in fundamental conflict with the basic principles of liberal democracy' (Turner 2003: 48). Understood as government by public discussion, liberal democracy should involve equal opportunity to participate in public discussion on politically relevant matters. However, because of their different epistemic circumstances it seems that the requisite equality cannot obtain in relations between experts and non-experts. Not only do non-experts lack knowledge of many things known to experts, but often non-experts also lack the training required to assess directly the grounds backing up many expert claims. Accordingly, experts and non-experts cannot deliberate on an equal footing with respect to certain matters. When matters pertaining to an expert's field of competence are at issue, some claims must be taken on trust in the authoritativeness of experts, because a competent evaluation of the relevant evidence is beyond reach. In such cases, there is an asymmetry of discursive standing that enable experts to persuade other experts as well as non-experts, while non-experts lack the capacity to sway the opinion of experts concerning the matter at hand.

As Turner sees it, this lack of reciprocity turns someone's epistemic superiority into a form of political inequality adverse to democratic law-making. In his view, accepting something as true or valid based on expert statements involves undue deference to expert authority and failure to use one's own reason.[10] Meaningful public discussion should be 'generally intelligible' and characterised 'by some degree of mutual comprehension' (ibid.: 5, 12). Because of epistemic inequality between experts and non-experts we cannot be equals as political reasoners. Instead, we are left 'with a picture of modern democratic regimes as shams, with a public whose culture and life world is controlled or "steered" by experts whose actions are beyond public comprehension' (ibid.: 23).

This diagnosis seems to overstate the link between epistemic and political dependence, as well as to rest on an excessively demanding ideal of public deliberation. Admittance of relatively esoteric expert knowledge in public deliberation can only constitute an inescapable dilemma if it somehow conflicts with the idea of an inclusive public sphere that is indifferent to social status hierarchies.

However, there seems to be no compelling reason to assume that there is such a conflict.

For one thing, no one is expert across all the disciplines and professions relevant to political decision-making. Because of knowledge growth and specialisation, all experts are laypersons with respect to many domains where others are expert. As Kant – often mistaken for an epistemic individualist[11] – puts it, human predispositions for the use of reason 'develop completely only in the species, but not in the individual' (Kant 2007: 109). Since everyone lacks sufficient knowledge and training to assess the relevant evidence in most fields, the worry that someone might dominate others simply in virtue of epistemic superiority regarding certain matters seems grossly exaggerated. If we consider that we can only deal adequately with many, if not most, political issues by drawing on knowledge from a variety of expert domains, then the problem for democratic government generated by epistemic asymmetry is at least attenuated by the fact that we are all close to equals in ignorance.

Moreover, and more fundamentally, adjusting political opinions based on expert advice does not imply acceptance of status hierarchy between persons. Political equality can go together quite well with yielding to expert judgements, even when one does not grasp in all respects the reasoning that supports the judgements. To accept an expert judgement as authoritative in an epistemic sense is simply to accept that there are reasons supporting certain views and that these reasons are accessible to everyone who has time and skill to investigate the matter on which the expert makes a judgement.[12] Such acceptance involves no conflict with the republican ideal. Acknowledging another's power of judgement does not make that other your master. Nor is there any obvious intellectual failure involved in accepting the epistemic authority of experts. Thinking for oneself, striving to form one's own judgement rather than uncritically accepting everything others tell us is, of course, a commendable ideal. Yet to insist on always making up one's own mind without deference to expert opinion can also indicate a serious lack of judgement. After all, the expert might have good reasons for saying what she says, and refusing to consider her advice is not only appallingly arrogant but can also have grievous consequences.

Note also that discussion need not be generally comprehensible in order to be public. For instance, in distinguishing between private and public uses of reason, Kant primarily focusses on the status of the speaker and the scope of the audience addressed by the speaker.[13] First, unlike private use of reason, which is reasoning in one's capacity as an official whose reasoning is subject to authority, public use of reason is speaking freely in one's own person. Second, public use of reason addresses, at least potentially, an unrestricted audience, which is 'the public in the strict sense, that is, the world' (Kant 1996a: 19). Reasoning qualifies as public if it is free from two constraints: the constraint of speaking in the name of another and the constraint of addressing an exclusive audience closed off from the wider public. There is no hint that all aspects of public use of reason should be comprehensible to everyone. In fact, Kant also refers to public reason as the use of reason in the capacity of a scholar, and elsewhere suggests that with respect to scholarly discussions, 'the people are resigned to understanding nothing about this' (Kant 1996b: 260–261).

Correspondingly, in Habermas's analysis, epistemic parity is absent among the common features of the central institutions of the bourgeois public sphere. Discussion within *Tischgesellschaften*, salons, and coffee houses tended towards disregard of status, questioning of formerly unquestioned topics, and general accessibility (Habermas 1989: 36–37). Parity of discussants, free enquiry, and universal accessibility characterised the ideology of the bourgeois public sphere, whereas general comprehensibility appears inessential. Of course, admission to the public sphere was based on education, and for this reason also on property ownership (ibid.: 85), but these conditions point towards the public sphere's quality as a reading public more than a demand for a superhuman capacity to scrutinise directly every contribution to public debate.

We can add to this that complete epistemic transparency does not typically appear in contemporary accounts of the ideals embodied in democratic deliberation. Normally, the emphasis is on rational persuasion resulting from an open deliberative process where differences in wealth and power do not frustrate participation on equal terms (Christiano 2008: 190; Cohen 1997: 74–75). The important thing is that public deliberation should let 'the authority of the better argument […] assert itself against that of social hierarchy' (Habermas 1989: 36). This requires an inclusive public sphere where participants are willing to listen and learn from others irrespective of social status, but not that all participants must fully comprehend every aspect of the issues under discussion. Accordingly, it is hard to see how epistemic asymmetry in itself challenges the idea of democratic procedures as the 'discursive rationalization' of political power (Habermas 1996: 300).

Democratic deliberation need not be equally transparent to everyone. With respect to formal decision-making, democratic equality implies one person, one vote, as well as meritocratic assignment of public offices. With respect to deliberation and opinion-formation, the more important thing is to bring the impersonal force of valid arguments to bear on the matters at hand. Certainly, we have no guarantees that the better arguments win the day, but epistemic asymmetry does not justify us giving up on the ideal of political self-legislation by the people. As with public laws and institutions in general, we can expect permanent tensions between actual expert arrangements and the republican ideal, but such tensions are not fatal. Popular sovereignty demands that all governments to the fullest approximate the idea of an institutional scheme where the subjects of laws also are the authors of the laws. As a regulative principle, the moral standard implicit in public criticism does not stand or fall with its actual realisation. Existing governments can conform to it to a greater or lesser degree, and it is by means of the ideal standard that we can assess to what degree a system of political rule is morally adequate.

Conclusion

In this chapter, I have argued that the conventional understanding of democracy as an institutionalised practice of political self-legislation gives us enough conceptual resources to justify political expert arrangements. Contrary to Pettit, I do not see such arrangements as remedies against electoral interests unduly influenced by poor popular judgements. Nor do I see them as adverse to the idea of an autonomous people giving laws to itself. Political expert arrangements provide knowledge indispensable for approximating a system of public and self-imposed laws that realises equal freedom for all. In this way, they empower the people conceived as a self-legislating and united whole. Accordingly, there is no need for a reinterpretation of democratic ideals in order to accommodate the need for expert knowledge in good government.

This is not to say that uniting reliance on political expertise and democratic law-making is frictionless or unproblematic. Recognition as expert within a policy-relevant domain comes along with the opportunity to exert undue political influence, and so might unjustifiably increase the expert's power in relation to others. At the same time, we should avoid the hasty conclusion that epistemic asymmetry between experts and non-experts necessarily undermines democratic processes. Epistemic asymmetries do not threaten the main political function of democratic deliberation, which is to bring the impersonal force of valid arguments to bear on matters at hand. Nor do such asymmetries unavoidably subvert our equality as citizens of a democratic republic. We can expect permanent tensions between actual practice and the republican ideal, but such tensions are not fatal. Hence, unelected political bodies are not inherently adverse to democratic self-legislation.

Notes

1 I would like to thank Erik Oddvar Eriksen and the participants at the REFLEX-workshop *Making non-majoritarian institutions safe for democracy* at ARENA Centre for European Studies, University of Oslo, June 2019, for valuable comments and suggestions, as well as for stimulating discussion.
2 Throughout this chapter, I use 'political expert arrangements' about any public body staffed by personnel employed because of their specialised knowledge. The term covers bodies that perform governmental functions as well as bodies that perform advisory functions.
3 By defining expertise in terms of the capacity to make reliable judgements, I take my cue from Daniel Viehoff (2016: 409).
4 As I point out below, there are also important differences, both with respect to how they conceive the idea of freedom and with respect to how they think about the relation between freedom and political institutions.
5 Pettit aligns his neo-republican theory with the idea of a mixed constitution. Traditionally, this idea signifies a constitutional mixture of monarchy, aristocracy, and democracy which aims at the common good through mediation of the conflict between popular and aristocratic interests. In Pettit's usage, 'mixed constitution' primarily refers to institutional sharing and balancing of power as a crucial measure for securing the rule of law and the equality of citizens.

6 It is also questionable whether expert knowledge *qua* expert knowledge can be value neutral, that is, even if we abstract from the political context within which expert officials work. See Torbjørn Gundersen's contribution to this volume (Chapter 9).
7 Note that expert disagreement does not mean that anything goes. Even when there is substantial disagreement, expertise can serve as a truth sensitive filter that narrows down which 'kinds of theories can actually go into the process of policy-making' (Christiano 2012: 42).
8 In order to balance between institutional independence and accountability, Eva Krick and Cathrine Holst suggest that ex ante and ex post measures are more suitable than ongoing policy control mechanisms 'that include stakeholders and politicians on a par with non-political experts or that emphasise close and direct control of expert bodies' activities' (Krick and Holst 2019: 125–126).
9 See Erik Oddvar Eriksen's contribution to this volume (p. 27).
10 Although he draws less dramatic conclusions concerning the consequences for democratic government, James Bohman similarly speaks of a 'surrender' of 'autonomy to experts' (Bohman 1996: 168).
11 On the social aspects of Kant's epistemology, see Gelfert (2006; 2010).
12 I here assume a simple expert/novice situation without significant disagreement among the experts. As pointed out in the previous section, another type of problem arises when experts disagree, because then we must make judgements about what expert to trust. This problem does not undermine the present line of argument, which addresses the claim that accepting the epistemic authority of experts involves a form of deference incompatible with political equality.
13 For a good discussion of Kant's peculiar way of drawing this distinction, see Peterson (2008: 226–230).

References

Aristotle (1981) *The Politics* [trans. T. Sinclair]. London: Penguin Books.
Bohman, J. (1996) *Public Deliberation: Pluralism, Complexity and Democracy*. Cambridge: MIT Press.
Brunkhorst, H. (2005) *Solidarity: From Civic Friendship to a Global Legal Community*. Cambridge: The MIT Press.
Christiano, T. (2008) *The Constitution of Equality. Democratic Authority and Its Limits*. Oxford: Oxford University Press.
Christiano, T. (2012) 'Rational Deliberation among Experts and Citizens', in J. Parkinson and J. Mansbridge (eds.) *Deliberative Systems: Deliberative Democracy at the Large Scale* (pp. 27–51). Cambridge: Cambridge University Press.
Cohen, J. (1997) 'Deliberation and Democratic Legitimacy', in J. Bohman and W. Rehg (eds.) *Deliberative Democracy: Essays on Reason and Politics* (pp. 67–91). Cambridge: The MIT Press.
Dahl, R.A. (1989) *Democracy and Its Critics*. New Haven, CT: Yale University Press.
Gelfert, A. (2006) 'Kant on Testimony', *British Journal for the History of Philosophy*, 14(4): 627–652.
Gelfert, A. (2010) 'Kant and the Enlightenment's Contribution to Social Epistemology', *Episteme*, 7(1): 79–99.
Goldman, A.I. (2001) 'Experts: Which Ones Should You Trust?' *Philosophy and Phenomenology Research*, 63(1): 85–110.
Habermas, J. (1989) *The Structural Transformation of the Public Sphere: An Inquiry into a Category of Bourgeois Society*. Cambridge: The MIT Press.
Habermas, J. (1996) *Between Facts and Norms*. Cambridge: Polity Press.

Holst, C. and Molander, A. (2017) 'Public Deliberation and the Fact of Expertise: Making Experts Accountable', *Social Epistemology*, 31(3): 235–250.

Kant, I. (1996a) *Practical Philosophy* [trans./ed. M. Gregor]. Cambridge: Cambridge University Press.

Kant, I. (1996b) *Religion and Rational Theology* [trans./ed. A.W. Wood and G. di Giovanni]. Cambridge: Cambridge University Press.

Kant, I. (2007) *Anthropology, History, and Education* [eds. G. Zöller and R.B. Louden]. Cambridge: Cambridge University Press.

Krick, E. and Holst, C. (2019) 'The Socio-political Ties of Expert Bodies: How to Reconcile the Independence Requirement of Reliable Expertise and the Responsiveness Requirement of Democratic Governance', *European Politics and Society*, 20(1): 117–131.

Maus, I. (1994) *Zur Aufklärung der Demokratietheorie. Rechts- und demokratietheoretische Überlegungen im Anschluß an Kant*. Frankfurt am Main: Suhrkamp Verlag.

Maus, I. (2011) *Über Volkssouveränität*. Berlin: Suhrkamp Verlag.

McCormick, J.P. (2013) 'Republicanism and Democracy', in A. Niederberger and P. Schink (eds.) *Republican Democracy. Liberty, Law and Politics* (pp. 89–127). Edinburgh: Edinburgh University Press.

Moore, A. (2014) 'Democratic theory and Expertise: Between Competence and Consent', in Cathrine Holst (ed.) *Expertise and Democracy* (pp. 37–71). ARENA Report No. 1/14. Oslo: ARENA.

Neuhouser, F. (2008) *Rousseau's Theodicy of Self-Love: Evil, Rationality, and the Drive for Recognition*. Oxford: Oxford University Press.

List, C. and Goodin, R.E. (2001) 'Epistemic Democracy: Generalizing the Condorcet Jury Theorem', *The Journal of Political Philosophy*, 9(3): 277–306.

Peterson, J. (2008) 'Enlightenment and Freedom', *Journal of the History of Philosophy*, 46(2): 223–244.

Pettit, P. (1997) *Republicanism: A Theory of Freedom and Government*. Oxford: Oxford University Press.

Pettit, P. (2001) *A Theory of Freedom: From the Psychology to the Politics of Agency*. Cambridge: Polity Press.

Pettit, P. (2004) 'Depoliticizing Democracy', *Ratio Juris*, 17(1): 52–65.

Pettit, P. (2013) 'Two Republican Traditions', in A. Niederberger and P. Schink (eds.) *Republican Democracy: Liberty, Law and Politics*. Edinburgh: Edinburgh University Press.

Rawls, J. (1993) *Political Liberalism*. New York: Columbia University Press.

Ripstein, A. (2009) *Force and Freedom: Kant's Legal and Political Philosophy*. Cambridge, MA: Harvard University Press.

Rousseau, J.J. (2001) *Collected Writings of Rousseau*, vol. 9 [eds. C. Kelly and E. Grace]. Hanover, NH: Dartmouth College Press.

Rousseau, J.J. (2011) *The Basic Political Writings*. Indianapolis, IN: Hackett Publishing Company.

Turner, S.P. (2003) *Liberal Democracy 3.0*. London: SAGE Publications.

Urbinati, N. (2012) 'Competing for Liberty: The Republican Critique of Democracy', *American Political Science Review*, 106(3): 607–621.

Viehoff, D. (2016) 'Authority and Expertise', *The Journal of Political Philosophy*, 24(4): 406–426.

Weinrib, J. (2016) *Dimensions of Dignity: The Theory and Practice of Modern Constitutional Law*. Cambridge: Cambridge University Press.

Zylberman, A. (2016) 'Human Rights and the Rights of States: A Relational Account', *Canadian Journal of Philosophy*, 46(3): 291–317.

9

VALUES IN EXPERT REASONING

A pragmatic approach

Torbjørn Gundersen

Introduction

The role of scientific experts in unelected bodies, such as agencies, expert panels, and ad hoc committees, in public policymaking is inescapable. These bodies are designed to serve an epistemic and a technical role of making public policymaking more knowledge-based and efficient. However, they are intimately tied to ethical and political values in a way that ordinary scientific research is most often not. Scientific advisory work in agencies has a direct, foreseeable, and intended *political impact*. Moreover, the mandates of agencies often involve an *explicit aim* of promoting certain political goals, such as sustainable development or climate change mitigation. In this chapter, I examine the proper role of ethical and political values in the reasoning of scientists when providing knowledge for political use within expert bodies.

Philosophers of science who have grappled with this issue over the last couple of decades tend to adhere to one of the two divergent views. Some adhere to a version of the *value-free ideal* by recommending that scientists should strive to minimise the influence of ethical and political values on the knowledge they communicate and to defer the value questions to the public and its representatives (Betz 2013). According to the alternative and now arguably more popular view among philosophers and science studies scholars, which I shall here refer to as transactionism (Hicks 2014), ethical and political values play a legitimate and required role in all parts of expert reasoning. To provide policy-relevant knowledge in a responsible way, so those who adhere to this view tend to argue, experts should not aspire to be value-free (Douglas 2009). The philosophical discussion has thus revolved around the choice between two apparently incompatible views of seeing ethical and political values as either unacceptable (the value-free ideal) or acceptable (transactionism) in the reasoning of scientific experts. This chapter reframes the discussion of the role of values in expert reasoning. Using the role of scientists in unelected bodies as a source of examples, my aim is to develop and defend a new view on the role of values in expert reasoning by taking a more pragmatic approach. Contrary to the approach of central contributors in the literature of articulating and defending *an overarching and categorical principle or distinction* that defines the proper role of ethical and political values in expert reasoning, I will show that articulating and defending *a set of principles* that together regulate the proper role of such values is a more feasible approach. According to the pragmatic view of values, scientific experts must interpret, balance, and weigh these principles on a case-by-case basis.

To this end, in the 'The value-free ideal for scientific experts in unelected bodies' section, I shall consider the value-free ideal as it applies to the expert role of scientists, and lay out two central ways in which the ideal can be justified. In the 'Three transactionist arguments against the value-free ideal' section, I shall assess three central objections that have been raised against the value-free ideal in expert reasoning. I shall pay particular attention to the argument from inductive risk, which is widely considered the most forceful argument for the idea that scientific experts – under certain conditions – have an *obligation* to make ethical and political value judgements owing to the possible detrimental consequences of error. In the 'A pragmatic view of values in expert reasoning' section, I articulate the central features of the pragmatic view of values and seek to integrate some of the insights of transactionism with those of the value-free ideal in a way that is not only desirable but also feasible.

The value-free ideal for scientific experts in unelected bodies

In this section, I will present the value-free ideal (hereafter in this section, VFI) by articulating its main content, how it applies to the role of scientists as experts in unelected bodies, and its epistemic and democratic justification. When taking on the role as experts on a given topic, such as toxic waste or climate change mitigation, in unelected bodies, the VFI is a normative expectation that scientists often meet.

This chapter considers the experts that are either employed by an expert body (e.g. the EU agencies) or contribute to an expert body (e.g. the Intergovernmental Panel on Climate Change (IPCC)) on a temporary basis.[1] The source of their legitimacy is mainly a function of their knowledge-providing capabilities (their 'rigour', see Vibert 2007) and the facilitation of effective governance. The government's rationale for delegating authority to unelected bodies, however, varies (for overview, see Geradin and Petit 2005: 9). It might stem from the need for more stable and predictable regulation of policies, from the need for improved cooperation between different public institutions, or from ulterior motives to 'shift blame for unpopular decisions from governments to other actors' (Geradin and Petit 2005: 6).

Many kinds of expert groups are relevant to the realisation of the mandates of unelected bodies. Experts might be recruited from different academic disciplines, professions, or fields of practice (business, industry, non-governmental organisations (NGOs), or politics). I will focus on the experts recruited owing to their skills and knowledge in the *natural sciences*. Particularly in policy areas such as agriculture and fisheries, energy, public health, transport, and environmental issues, natural science is indispensable.[2] The role of scientists as experts in unelected bodies is best understood as a proper scientific role. This means that they should not only be held accountable to democratic principles but also scientific constraints and standards. In this respect, the role of scientists in unelected bodies is similar to that of professionals such physicians and lawyers who have a public mandate to perform a specific task in an autonomous way according to a set of epistemic standards and its own code of conduct (for a systematic account of the expert role, see Gundersen 2018).

It is fair to assume that some *aspects* of the work done within scientific expert bodies cannot reasonably be expected to comply with scientific standards. In the agencies where natural science is crucial, such as the European Environment Agency (EEA), European Fisheries Control Agency (EFCA), or European Food Safety Authority (EFSA), the governance and administration of the agency need not be regulated by scientific standards. The role of scientists as experts and the mandate of the agency within which they work need not be co-extensive: some of our normative expectations of scientists as experts do not apply to the unelected body as a whole and vice versa. This chapter considers the parts of the work performed by scientific experts within the agency that concern *the provision of knowledge* to other democratic institutions and the public, such as knowledge assessments, risk assessments, planning, or cost-benefit analysis (Dryzek 2013: 83–84).

In short, according to the philosophical literature, the VFI prescribes that ethical and political values should not play a role in the evaluation and acceptance of hypotheses (Douglas 2009: 45). In the case of experts, this means that ethical and political values should not influence the content of the claims that they provide to policymakers and other relevant audiences, such as interest groups or the general public. The contribution of experts is to inform, clarify, and improve the knowledge on which a policy can be based. Note that this definition amounts to a narrow ideal. Ethical and political values are deemed unacceptable. The VFI allows that *epistemic* values, such as predictive accuracy and consistency, can play a legitimate and required role in the evaluation and acceptance of hypotheses. Moreover, ethical and political values can play an acceptable role in problem selection or application of science as long as they do not influence the acceptance and evaluation of hypotheses, empirical claims, and general theories.

Let me now turn to the appeal of the VFI. Why is approximating the VFI desirable? The underlying motivations of the VFI are often briefly mentioned or tacitly assumed in philosophy and science studies. However, only few attempts have been made at explicitly formulating the normative arguments that support it. The aim here is to tease out some of the appeal of the VFI by providing a justification for it. I suggest an epistemic argument and a democratic argument for the VFI, which both focus on how it can play a beneficial role in the reasoning of scientists.

The epistemic argument for the value-free ideal

The *epistemic argument* for the VFI is based on the idea that the core of scientific knowledge production and dissemination requires protection from ethical and political values. As de Melo-Martín and Intemann (2016) argue, the VFI is motivated by 'the desire to protect the epistemic integrity of science against the problem of wishful thinking'. The argument can be formulated as follows. The proper role of scientific experts is to provide objective and reliable knowledge to policymakers. Ethical and political values can be a source of harmful cognitive distortion that undermines the ability of scientists to provide knowledge in an objective, reliable, and trustworthy way. To avoid such cognitive distortions, the proper role of scientific experts requires that the influence of ethical and political values is minimised. Hence, by seeking to minimise the influence of ethical and political values, the VFI reduces an obstacle to the proper role of scientific experts. Thus, an appeal of the VFI is that it serves as a safeguard against politicised and biased experts, which can come in the form of wishful thinking or brute manipulation and fraud. Scientific experts who communicate their results in a way that is tailor-made for supporting a political view or select data to benefit certain commercial interests run counter to the common expectations of sound science.

Values can influence the judgements of experts in more tacit ways or through explicit normative considerations. According to the VFI, both are unacceptable. A case of tacit value influence is preference bias, which can arise from the personal values of scientists or the institutional contexts in which they work. Wilholt (2009) argues that preference bias, which 'occurs when a research result unduly reflects the researchers' preference for it over other possible results', counts as an 'epistemic shortcoming'. Using examples from biomedical research, Wilholt (2009: 93–94) shows how scientists' preferences for some outcomes – owing to economic interests and institutional constraints – can unduly influence experimental design, interpretation of data, and dissemination of results. Because such cases of value influence can be unintended and tacit and can lead to rather subtle forms of skewing of the results, it is often difficult to ascertain whether the influence of ethical and political values is tantamount to scientific misconduct. Equally bad, as those who hold the VFI tend to argue, is the intrusion of ethical and political values that occurs owing to the experts' intended efforts to take ethical and political values into consideration as part of their reasoning in expert bodies. Examples of such value judgements include allowing the precautionary principle, economic growth, or sustainable development to influence the content of the knowledge they communicate to their audience, such as other democratic institutions, other stakeholders, or the public. For instance, if scientists downplay the epistemic uncertainty over some environmental risk to alarm the public, this might count as an epistemic shortcoming of the advice provided. Indeed, the idea that ethical and political values can lead to cognitive distortion that undermines the epistemic status of knowledge is rather uncontroversial.[3]

Now, if we agree that ethical and political values can influence the work of scientific experts in unacceptable ways, this suggests that it is desirable for scientists to exclude such values from their work, as recommended by the VFI. This recommendation, in turn, requires that we formulate professional guidelines and mandates to regulate expert practice to diminish the influence of ethical and political values. The VFI can thus be understood as an adequate response to the concern that different kinds of political, social, and commercial values skew and distort scientific knowledge. This concern, in turn, can justify the need for developing procedures, methods, and policies that can minimise such influences.

The democratic argument for the value-free ideal

The epistemic argument states that science requires protection from ethical and political values. However, it is also common to justify the VFI in the opposite way, as it were, by arguing that democratic policymaking and morality require protection from science (see, for instance, Betz 2013: 207; de Melo-Martín and Intemann 2016; Hudson 2016; Longino 2008: 128; Weber 2013[1917]). The democratic argument for the VFI can be formulated as follows. Democratic ideals require that all citizens are equally involved in defining the values on which policymaking is based. If scientific experts make ethical and political value judgements in a way that influences the knowledge they communicate to policymakers, they have an undue influence on the direction of policymaking. Hence, to avoid undue influence of science on democracy, the role of ethical and political values should be minimised, constrained, and limited in the way prescribed by the VFI. Longino (2008: 128) illustrates the rationale for the democratic justification of the VFI in the following quote.

> In a culture where so much rests on the sciences we fear that certain kinds of values will lead to acceptance of representations of the natural and social worlds in theories, hypotheses, and models that favor the interest of certain members of or groups in society over those of others.

Therefore, the democratic argument for the VFI is based on the worry that if scientific experts include ethical and political values in the communication of knowledge, they and the institutions within which they work will have excessive influence over democratic decision-making. That is, including ethical and political values gives them 'disproportionate power' (de Melo-Martín and Intemann 2016) and unjustifiable influence over the outcome of democratic policymaking and moral reasoning. This way of justifying the VFI is closely tied to a fear of technocracy, where experts have authority to make political decisions independent of democratic representation and participation. The power that experts wield in a technocracy can be defined in many ways; one interpretation is that experts in a technocracy have a mandate *both* to provide knowledge and to define the political goals that policymaking should be based on.[4]

In summary, I have provided a charitable interpretation of the VFI. Because the epistemic and democratic arguments arguably resonate with rather deeply entrenched intuitions about the proper relation between science and politics, I shall assume that they should be taken into consideration when formulating a new proposal for the role of values in expert reasoning. In the next section, I assess three central objections to the VFI for scientific experts.

Three transactionist arguments against the value-free ideal

The alternative to the value-free ideal is that ethical and political values are acceptable, legitimate, and even required in all parts of expert reasoning. Hicks (2014) has referred to this view as transactionism: '*transactionism* is the view that some ethical and political values may legitimately influence the epistemic phase of scientific inquiry – that is, they may legitimately make a difference to the content of the standards of acceptance and rejection' (Hicks 2014: 3274, italics in original). There are several objections to the value-free ideal available in the literature. In the case of scientific experts, I find three objections to the value-free ideal particularly influential and interesting: (i) an empirical objection, (ii) a political mandate objection, and (iii) an argument from inductive risk. These three objections will inform the pragmatic view of values that I flesh out in the 'A pragmatic view of values in expert reasoning' section.

The empirical objection

The empirical objection against the value-free ideal is rather common in philosophy and science studies, and is fuelled by the findings of empirical studies of science. As opposed to the idealised versions of science often found in scientific textbooks, social scientific and historical studies show how scientific expertise is entangled with ethical and political values owing to personal, contextual, and institutional factors (for a systematic account of such 'socio-political ties' of expert bodies, see Krick and Holst 2019). The strategy of the empirical objection is to show that the value-free ideal is untenable because it is based on a false view of science as value-free, impartial, or neutral. In different ways, versions of the empirical objection purport to show that the value-free ideal fails because the idea that science is or can be value-free fails. I think this line of reasoning tacitly informs much of the scholarly criticism of the value-free ideal. It can be found in both the science studies literature and the philosophy of science. For instance, a version of this argument can be attributed to Jasanoff (1990: 249), who states: 'The notion that scientific advisers can or do limit themselves to addressing purely scientific issues, in particular, seems fundamentally misconceived'.[5]

However, a reasonable interpretation of the value-free ideal is that it is a regulative ideal articulating that scientists should *aspire to* and *strive to* be value-free.

In this view, the feasibility of the value-free ideal does not rest on the implausible presumption that scientists can ever be completely free from ethical and political values, as some authors seem to imply (see, for instance, Kourany 2008). The VFI is compatible with the plausible assumption that scientists, like the rest of us, are influenced by ethical and political values in their work. Even if completely setting aside all ethical and political values in expert reasoning is impossible, the value-free ideal can be a meaningful ideal if there is a realistic possibility for scientists to *constrain*, *limit*, or *minimise* the influence of ethical and political values. This way of interpreting the value-free ideal can be found in the following quote from de Melo-Martín and Intemann (2016: 502):

> Clearly, the fact that an ideal might be unattainable does not necessarily mean that it cannot be useful in practice, so long as there are practical ways to promote or strive for the ideal. That is, even if value judgments are unavoidable, insofar as they are thought to negatively influence science, we can strive to minimize their presence. We take it then, that challenging the VFI requires showing that even attempting to approximate the ideal would be undesirable.
>
> *(2016: 502)*

In sum, while the empirical objection points to the all but inevitable entanglements between scientific expertise and ethical and political values, it does not entail that scientists cannot and should not aspire to be value-free.

The political mandate objection

Although scientific experts can limit the role of values in their work to comply with the value-free ideal, one might object that this runs counter to their public mandate. Indeed, the role of scientists in expert bodies differs from that in ordinary scientific research; their explicit aim in expert bodies is policy-relevance and to promote political goals, such as improving public health or protecting the environment. A case in point is the EEA, which provides scientific assessments and information about the environment to policymakers, particularly to the European Commission, the European Parliament, and the Council of the European Union as well as actors such as NGOs and the public. The EEA is an unelected body that is not directly controlled or governed by other EU institutions, and its authority stems from its expertise and ability to improve the epistemic basis of policymaking in the EU:

> [The EEA] is an agency of the European Union, whose task is to provide sound, independent information on the environment. The EEA aims to support sustainable development by helping to achieve significant and measurable improvement in Europe's environment, through the provision

of timely, targeted, relevant, and reliable information to policymaking agents and the public.

EEA 2019

As the quote from the EEA's mandate indicates, the role of the EEA is political as it aims to realise political values and goals such as an improved environment and sustainable development. Hans Bruyninckx, executive director of EEA, states that the EEA aims to 'contribute to Europe's ambition to make the transition towards a low-carbon, resource-efficient, and ecosystem-resilient society by 2050' (EEA 2015). Moreover, the mandates of agencies entail that experts must at interpret the meaning of political values (Eriksen 2020). For instance, the EEA's mandate of promoting sustainable development must involve an interpretation of that concept by the agency. This process is also likely to have a political impact. In other words, one might object to the value-free ideal that because the mandate of such unelected bodies is to promote and interpret political aims, demanding that the experts should aim to be value-free does not make much sense.

However, one could argue that an unelected body's political mandate need not imply that the scientific experts working within the EEA must make political value judgements in the very process of gathering and providing knowledge to policymakers and the public. Indeed, the EEA aims to realise its political mandate by providing relevant, reliable, and independent *information* on the environment. Moreover, since its establishment in the early 1990s, the EEA is expected to provide policy-relevant knowledge about the environment to the EU but to avoid making policy recommendations (Waterton and Wynne 2004: 90). Thus, it is fair to interpret the mandate of the EEA as implying some version of the value-free ideal.

In my view, the political mandate objection shows that the value-free provision of knowledge is not *sufficient* for the expert bodies such as the EEA to properly fulfil their mandate. This does not, however, entail that the value-free ideal cannot play a useful role in certain aspects of expert reasoning within agencies, such as collecting data and establishing empirical claims.

Having briefly considered two kinds of objections against the value-free ideal, I will now examine the argument from inductive risk, which is widely considered the strongest argument against the value-free ideal in the literature. According to this argument, scientists cannot and should not avoid making value judgements even when accepting and evaluating the empirical claims they communicate to policymakers and the public.

The argument from inductive risk

Let me lay out the argument from inductive risk (referred to as AIR in this section) using Rudner's (1953) seminal version of the argument as a starting point. His argument purports to show that scientists must make ethical and political value judgements in the very 'methods and procedures of science' (Rudner 1953: 1).

While later contributions have refined and developed Rudner's argument, the core idea can be found in Rudner's original version.

Rudner's argument goes as follows. First, he assumes that scientists, at a certain point, are faced with the choice of accepting or rejecting hypotheses. Rudner notes: 'No analysis of what constitutes the method of science would be satisfactory unless it comprised some assertion to the effect that the scientist as scientist accepts or rejects hypotheses' (Rudner 1953: 2). Second, owing to uncertainty and the lack of complete evidential support, scientists can make a mistake. In Rudner's terms, hypotheses are never 'completely verified' (ibid.) and therefore there is a risk that scientists can be wrong. Third, scientists must decide whether the evidence is sufficiently strong to justify the acceptance of a hypothesis. This decision cannot be resolved without the scientists using their judgement in deciding where to set the evidential standards required for accepting and rejecting that hypothesis. Fourth, the decision of where to set the evidential standards involves a value judgement of the ethical consequences of making a mistake:

> Obviously our decision regarding the evidence and respecting how strong is 'strong enough', is going to be a function of the *importance*, in the typically ethical sense, of making a mistake in accepting or rejecting the hypothesis.
> *Ibid. (italics in original)*

The AIR can be given a descriptive or normative interpretation (Betz 2013). The descriptive version of the AIR shows that it is *impossible for scientists to avoid making* ethical and political value judgements when they accept or reject hypotheses. This version of the argument can be attributed to Rudner, who concludes his article by saying that scientists 'must' make value judgements (Rudner 1953: 6).[6] According to the normative interpretation of the AIR, the argument purports to show that it is *undesirable* for scientists to try to avoid making ethical and political value judgements when accepting hypotheses. Because making a mistake can have severe consequences, ignoring moral reasoning as a part of the scientific process is undesirable. Douglas (2009: 87) explicitly interprets the AIR in a normative sense:

> Even when making empirical claims, scientists have the same moral responsibilities as the general population to consider the consequences of error [...] It means that scientists should consider the potential social and ethical consequences of error in their work, that they should weigh the importance of those consequences, and that they should set the burdens of proof accordingly.

According to Douglas (2009: 104), where to set the evidential standards for making empirical claims is partly based on a moral evaluation of the consequences of false positives and false negatives.

The AIR is highly relevant to the role of scientists as experts. Uncertainties and direct societal impacts are endemic to expert practice, and we might reasonably expect major inductive risk in the performance of that role. Some even argue that the AIR has limited scope and *only* applies to the context of applied and policy-relevant science, where science is communicated and used in policymaking contexts. A case in point is Steele's (2012) argument that Rudner's version of the AIR is not applicable to the context of scientific research as Rudner intended it to. Steele argues that the AIR fits better to the role of scientists as experts in policymaking. According to Steele, Rudner's 'points are arguably more compelling [...] when applied to the science-for-policy domain' (Steele 2012: 894). The reason for this is tied to the idea that scientists who inform policymakers must translate complex, technical, and uncertain knowledge to an audience of non-experts. Steele (ibid.: 898) illustrates this with the categories used by the climate scientists of the IPCC to report uncertainties, such as 'extremely likely' and 'likely'; these are coarse and leave the expert with a considerable discretionary space. The experts of the IPCC must therefore translate their beliefs about the current state of knowledge into these rather coarse confidence categories. The translation requires that scientists as experts make value judgements in the sense put forth by Rudner:

> In short, while Rudner's assumption that scientists must report certainties to policymakers is not convincing, there is a more plausible general assumption that delivers Rudner's conclusions: scientists must often, for pragmatic reasons, deliver advice to policymakers in terms of a standardized evidence/plausibility scale that is cruder than the scale appropriate for representing their beliefs. In other words, the structure of the beliefs of scientists is often more complex than the predefined evidence scales, and there is no canonical projection. In these situations, scientists cannot avoid making value judgements, at least implicitly, when deciding how to match their beliefs to the required scale.
>
> *Steele (2012: 899)*

Based on this view, the expert role of scientists demands that they communicate their knowledge in an effective manner to enable policymakers to make better and informed decisions. This requires that they translate complex and uncertain empirical claims into a form that can be understood and utilised by policymakers, who tend to lack the required knowledge for understanding and properly evaluating the claims. It does not suffice for scientific experts to approximate epistemic values such as consistency and empirical accuracy. They must take the perspectives, values, and level of scientific literacy of policymakers into account. Insofar as there is an epistemic asymmetry between the scientific experts and the policymakers and public for whom the reports are written, representing their beliefs as accurately as possible might run contrary to effective communication

(John 2015). Providing a mere presentation of existing uncertainties would therefore be a misleading interpretation of the public mandate of experts.

In sum, the AIR successfully shows that scientists in their role as experts ought to make ethical and political value judgements when translating and communicating the current state of knowledge to policymakers. In the next section, I will lay out the central aspects of the pragmatic view of values in expert reasoning, beginning with the implications of the three transactionist arguments against the value-free ideal.

A pragmatic view of values in expert reasoning

The three arguments against the value-free ideal – the empirical objection, political mandate objection, and argument from inductive risk – are worth serious consideration for those who adhere to the value-free ideal. However, instead of seeing them as *refuting* the value-free ideal, as central authors such as Douglas (2009) and Steel (2014) do, my approach here is to view them as providing us with insights and principles that can *supplement* the value-free ideal. First, my assessment of the empirical objection shows that ideals can be meaningful and feasible without presupposing perfection. Second, the assessment of the political mandate objection shows that scientific experts must take a broader set of political values into account to interpret their mandate. Third, the argument from inductive risk shows that scientists under certain conditions should make ethical value judgements owing to the risk of error. I find the argument from inductive risk to be the most forceful argument and will therefore elaborate on it.

The argument from inductive risk in the literature on values in science has two main responses. On the one hand, there are those who argue that the argument is unsuccessful and adhere to a version of the value-free ideal (Betz 2013; Hudson 2016; Jeffrey 1956; McMullin 1982). On the other hand, there are those who find the argument from inductive risk successful in undermining the value-free ideal and adhere to a brand of transactionism. Thus, the value-free ideal and transactionism are seen as competing and conflicting standards, which tend to be based on a diverging assessment of the success of the argument. There is, however, a largely unnoticed agreement between those adhering to the value-free ideal and transactionism. First, both assume that *if the argument from inductive risk is valid, it implies that the value-free ideal must be untenable*. Second, both camps aim to formulate *one fundamental, categorical, and overarching principle* for the role of values in science. The pragmatic view departs from these two views.

First, regarding the implications of the argument from inductive risk, the pragmatic view assumes that the value-free ideal can be interpreted as compatible with the argument from inductive risk. A successful version of the argument from inductive risk need not be interpreted as *refuting* the value-free ideal (I will elaborate on this in the next section).[7] Second, the pragmatic view departs from the (more or less tacit) view that the aim of philosophical inquiry is to formulate one fundamental principle on the status of ethical and political values.

It assumes that the quest for one single principle for how scientists ought to perform their role as experts in cases involving highly complex, uncertain, and impactful knowledge is misguided. This is mainly because the value-free ideal and its proposed alternatives are all insufficient in defining how scientists should consider ethical and political values in concrete cases. Because the value-free ideal is a proscription, it does not mention the many legitimate ways in which ethical and political values can play a role in expert bodies. As Resnik and Elliot (2019) point out, the alternatives to the value-free ideal suffer from the similar problem as the value-free ideal itself: they 'do not adequately address all of the ways that ethical and political factors may bias or corrupt research [...] they are incomplete' (Resnik and Elliot 2019: 6). Consequently, the pragmatic view assumes that the value-free ideal and transactionism together generate a set of valid principles for scientific experts.

Even more problematically, the ambition of formulating a fundamental principle neglects a central feature of the application of values and ideals in expert reasoning. Contrary to simple rules and algorithms, the application of normative principles and professional ideals requires the use of judgement and interpretation (Kuhn 1977). Principles are imprecise and must be interpreted, applied, and balanced in the choice situations that scientists find themselves in. I think it is highly plausible that the value-free ideal requires the use of judgement about how principles should be applied in concrete contexts, how they should be understood, and how they must be balanced against moral and political values. Hence, neither the value-free ideal nor the transactionist alternatives ought to be understood simply as a rule scientists have to obey.

Sketching out the pragmatic view

Having reassessed the implications of the arguments against the value-free ideal, I will now flesh out the pragmatic view of values in more detail.[8] The view is partly based on identifying reasonable principles in the discussion of the value-free ideal. Moreover, the pragmatic view is based on taking feasibility more thoroughly into consideration than what has been the case in the science and values discussions. So understood, when defining ideals for the role of values in expert reasoning, we are engaging in an attempt at formulating what scientists ought to do given certain facts about the decision situation they find themselves in and the principles we find desirable.

In short, the pragmatic view recommends that scientific experts must interpret and apply a *wider set* of epistemic, democratic, and moral principles on a case-to-case basis. The recommendation can be broken down into the following three claims: (i) The role of ethical and political values in expert reasoning should not be considered as always legitimate or illegitimate; (ii) both the value-free ideal and the central objections to it provide us with a set of considerations that scientists should take into account as experts; and (iii) in their role as experts, scientists must use their judgement in interpreting and balancing these considerations against each other in a context-sensitive and transparent manner. These claims are explained in the following paragraphs.

The first claim is that the influence of ethical and political values is neither only good nor only bad. Instead, the influence of ethical and political values in expert reasoning is more like a *double-edged sword*. On the one hand, it *can* be detrimental to the knowledge-producing abilities of scientists and can undermine democratic ideals and moral autonomy. The value-free ideal provides us with a normative response to these unsettling effects of the influence of ethical and political values in expert reasoning and resonates well with our intuitions about the role of scientists as providers of genuine knowledge to society. On the other hand, ethical and political value judgements can be required for scientists to provide knowledge to policymakers and the public in a morally responsible manner. The argument from inductive risk shows that in policy-relevant contexts wherein human well-being is at stake, scientists should consider the possible consequences of making a mistake. Moreover, to translate knowledge to policymakers and the public, scientists must make ethical and political value judgements (at least implicitly) when making coarser claims about confidence and probability. Reducing the risk of error by hedging, conditioning, and making uncertainties explicit so as to avoid making value judgements (Betz 2013) may come at the cost of making the output to policymakers and the public less relevant. To ignore and deny the role of ethical and political values even in the core of science can then lead to irrelevant and ineffective communication of knowledge.

Second, rather than presenting the discussion over values in expert reasoning in terms of being for or against the value-free ideal, the strategy of the pragmatic view is to *unpack the underlying normative arguments* in the debates. In my interpretation of the value-free ideal in the 'The value-free ideal for scientific experts in unelected bodies' section, I identified two important arguments for it: the epistemic argument and the democratic argument. I suggest that the value-free ideal should be considered as a regulative ideal that plays a useful role in steering scientists away from cognitive distortion and undue influence on democratic decision-making. Yet in some contexts where there is significant uncertainty and significant external impact, the argument from inductive risk shows that scientists should take the potential harm of making a mistake into account when providing empirical claims for practical use. This is because, as the argument from inductive risk shows, scientists, like the rest of us, are morally responsible for making an error and the expert role requires them to make value judgements when translating knowledge to policymakers.

In sum, the discussion over the value-free ideal has yielded four central principles that scientific experts need to take into account: (i) avoid epistemic distortions; (ii) avoid undermining democratic and moral autonomy; (iii) take moral responsibility for impact; and (iv) aim for relevance and usefulness to policymakers. This means that rather than deciding between the value-free ideal and transactionism on level 1 in Figure 9.1 on next page, the pragmatic view recommends that experts must apply the underlying principles on level 2:

Level 1: Ideals (philosophical)	
Value-free ideal ethical and political values are unacceptable	**Transactionism** ethical and political values are acceptable

Level 2: Principles for experts			
Epistemic principles	Avoid undue influence on democracy	Moral responsibility for impact	Policy-relevance
(Accuracy)	(Accountability)	(Precaution)	(Efficiency)

FIGURE 9.1 Ideals and principles for values in expert reasoning.

Although this does not mean that the principles on level 1 are irrelevant to expert reasoning, the pragmatic view assumes that scientists must ask themselves how the principles on level 2 indicate whether they should include ethical and political values.

The third and final claim of the pragmatic view is that scientists must balance and weigh these considerations against each other in *a context-sensitive manner*. In the professional ethics and bioethics literature, such balancing between conflicting moral norms is considered central to the moral reasoning of professionals such as doctors and lawyers. As Beauchamp and Childress (2009: 303) note, doctors' obligation of veracity is 'prima facie binding, not absolute'. Rather, veracity must be balanced against other professional obligations:

> Careful management of medical information—including limited disclosure, staged disclosure, nondisclosure, deception, and even lying—is occasionally justified when veracity conflicts with other obligations such as those of medical beneficence. As contexts change, the moral weights of veracity and beneficence will be heavier or lighter, and no decision rule is available to determine that one outweighs the other when we have to determine whether to disclose or withhold information. Accordingly, the weight of various obligations of veracity is difficult to determine outside of specific contexts.
>
> *Beauchamp and Childress (2009: 303)*

In a similar manner, scientists must *balance a set of principles* that applies to their role as experts. For instance, when assessing the current state of knowledge about climate change, scientific experts are mandated to perform their task in terms of not only epistemic accuracy but also effective communication and moral responsibility (Gundersen 2020). The epistemic caution of avoiding errors by accurately reporting uncertainties might have the potentially harmful consequences of failing to warn of dangerous climate change. Exaggerated environmentalist precaution might undermine the reliability of their claims or, worse, lead to radical climate policies without a factual basis. In sum, a central assumption of the pragmatic view of values is that scientific experts face conflicting normative standards and constraints, which must be balanced. The balancing of these considerations points to an integrative use of judgement.

Now, one might argue that the appeal to judgement in the sense laid out here fails to provide any useful guidance in difficult normative questions that scientists face. Those who share the ambition of developing a fundamental principle might feel that the pragmatic view does not convey much normative insight or any crucial guidance for scientific experts. In my view, however, the development of the principles that scientists need to interpret and apply in concrete contexts is about as far as we can get. The pragmatic view of values thus takes the feasibility of principles and contextual factors thoroughly into consideration and aims to develop principles that can 'actually guide people in their behavior' (Musschenga 2005: 468).

Finally, given the fact that epistemic, ethical, and political value judgements are integral parts of expert reasoning, the pragmatic view of values recommends that scientific experts should aim to be transparent about what kinds of value judgements they have made when deciding the empirical claims they communicate to policymakers. Insofar as scientific experts make value judgements when translating knowledge, they must be clear about the value judgements they make. This resonates with how Rudner saw the implications of his argument. Although Rudner says very little about how to tackle the issue, he does provide some hints by stating that 'objectivity in science lies at least in becoming precise about what value judgements are being and might have been made in a given inquiry' (Rudner 1953: 6). Rudner thus suggests the reasonable demand that, insofar as they must make value judgements, scientists should strive to articulate those value judgements. Epistemic, ethical, and political values can sometimes pull in different directions – that is, towards epistemic caution and environmental precaution, respectively. For instance, if scientific experts in the EEA lower the evidential standards for communicating that particulate matter causes premature death, owing to the possible detrimental consequences of making a false negative, they ought to make this explicit. To deny this kind of transparency runs the risk of technocracy and scientism, which the value-free ideal wisely seeks to avoid.

Conclusion

In this chapter, I have proposed a pragmatic view of values for scientific experts, according to which the scientists who work in unelected bodies must take a broader set of normative standards into account – epistemic, ethical, and political – to provide accurate and useful output to policymakers in a morally responsible manner. This *incorporates* the value-free ideal and the normative lessons that can be drawn from the central objections to that ideal. I have argued that the argument from inductive risk successfully shows that it is, under certain conditions, *ethically desirable* that scientists take into account the possible detrimental consequences of making a mistake when accepting hypotheses. Second, it is a *pragmatic requirement* that scientific experts make value judgements so as to provide policymakers and the public with relevant, useful, and applicable knowledge in accordance with the political mandate. The way in which scientists communicate knowledge to policymakers must be effective in the sense that it enables policymakers to make better decisions. However, the argument from inductive risk does not refute the normative reasons I identified for the value-free ideal in the "The value-free ideal for scientific experts in unelected bodies" section. The value-free ideal should be balanced against the moral and pragmatic concerns raised by the argument from inductive risk.

The pragmatic view resembles transactionism in the sense that ethical and political values can be legitimate when scientists provide empirical claims to policymakers and the public. Why not, then, simply see it as a form of transactionism? I have attempted to show that there are two main reasons for this. Even if scientific experts ought to include ethical and political values in their provision on knowledge, this does not refute the arguments for the value-free ideal. The pragmatic view states that the choice situation of the scientists who are to inform policymakers about the state of knowledge on some topic must take a broader set of considerations into account. The other reason is that the pragmatic view cannot be reduced to one overarching principle for the proper role of values in expert reasoning. Taking seriously the complexities of the tasks of scientific experts in policymaking – owing to uncertainties, risks, and policy-relevance – undermines the feasibility and desirability of one single normative principle.

Notes

1 Unelected bodies can have different mandates. They can play an advisory, monitoring, or regulatory role. Despite these differences, they are all given authority in democratic policymaking, regardless of how remote it might be from decision-making.
2 Some agencies such as ESMA or Frontex in the EU operate without leaning on experts from natural science in any substantial ways.
3 Even those who seek to replace the VFI accept this idea and incorporate it in their alternative proposals in some form or another (Douglas 2008, 2009; Kitcher 2011; Steel 2014). This could be considered to indicate that the epistemic argument is not unique to the VFI and that it does not discriminate between the VFI and its alternatives.
4 Recently, Sunstein (2018) has *defended* a 'technocratic conception of democracy' based on the significance of cost-benefit analysis, which states, 'the public is ultimately sovereign, but, for good reasons, technocrats are given a lot of authority – by the public itself. Most citizens know that they do not have the background or time to answer hard questions about food safety, about air pollution, and about carcinogens in the workplace. Cost-benefit insists that difficult questions of fact should be answered by those who are in a good position to answer them correctly' (Sunstein 2018: xi). This view departs from the VFI in that experts can make value judgements (e.g. over the value of human lives, nature, and the economy) without input from policymakers or the public. Insofar as this is the case, experts define not only the means but also the ends of policymaking.
5 For a similar argument, see Brown (2009: 2).
6 By saying that it is *impossible* for scientists to avoid making ethical and political value judgements, the descriptive version of the AIR can be given a more metaphysical formulation. It is not always clear whether it is understood in terms of the idea that scientists *as a matter of fact* must make value judgements or that it is *impossible* to avoid

making value judgements. I do, however, find the former version more plausible and shall here understand the descriptive version of the AIR in that sense.

7 That the AIR does not refute the two arguments for the VFI is underscored by the fact that the epistemic argument fits with a central commitment in Douglas's form of transactionism. Her normative proposal is based on the view that values should not be unconstrained in the core of science (Douglas 2009: 87). To prevent the harmful effects of ethical and political values, she limits the role of values to an indirect role, thus recognising something akin to the epistemic argument for the value-free ideal. De Melo-Martín and Intemann (2016) argue that Douglas's alternative to the VFI – *the indirect role of values* view – assumes a central idea of the VFI that values cannot serve as evidence, which, in their view, is untenable.

8 This is not tied to the philosophical views under the umbrella of pragmatism or neo-pragmatism. The view is pragmatic in the sense of being practical and taking the application of values, ideals, and standards we are considering here more seriously into account.

References

Beauchamp, T.L. and Childress, J.F. (2009) *Principles of Biomedical Ethics*, 7th ed. New York: Oxford University Press.

Betz, G. (2013) 'In Defence of the Value Free Ideal', *European Journal for Philosophy of Science*, 3(2): 207–220.

Brown, M.B. (2009) *Science in Democracy: Expertise, Institutions, and Representation*. Cambridge: The MIT Press.

De Melo-Martín, I. and Intemann, K. (2016) 'The Risk of Using Inductive Risk to Challenge the Value-Free Ideal', *Philosophy of Science*, 83(4): 500–520.

Douglas, H. (2008) 'The Role of Values in Expert Reasoning', *Public Affairs Quarterly*, 22(1): 1–18.

Douglas, H. (2009) *Science, Policy, and the Value-Free Ideal*. Pittsburgh, PA: University of Pittsburgh Press.

Dryzek, J.S. (2013) *The Politics of the Earth: Environmental Discourses*. Oxford: Oxford University Press.

EEA (2015) 'The European Environment Agency: Who We Are, What We Do, How We Do It', *General Brochure*, No 2/2015. Available at: https://www.eea.europa.eu/publications/eea-general-brochure [accessed 17 December 2020].

EEA (2019) *About Us*. Available at: https://www.eea.europa.eu/about-us [accessed 17 December 2020].

Eriksen, A. (2020) 'Accountability and the Multidimensional Mandate', *Political Research Quarterly* [online first]. https://doi.org/10.1177/1065912920906880.

Geradin, D. and Petit, N. (eds.) (2005) *Regulation Through Agencies in the EU: A New Paradigm of European Governance*. Cheltenham: Edward Elgar Publishing.

Gundersen, T. (2018) 'Scientists as Experts: A Distinct Role?', *Studies in History and Philosophy of Science Part A*, 69: 52–59.

Gundersen, T. (2020) 'Value-Free yet Policy-Relevant? The Normative Views of Climate Scientists and Their Bearing on Philosophy', *Perspectives on Science*, 28(1): 89–118.

Hicks, D.J. (2014) 'A New Direction for Science and Values', *Synthese*, 191(14): 3271–3295.

Hudson, R. (2016) 'Why We Should Not Reject the Value-Free Ideal of Science', *Perspectives on Science*, 24(2): 167–191.

Jasanoff, S. (1990) *The Fifth Branch: Science Advisers as Policymakers*. Cambridge, MA: Harvard University Press.

Jeffrey, R.C. (1956) 'Valuation and Acceptance of Scientific Hypotheses', *Philosophy of Science*, 23(3): 237–246.

John, S. (2015) 'The Example of the IPCC Does Not Vindicate the Value Free Ideal: A Reply to Gregor Betz', *European Journal for Philosophy of Science*, 5(1): 1–13.

Kitcher, P. (2011) *Science in a Democratic Society*. Amherst, NY: Prometheus Books.

Kourany, J.A. (2008) 'Replacing the Ideal of Value-Free Science' in M. Carrier, D. Howard, and J.A. Kourany (eds.) *The Challenge of the Social and the Pressure of Practice: Science and Values Revisited* (pp. 87–111). Pittsburgh, PA: University of Pittsburgh Press.

Kuhn, T.S. (1977) 'Objectivity, Value Judgement, and Theory Choice', in *The Essential Tension: Selected Studies in Scientific Tradition and Change*, 320–339. Chicago, IL: University of Chicago Press.

Krick, E. and Holst, C. (2019) 'The Socio-Political Ties of Expert Bodies. How to Reconcile the Independence Requirement of Reliable Expertise and the Responsiveness Requirement of Democratic Governance', *European Politics and Society*, 20(1): 117–131.

Longino, H.E. (2008) 'Values, Heuristics, and the Politics of Knowledge', in M. Carrier, D. Howard, and J. Kourany (eds.) *The Challenge of the Social and the Pressure of Practice, Science and Values Revisited* (pp. 68–86). Pittsburgh, PA: University of Pittsburgh Press.

McMullin, E. (1982) 'Values in Science', *Proceedings of the Biennial Meeting of the Philosophy of Science Association*, 2: 3–28.

Musschenga, A.W. (2005) 'Empirical Ethics, Context-Sensitivity, and Contextualism', *Journal of Medicine and Philosophy*, 30(5): 467–490.

Resnik, D.B. and Elliott, K.C. (2019) 'Value-Entanglement and the Integrity of Scientific Research', *Studies in History and Philosophy of Science Part A*, 75: 1–11.

Rudner, R. (1953) 'The Scientist Qua Scientist Makes Value Judgements', *Philosophy of Science*, 20(1): 1–6.

Steel, D. (2014) *Philosophy and the Precautionary Principle*. Cambridge: Cambridge University Press.

Steele, K. (2012) 'The Scientist Qua Policy Advisor Makes Value Judgements', *Philosophy of Science*, 79(5): 893–904.

Sunstein, C.R. (2018) *The Cost-Benefit Revolution*. Cambridge: MIT Press.

Vibert, F. (2007) *The Rise of the Unelected: Democracy and the New Separation of Powers*. Cambridge University Press.

Waterton, C. and Wynne, B. (2004) 'Knowledge and Political Order in the European Environment Agency', in S. Jasanoff (ed.) *States of Knowledge: The Co-Production of Science and Social Order* (pp. 87–108). Abingdon: Routledge.

Weber, M. (2013[1917]) 'Der Sinn der "Wertfreiheit" der Soziologischen und Ökonomischen Wissenschaften', in M. Carrier, and Schurz, G. (eds.) *Werte in den Wissenschaften. Neue Ansätze zum Werturteilsstreit* (pp. 33–56). Berlin: Suhrkamp Verlag.

Wilholt, T. (2009) 'Bias and Values in Scientific Research', *Studies in History and Philosophy of Science Part A*, 40(1): 92–101.

10
EXPERTS
From technocrats to representatives

Erik O. Eriksen

Introduction

The previous chapters have made clear that knowledge-based decision-making is indispensable to modern democracies, but also that there is a tension between democracy and depoliticised expert arrangements. Where democracy requires egalitarian and inclusive law-making procedures, expert deliberation is, in important respects, exclusive. It privileges the knowers with regard to truth. This is a problem, in particular when experts with decision-making power operate within large zones of discretion. Inevitably, they deal with values and *policy ends*, and not just *means* when they handle controversial issues, and hence they wield political influence. They affect who gets what, when and how. The general problem of the discretionary powers of unelected bodies is that they are in tension with the requirements of the democratic *Rechtsstaat*. There is a tension between discretion and the formal demands of the rule of law – the principles of predictability, legality, and equal treatment, and there is a tension between discretion and democratic authorisation, raising the prospects of arbitrary rule.

Unelected bodies or *non-majoritarian institutions* (NOMIS) with specialised authority, neither directly elected nor directly managed by elected officials, are, as demonstrated, difficult to hold to account through delegation models of control. Accountability entails the obligation to justify and thus to ensure that discretionary decision-making power is used in a reasoned and justifiable manner. It has been argued that accountability and hence the conditions of legitimacy can be captured in *the public reason model*.

This assumption finds its basis in *the right to reasons*, which is an independent human right as well as a constitutional right. To be subject to unreasoned or unjustified administrative law is to be treated as the mere object of political power, not as a subject, that is, not as a co-legislator, that is as a citizen with political rights. There is a moral right to be given reasons for consequential decisions (Forst 2012). This right to justification, then, is not merely an instrument for protecting other rights, but is a right that expresses everybody's equal worth and membership in the sovereign body responsible for the wielding of political power. It is the manifestation of the moral principle of equal citizenship.

The right to justification confers a duty on public institutions to provide reasons. And, as indicated, reasons are, in fact, legally requested whenever an administrative decision is subject to judicial review. The requirement to give reasons is entrenched as positive law both in Europe, especially in the EU,[1] and in the United States. Reasons apply, however, only when they can be contested. Reason giving involves explanation and justification, the subjection of reasons to a *critical test*. 'Without some assessment of whether agency reasons are legally sound, factually accurate, and logically coherent, the reasons requirement would become an empty formality' (Mashaw 2018: 70). Effective accountability regimes are required to subject the reasons to a critical test, namely, the exposure to the scrutiny by the affected parties in free and open public debate.

According to standard theory, administrative bodies act instrumental rationally on political and legal instructions. Ample evidence testifies to the contrary, that this is not the case. Implicitly or explicitly, NOMIS deal with extra-legal and extra-scientific values and commitments due to their discretionary powers. However, arbitrariness is not necessarily the consequence when the reasons for their discretionary power are subjected to a public test. Experts are 'technocrats' when they illegitimately interfere in the domain of politics. When properly constrained experts can, however, be 'representatives'. To see that this is possible requires a shift in basic categories.

A theoretical shift is needed in order to provide a justificatory account of NOMIS' discretionary powers. One can see power-wielding experts as 'representatives' when one is able to conceive of decisions about ends as resting on reasonable grounds. Otherwise, there would be no way of assessing them, of subjecting them to a critical test. To see that agency reasons can be based on true representations of facts and values requires a move beyond the contractual concept of representation, which is underlying the delegation principle as specified by the principal agent model. It also requires a move beyond decisionism, which conceives of goals and aims as simply a matter of sovereign enactment. In the latter perspective, values are seen as incommensurable and laws as not fit for truth testing. It is, however, the possibility of reasoning intelligibly about normative questions that makes epistemological space for NOMIS' involvement in rule-making and end-setting.

Drawing on the insights established by the previous chapters, this chapter clarifies the need for a theoretical shift; first, with reference to the concept of representation, and then with reference to epistemology. It suggests that *the mechanism of truth-based claims-making* explains how epistemic claims can legitimately be turned into political claims. Thereafter, the chapter takes issue with decisionism premised on non-cognitivism, and advocates a political conception of truth. Justice is a claim of truth. Even though there are different conceptions of justice, it is assumed that affected parties can agree on non-arbitrary institutions when they are given reasons for decisions which affect their rights and duties and are given the possibility to respond. Lastly, a normative framework for unelected bodies is identified, which ascribes them an important democratic function: as unelected bodies do not seek re-election or popularity, they can speak truth to politics as well as to the citizenry at large.

Beyond delegation

NOMIS are prototypically called on in the name of knowledge, when independent assessment based on specific expertise is needed to safeguard long-term interests, and when effective implementation requires participation from civil society. Decision-makers need to know the nature of problems as well as of the task environment before political initiatives can be carried out. What is more, the problems which citizens and politicians call on expertise to solve are not merely technical. They are 'ill formed' or *wicked problems* that do not lend themselves to precise treatment by the disciplinary standards of basic science. Unelected bodies are there to handle questions to which there are no predetermined, correct answers. In order to reach a qualified decision on such problems, epistemic agents have to draw on extra-scientific sources, be they commonly shared values and norms or private, non-epistemic values, esoteric knowledge, or other contingent factors. What is of principled interest is not *phronesis*, the type of knowledge of context and practical judgement, which is needed to apply general rules – justified norms, but the import of *extra-scientific support factors*, of values and norms. Values and norms are, for example, needed for defining what matters as harms, what constitutes a risk, what counts as beneficial effects of policies, which criterion of optimality should be applied, and in deciding whether citizens' preferences should be included in assessments. Regulatory polices involve norms and values that are both extra-scientific and extra-legal. Still they are needed to reach a qualified decision, to wit, abolishing one fact-value pair only serves to create another fact-value pair (Finkel 2018: 22). When this is the case, how can we *know* that NOMIS are doing *the right thing*?

It is necessary to challenge the established view that NOMIS are legitimate only when they comply with instrumental means-end rationality and when they are accountable to the legislature. Due to the nature of their problem portfolio and tasks, their autonomy and their knowledge base, NOMIS inevitably make political value judgements and *wield political power*. They act on the basis of political inputs, of statutes and policy statements, which, due to their vagueness and indeterminacy, must be interpreted, given an objective meaning, be organised, specified, operationalised with the help of knowledge of experts. This task is a prerogative of administrators, who 'exercise considerable discretion in giving content to ambiguous laws' (Sunstein 1997: 289).

NOMIS operate within large zones of discretion and are often involved in the preparing of legislation, in formulating statutes and the constituent regulations of their own operations. NOMIS are not merely implementing bodies even where there are prescriptions to separate policy and operations. Often NOMIS are involved in rule-making and end-setting, in setting the norms by which they themselves are to abide. For example, it is the ECB that sets the monetary target itself, not the European parliament. In Chapter 7, the authors, in a study of parliamentary committee hearings with the ESMA, find that 'the elected politicians want to know what agency representatives think of the Council's position on political questions'. The authors find it conceptually impossible to be "purely technical" with the kinds of mandates they have. Often NOMIS' decisions make a difference. Standard setting power is *agenda setting power* when new measures trigger political initiatives.

A change in approach from the prevailing principal-agent theories, which see the accountability of NOMIS as a question of how the elected can have adequate *partisan control* over expert bodies, is needed. Control for partisan advantage scored by a governing majority power is inappropriate for expert bodies that are mandated to be impartial and non-biased. Truth is not a partisan position.

Agencies and central banks, which, in contrast to bureaucratic bodies, prototypically act on a wide discretionary basis, cannot simply defer to the legislator's command, or instrumental rationality. When the legislator assigns competences to agencies that it does not possess itself, as is the case with some EU agencies, there is not only a question of accountability but also a question of whether there is delegation. The relevance of mandate delegation is limited as the legitimacy of the EU does not solely rest with the member states, but also with the representation of its citizens in the European Parliament (Art. 10(2) TEU). The political role of agencies has been discussed throughout the book. Chapter 6 suggests the *recognition model of accountability* premised on the public-reason perspective. The delegation model and, in particular, the way in which it has been conceived by principal-agency theory, relies on a contractual model of representation. In order to account for the normativity of the new grammar of politics, in which NOMIS have been given *policymaking discretionary powers*, and where a plethora of accountability regimes are in place, we need to re-visit the conception of representation.

Forming the common will

Usually representation is called for only when values and interests are involved, not when it is a question of facts. But as we have seen experts deal with values too. We should, however, not see representation as merely 'transmission belts' for constituent opinion, as corresponding to pre-existing state of affairs. The idea that political decisions should correspond to a pre-existing reality of either objective interests (as elite democrats hold) or popular will (as participatory democrats hold) overlooks the fact that the process of representation is itself *creating* a political reality.

Representation is relational and cannot be reduced to contractually responsive statements (Mansbridge 2011).[2] Neither the 'mandate' nor the 'trustee' model suffices. Representation is not about reflecting or responding to pre-political wills; it is about the process of forming opinions and will, of establishing the public interest, through a complex procedural arrangement. Representation is about making present something that is not present (Pitkin 1967: 241). It is about the active mobilisation and mediation through institutions, procedures and political processes of contestation, persuasion, deliberation and learning. Conceiving of political representation as a contractual relationship neglects how far decision-makers actively shape opinions and decisions through, for example, political mobilisation and campaigning; that representation has *demos*-shaping effects; and that different types of accountability relationships are involved.

The representative is then not merely 'standing for' or mirroring the electorate, but is 'acting for' it; hence, the representative 'needs to be constantly recreated and dynamically linked to society in order to pass laws' (Urbinati and Warren 2008: 20; cp., Vieira and Runcimann 2008). Representation itself is interpretive and an act of constituting. It is a *performative act of constituting* that cannot be reduced to responding to what is already there. A political candidate is actively shaping demands and opinions through *representative claims-making* (Saward 2010). Representation is an act of claiming the right understanding of an issue as well as of legitimate interests. Through speaking in the name of someone's wants and beliefs, representatives, in fact, establish common interests, shared understandings, and opinions. Representation is thus not merely a discursive squaring of the circle between common sense and objective knowledge (Dryzek and Niemeyer 2008). Representation is about *forming and commanding the common will*. This is the case, for example, when representatives succeed in establishing that the working class has a common interest supportive of a particular policy advocated by a particular party.

Representing facts and values

As reality is only known to us through representations (Peirce 1958) expert advice is a form of representative claims-making. The world is linguistically structured and hence is accessible to us through symbolic categories. It is only through speech acts that competent actors can come to a common understanding over something. Communication is the indispensable condition of possibility for thought and knowledge.[3] The linguistic medium gives us access to a common reality where we can comprehend and cope with exigencies through representations.

Also experts are involved in representative claims-making. Science discovers facts and validates findings. Still, '[D]iscovering "scientifically true answers" does require value commitments, decisions and judgements' (Brown 2009: 257). It is, however, one thing that the scientific discovery process itself is normatively charged, but quite another that, whenever experts represent a scientifically true answer, they infuse it with values, commitments, and specific interests. Expert advice is a form of representative claims-making because representing facts or nature involves representing humans as well. By referring to an objective state of affairs, epistemic agents make sense of something and make claims on its behalf. Epistemic agents do not establish new factual knowledge, but 'produce a basis for public policymaking knowledge by providing vital observations and measurements, causal knowledge, and a risk analysis of natural phenomena, technologies, and human activities' (Gundersen 2020: 92). The very act of establishing *valid and useful knowledge* involves adding a value component, which is what makes the facts socially and politically relevant. It involves the adding of normative premises in a syllogism.[4] Without a value component, experts would be impotent; they would not be able to reach a decision or give pertinent advice.

By claiming knowledge constructs, epistemic actors 'act for' something seen as important, some vital interests or values to be protected. They take on the performative attitude of communicative actors who try to achieve something in the world by reaching agreement with one another.[5] Claiming knowledge constructs is *a performative act* and one with implications and consequences for interests and statuses. However, such claims are fallible. Both new factual information and the articulation of other normative concerns may invalidate them.

Expert representation should be seen as practices of mediation that engage and transform the state of affairs. However, experts do not interpret and represent at will. Their knowledge constructs, their interpretations and representative claims, are directed to others for recognition, validation, justification – to the professional, scientific, democratic and moral community. Facts, data, and information are only knowledge when they form part of an organised and specified validating system. Facts, as part of a cognitive system, are *knowledge constructs* infused with values; they are structured, politically institutionalised and culturally patterned (Parsons 1951: 336). A claim is a speech act that is related to others but is not a claim unless it is related to truth conditions. Claims have the *cognitive function* of representing a state of affairs. They also have the *expressive function* of making the experiences of the speaker known, and the *appellative function* of directing requests to addressees (cp. Habermas 1984: 275).

From these premises, we derive the claims-making proposition of epistemic agency: when epistemic agents obtain new information and become aware of problems, they act by making claims. Situated in a systematic body of knowledge, epistemic agents make their *nous* known to others. When they, for example, discover climate change and identify its putative effects, they turn epistemic claims into representative claims. They do so by seeking *public approval* and hence corroboration for their representation of facts, through giving accounts and grounds. By referring to an objective state of affairs, experts make sense of something and make claims on its behalf. Since claims-making is an action, which transforms initiatives into practical results it can be conceived of as a mechanism. Mechanisms are *hypothesizing devices* that explains events; they intermediate between an input and an output. The mechanism of *truth-based claims-making* explains how epistemic claims through public reason-giving processes putatively are transformed into legitimate political claims. It ensures that claims based on established truths are put to the test of public reason, involving the affected parties. The mechanism of *truth-based claims-making* explains how the circle between the participatory and epistemic dimension of democracy can be squared.

The very act of establishing *knowledge constructs* involves more than the compilation of empirical facts. To reiterate, when experts handle problems, they do not merely discover facts, but also their relation to norms and values. When, for example, they represent climate change, when they deal with pandemics, GMOs or the financial crisis, they relate to 'ought questions' – a fact-value pair – about what should be done. Epistemic agents prototypically seek public approval for their representation of facts through reason giving. There is an obligation to inform stemming from basic rights and the principles of administrative law. Moreover, as we return to, they can defy technocratic solutions and ensure justified outcomes only by referring their resolutions to the trial of public debate. However, one must switch from a non-cognitivist to *a cognitivist approach* in order to establish the epistemological basis for claiming truth for representations.

Beyond decisionism

In order to provide a justificatory account of NOMIS, a second theoretical move have to be undertaken: we need to break with the idea that only scientific claims can be true, while value claims cannot. We must thus break with Max Weber's decisionistic approach, where normative questions are considered rationally irresolvable, as a fight between devils and gods, as a question of faith and preference. In this sceptical conception, the political realm consists of unresolvable, incommensurable or incompatible value schemes. In moral philosophy, decisionism is associated with non-cognitivism, which asserts that moral judgements are not truth apt – neither true nor false. It is not the substantive content of the decision that determines its validity, but rather the authority that made it. Classical non-cognitivism holds that political argument is a matter of decisions seen as expressions of attitude or brute preference. This is evident in emotivist ethical theories[6] as well as in hard-nosed realism.

In political theory, decisionism is associated with Carl Schmitt's conception of the political will as the unalienated manifestation of own *existence*. For him, the political realm is, so to speak, irrational, constituted by irresolvable conflict between friends and foes. In Schmitt's constitutional theory, the idea of homogenous peoples figures as an extra-legal entity that makes those fundamental 'existential' decisions of making and amending the constitution. In this theory, the people exist as an ethno-political community in the state of nature where it has a natural right to act as the constituent power. The people need no legitimation when they act as sovereign (Schmitt 1932).[7]

Another variant of decisionism is found in Hobbes's positivist credo that the authority – the sovereign – makes the law without any claim to truth: *Auctoritas, non veritas, facit legem*. For positivists, legal validity is simply an act of authority, and hence justice is fixed by the social facts of sovereign enactment.[8] When this is the case, it would not be hard 'to deny the proposition that individuals have a right to liberty of conscience is true' (Cohen 2009: 18). Decisionism thus has far-reaching consequences for the understanding of democracy. Contrary to decisionism, moral cognitivists claim that normative questions can be settled objectively – that they are 'fact stating' or 'truth apt'. Norms are capable of being true or right; hence, there are truths about rightness.

Truth is a reason for accepting propositions. Agreement on propositions about the truth of some freedom rights is a pre-condition for any viable human community. To assess injustices and instances of domination itself requires practices that are autonomous and non-dominating. Separating truth from error is essential for interpretation, reasoning, arguing, for getting things right, which, however, is intrinsically connected to the ability to get to a reasoned agreement with others, hence the normativity of the democratic procedures of opinion- and will-formation. The principle of democracy itself presupposes the validity of moral judgements (Habermas 1996: 110). The democratic *Rechtstaat* builds on the presupposition of moral truths, and that these can ensure justice. According to the democratic principle, truth makes justice. One can thus reverse Hobbes's credo into *Veritas, non auctoritas, facit legem*. The political concept of truth is made up of propositions about justice, as some agreement in conceptions of justice is a prerequisite for a democratic community. Even if people disagree and there are different conceptions of justice, they can 'still agree that institutions are just when no arbitrary distinction between persons are made in the assigning of basic rights' (Rawls 1971: 5). Basic rights, resting on deontological norms, can only be outweighed by other basic rights. Among these basic rights is the right to freedom of thought and expression, resting on the right to justification, which corresponds to the reason-giving duty of power-holders.

A political conception of truth is built into the very constitutional set-up of modern democracies. A series of 'self-evident truths' make up the political realm, which attest to the cognitivists' claim that some normative questions are rationally resolvable. Positivised, bankable basic rights are a product of public reasoning, justification, and decision-making. Although the idea of public reason – according to Rawls – does without the concept of truth, public reason is an exercise of practical reason, of reflection, and judgement:

> So if the idea of reasoning and judgment applies to our moral and political statements, as opposed simply to our voicing our psychological state, we must be able to make judgments and draw inferences on the basis of mutually recognized criteria and evidence; and in that way, and not in some other way, say by mere rhetoric or persuasion, reach agreement by the free exercise of our powers of judgment.
>
> *Rawls (1993: 110–111)*

The Rawlsian position with regard to a conception of truth in political liberalism is controversial.[9] Rawls' 'method of avoidance' so to say trades truth for pluralism. I will side with Joshua Cohen (2009), who claims that a conception of justice involves the concept of truth. *Justice is a claim of truth*. Legal and political validity depends on truths about rightness. A political conception of truth, which includes the proposition that justice requires equal basic liberties, is at work in democracy's public reason. It cannot then be that democracies consist of people who believe "in reason and in human individuals" – and who consequently agree on the principle of equal rights – and people who do not share this belief, and who will only comply on unwarranted grounds such as prudence or fear of sanctions (Popper 2012: 16). The latter ones raise a self-defeating claim that rejects what has already been agreed to, what has been presupposed, when taking part in a legally structured political process; when entering a public discourse. However, as we will see, the political conception of truth has to be a pragmatic one, relating to how truth works in action on problems.[10] Here true beliefs are assumed to be accepted as the result of inquiry. This pragmatic-political conception of truth includes the propositions that justice requires equal basic liberties, a fair scheme of co-operation among persons understood as being free and equal.[11] There would be no conception of justice – no metric according to which one can assess what is equally good for all – if the proposition of the truth of equal basic liberties was not agreed on.

Getting it right

The very communicative practice of making assertions, of stating propositions, of claiming knowledge of something is one related to truth. Pragmatism has highlighted how truth functions in the practices people co-operatively engage, namely, how it functions in problematic situations (see e.g. Dewey 1927). We figure out what people mean by assuming they are right, that they are saying something true. We solve conflicts and disagreement by checking the facts and the rightness of the norms applied. Asserting something is to claim it is true; hence, a claim is not a claim unless it is amenable to truth testing, unless it is related to truth conditions. Unlike all other predicates, truth 'is always asserted when anything at all is asserted', and this also holds for normative statements.

> Truth is connected as well to norms of thought and interaction that call for accuracy in representation, sincerity in expression, consistency, 'getting it right', and being attentive to how things are and not simply how we wish them to be.
>
> *Cohen (2009: 14)*

Truth is a concern for getting things right. The reason-giving principle itself is premised on a procedure with normative credentials concerning how to get things right by consensually solving problems and resolving conflicts, that is, through the give and take of reasons in a deliberative process where force and bargaining power are excluded. The political realm is made up of procedural arrangements constituted by a series of moral 'facts' revolving around the freedom and equality of the citizens, whose aim is to ensure a correct result. When the prescribed procedures are followed, when the case is clarified in factual and normative terms, when the affected parties or their representatives are included in inclusive and legally regulated processes of deliberation and decision-making, the results may enjoy the presumption of being legitimate.

Deliberation is a cognitive process for the assessment of reasons in a practical situation oriented towards reaching fair or good decisions. Discourse theory assumes that some value controversies can be rationally resolved under the proviso that a solution is right if it withstands all attempts to invalidate it under conditions of a rational discourse. In a decision-making context, rightness is a condition for agreement and faultiness for disagreement. When each side during the deliberative process tries to create consistent representations of facts and schemes of values, one side becomes indefensible. Fault may be either due to the poor epistemic quality of the representations or to the poverty of the value schemes (Kitcher 2011: 36ff). However, deliberation only works in a normative context in which the forceless force of the better argument has a legal backing, where non-compliance is sanctioned, where moral action is not expensive and where there is protection of basic rights.[12] As established, this basic structure rests on a set of propositions that constitute the political conception of truth

Discourse theorists contend that we cannot – on pain of performative contraction – but hold basic rights true. Basic equal basic rights are pragmatic presuppositions for the possibility of joint assessment and critique; for democratic opinion-formation and will-formation. To deny them will bring contestants into a performative contradiction, in that they have already confirmed them in the very act of contesting them (Apel 1976: 267ff). Such a denial is *self-defeating*. One cannot make a claim that basic equal rights do not exist because, already, by making this claim, one has confirmed that they exist. Without them, you would not be able to make the claim. The principle of equal basic rights is constitutive of the democratic procedure and those who object to it are, in a way, presupposing it already when they contest it, because it is only in the light of this principle that the contestants can make claims to the contrary at all.

Taken together then, basic human rights are self-evidently true, they are inalienable by morality as well as by the laws and the international covenants that we have sworn to uphold. They are moral truths constitutive of the political realm in modern societies. However, how can they be corroborated? To what *publicly observable surroundings* do moral claims correspond? Here, one may follow Jürgen Habermas (2003), who, while being a cognitivist, nonetheless, upholds a strict separation between facts and values, between a world of objects and the world of norms and values.

Dimensions of practical reason

According to the political conception of truth, there is an intersubjective basis for reaching agreement through reason giving, which also applies to normative questions. This is not an argument in favour of *moral experts* deciding which norms apply. The idea of moral experts rests on moral realism and fails to respect the difference between assertoric and normative claims. It runs counter to the very idea of (Kantian) morality premised on autonomous self-legislation. Rather, reason giving is an argument in favour of a procedural approach to normative questions based on the different knowledge claims they raise. This approach classifies different knowledge claims and their corresponding validating procedures. The question of what to do raises different queries and concerns in different issue areas; in different normative domains.

As different knowledge claims are raised by regulatory politics it is necessary to differentiate between different validating procedures. Sometimes, considerations of feasibility, cost-benefit and prudence are called for; other times, when identities and interests are affected, other normative considerations are called for. Pragmatic, ethical, moral, and legal norms all apply to policymaking, as there will be questions of the efficiency and value as well as of the moral and legal correctness of proposals. Pragmatic questions pertain to what is prudent or efficient, ethical questions to what is good for us and moral questions to what is just or fair – equally good for all, while legal questions pertain to what is legal or not legal – to what is judicially required (see Habermas 1996: 151ff).

When dealing with 'wicked' or ill-formed problems, the question of what do in regulatory fields involves concerns which cannot solely be handled through means-end calculations, cost-benefit analysis, the weighing and balancing of instrumentally rational action against alternative goals. An agency may, for example, not only assess the economic aspects of GMOs but also their ethical and moral aspects relating to health issues, sustainable development and the precautionary principle. The answer to the question of what to do is increasingly not given, nor can it be provided by data collection or the reasoning that takes place within the horizon of instrumental rationality.[13] As already Platon knew, the more we know, the more we know that we don't know. Knowledge in itself produces knowledge gaps. In the times of Covid 19, it became clear that never has our knowledge of *non-knowledge* been bigger at the same time as the necessity to act and to live under uncertainty prevailed.

Due to technological developments and new risks scenarios in policymaking, new levels of hazard, uncertainty, and ambiguity, ethical, moral and compounded legal questions increasingly make up the political agenda of NOMIS. Often the value-ladenness of the issues is not recognised, or covered up, and NOMIS and their agents proceed as though it is only a question of discovering the appropriate techniques, stratagems and programmes on a neutral and value-free basis. Inevitably, value questions are involved. Adam M. Finkel (2018: 21) identifies about 65 different value judgements in risk regulation that are routinely made, but hidden, in cost-benefit analysis. As discussed in Chapter 2, NOMIS deal with delicate security and military policies with deep ethical and moral implications. Complex monetary and financial policies with distributive effects, with consequences for public revenues, taxes and citizen well-being, are handed over to central banks. When it comes to health and safety, embryology and genetics agencies are required, by their mandates, to base their advice on ethical norms.

World reference – truth and rightness

Whether political ends are good, beneficial, or just are among the issues that NOMIS deal with. The fact that normative questions can also be assessed and criticised, that they can be deemed right or wrong, according to intersubjective standards, makes NOMIS reasoning on norms rationally accessible. Normative statements have, however, no objective-world correlation and are, consequently, only true by means of reason and reasoning.

> Facts owe their facticity to their being rooted in a world of objects (about which we state facts) that exist independently of our discretions of them. This ontological description implies that no matter how carefully a consensus about a proposition is established and no matter how well the proposition is justified, it may nonetheless turn out to be false in light of new evidence. It is precisely this difference between truth and ideal warranted assertibility that is blurred with respect to moral claims to validity.
>
> *Habermas (2003: 257)*

With regard to facts, what is true is not a function of what we know, but how the world is. A proposition is not true simply because it survives a discourse. Agreed-on truths can turn out to be false when confronted with new information, with new evidence. What is true is an objective matter. Truth is not an epistemic concept. The world may surprise us (Davidson 2001). The world of objects and facts constitutes an objective reference-point for truth claims.

Moral knowledge cannot meet this non-epistemic validity claim. There is no spatio-temporal location of this kind of knowledge. This does not imply that normative matters constitute an inaccessible terrain (Scanlon 2014: 70). As moral nous is linguistically represented, we have access to such knowledge through language. We discover the 'truth' of normative matters not through scientific confrontation, but through argumentation. We should, however, shift the focus from truth to *rightness*. While truth is a question of objective validity – of testable propositions – rightness is a question of normative validity, which can only be redeemed through argumentation.[14] The predicate 'right' is a question of ideal justified acceptability. It refers to *normative rightness* itself as the worthiness of recognition. There are truths about rightness, which is, however, an epistemic concept. Rightness depends on knowledge of the consequences of norm-compliance for actors' statuses, interests and values.[15]

In the social world, the normative question relevant for validity claims has to do with establishing well-ordered, legitimate, interpersonal relationships. These relationships exist only as long as people attach meaning to them, recognise, support and uphold them through norm-abiding actions. Acknowledging the worthiness of recognition of norms requires conditions of freedom, that is, that citizens are permitted the performative attitude of the first-person perspective to take a stand on them – to say yes or no. A coerced agreement is of little value, neither is enforced compliance. Moral norms regulate interpersonal relationships between persons who are supposed to recognise one another as equals. They owe their validity to the principle of *universalisation*, namely, that all affected parties can accept them in a free and open rational debate. The validity of moral judgements can then only be assessed in terms of how inclusive the normative agreement, which has been reached through a reason-giving process, is. Nevertheless, how to understand that people act, solve problems, and resolve conflicts, when validity claims are not cashed in, when truth claims are not corroborated and when it is impossible to involve all those affected in a moral discourse?

A pragmatic concept of truth

It is impossible to bridge the gap between truth and (ideal) rational acceptability through a scientific discourse. The gap can only be overcome pragmatically, according to Habermas, because interacting actors cannot suspend their truth claims, but must let their actions be directed by them. In everyday life, we cannot act from the falsifiable reservation that what we take to be true or right could be false or wrong.

Habermas (2003) suggests *a pragmatic concept of truth*, which refers to how truth claims function in everyday life. In a real-world context where action must be undertaken, where decisions must be made, the suspension of truth-claims are ruled out. Actors must act on what they know to solve pertinent problems and conflicts. When uncertainties arise, when knowledge is problematised and when there is conflict over courses of action, but there is need for action, one cannot wait for the evidence – for the eventual validation of truth claims. Correspondingly with reference to moral claims, 'The need to act before moral truth can be established provides reasons to act that outweigh the reasons for doing what would otherwise be correct action' (Soper 2002: xii).

In pragmatics, truth relates to *action on problems*. What is true is what is working, what turns out to be successful solutions to the problems and conflicts requiring immediate attention. Truth claims in such a context are corroborated by *the success of goal-oriented behaviour* in the objective world of facts. They are corroborated when their recommended actions realise goals effectively. Moral claims require another type of corroboration. They are corroborated when they enable *peaceful conflict resolution*, when they resolve conflicts of interaction consensually. Conversely, they falter against the inability to solve normative disagreement.

The question is then how normative rightness can be an unconditional validity claim. How can moral statements be binary coded – yes/no related to true/false; right/wrong – when what is true in this domain is not a function of how 'the world' is (but rather on how the world 'ought be')? The question is how the social world can be the same for all when there is no objective reference-point. It must be 'the same for everyone', but the identity or sameness is not given – as the objective world is. This social world is a task of practical reason, of our moral convictions: it must be created by participants who involve themselves in a process of *mutual role-taking* and thereby establishing a "We perspective" – a common world of intersubjectively shared norms. 'The unconditional nature of moral validity claims can then be accounted for in terms of the universality of a normative domain that *is to be brought about*' (Habermas 2003: 260–261). Humanity – the presupposed republic of world citizens – make up the reference system for justifying regulations in the common interest of all. The publicly observable surroundings to which moral claims correspond are thus not (yet) fixed. It is, so to speak, a world under construction – the projection of a universal communicative community.

Warranting correctness

In constitutional democracies, there are two procedures, a division of labour in determining the right thing to do: the scientific, and the democratic one. We do not call on the people, their opinions and reasons, to establish that there is climate change, but we do when it comes to the normative question of what to do about it. However, as we cannot know reality except through our representations, we cannot know whether factual statements are provisionally true unless they are open to public scrutiny, to the further testing of fallible claims. Only the scientific community, *the infinite community of investigators*, can warrant truth claims (Peirce 1958). We cannot know whether factual statements are valid unless they have been examined through trusted scientific procedures. Different types of political questions raise different validity claims, and hence require different procedures for redeeming them. The seriousness of pandemics are for scientists to decide, but the measures undertaken to combat them, which involve more than cost-benefit balancing, are political questions. Whether there is inflation or unemployment is not a political question, but one to be settled by the scientific community. Conversely, the validity of political ends such as full employment or price stability linked to inflation targets involve normative evaluations. When experts settle such questions they are technocrats. Science can decide what is true and false, not what is good or just/right or wrong.

Democracy does not trump science, and scientific truth does not dictate democracy (Galston 2012: 131). However, like science, democracy revolves around an inclusion principle. *Knowledge is universal and so are basic rights*. Scientific propositions aim for universality, and publicity is the test of the legitimacy and fairness of politics.[16] The democratic principle refers not simply to electoral systems embedded in a unified people but to the complex procedural arrangements that involve people in the making of the laws to which they are subjected. Democratic procedures enable those subjected to choose the ends of the political community through the legislature, through voting and deliberation. Only by justifying the decisions towards those affected by them and by involving them in a dialogue will there be a reason to believe that they are correct.

In order to account for the reason-giving principle and the right to justification, we must, thus, adjust for the moral value of deliberation. Because citizens have the right to justifications for officials' decisions, actions and judgements, decision-makers are obligated to provide them. The ideal of freedom puts governments under the burden of legitimation. The obligation to justify the use of political power to those affected by it is an expression of equal membership for everyone in the sovereign body that is responsible for authorising the use of power. The idea of deliberative democracy thus expresses a moral principle: unconditional respect for every person's autonomy and integrity.

The internal relation between knowledge and democracy

As argued, in constitutional democracies, a set of norms, institutions and procedures grounds the presumption of legitimate outcomes. They aim at ensuring correct reasoning. Procedural constrains aim to make NOMIS' resolutions non-arbitrary. They seek to guarantee that NOMIS' expert reasoning operates within procedures and with a mandate, which authorises the undertaking, selects topics, and questions, limits access of the premises for solutions and enables assessment of the validity/feasibility of proposals and connects to public deliberation prior to authoritative decision-making. Different institutions such as hearings, constitutional and ethical reviews, complaint and appeal procedures, professional communities, all serve to constrain the deliberations. They serve to exclude special interests and party politics from the reason-giving process. They aim at securing effective standards for qualified public approval (see Eriksen and Molander 2008). These procedures as well as prescriptions about impartiality, professionalism, integrity, responsibility, explanation, and justification provide an autonomous basis for decision-making and for speaking truth to power. They make up NOMIS' legitimacy basis, and hence for being entities in their own right.

The legitimacy of NOMIS depends on reasoning about the means and ends of policy in such a way that justifiable, mutually acceptable resolutions are made. The mechanism of *truth-based claims-making* explains the inherent connection between knowledge and participation: claims are only pragmatically true or right when they command scientific and democratic approval. Only knowledge-based decisions can be rational, but since we do not know the knowers, we cannot know whether they are right without hearing them out. That is, unless their nous are exposed to the trial of critical scrutiny by the affected parties in free and open public debate. Modern democracy, which is premised on the presumption that it is possible to reach agreement on factual and normative questions, needs science to validate knowledge claims. Science, which is premised on the free exchange of information, needs democracy to secure unconditional freedom and the autonomy of professional work.

Science and democracy, which mutually support each other and are one another's prerequisites, require open and free communication over claims and proposals. Public deliberation is procedure for cashing in validity claims. It tracks, generates and tests reasons. Also because disagreement prevails among experts, democratic legitimacy would seem to require that political authority is involved in some way. There is no lingua franca among experts. Procedurally regulated participation is needed to 'get things right' in politics.

There is thus an *intrinsic connection* between knowledge and democracy. Without presuming that laws are well-reasoned, we would say that they do not deserve recognition. A law that is based on false assumptions will, under favourable conditions, be opposed; a representative that is plainly wrong would not be able to convince audiences under conditions of freedom and equality – in an open and free debate. Public reason requires that political principles be justifiable to all persons to whom they apply. These principles includes constitutional arrangements, institutional designs, and rule of conduct, as well as of outcomes. In democracies, the wielding of political power must be justified by reasons that all reasonable people will be expected to endorse (Rawls 1993: 217). If reasonableness includes that 'reasonable people take into account the consequences of their action on others' well-being' (Rawls 1993: 49), it must also include hearing the voices of the affected parties in the regulation of practical matters. Otherwise, we would not know that reasonable outcomes were legitimate.

Building on the presumption that only public deliberation can ensure reasonableness, we can identify a normative model of NOMIS, one which goes beyond instrumental means-end scheming. However, not only the instrumental agency model, which sees agencies as neutral transmission belts for the statues, but also *the specification model* of Richardson, in which 'ends can be revised via specification' (Richardson 2002: 218), suffer from shortcomings. The latter overlooks the form of public duty towards the citizenry at large, the impartial concern for the freedom and welfare for all affected parties (Eriksen 2020). Arbitrary rule is the case when those affected are not heard, not merely when NOMIS do not track the political will (statutes), executive orders, and agency rules. Yet how can we know that agency action is right?

Reasonable or rational outcomes?

The standard of rationality is, as Mashaw (2018: 15ff) underscores, one that administrative law has long since abandoned. There is no absolute standard of correctness to apply also because administrative discretion comes from the statute – it is delegated by majority vote. Thus, the standard of reasonableness, which depicts that it is the weighing and balancing of different concerns and interests in interpreting statutes that confers legitimacy on resolutions. An agency decision is acceptable when it falls within a range of possible reasonable outcomes.[17] Since NOMIS possess discretionary, expertise-based powers to achieve goals they cannot simply defer to the judgements of courts (and hence the limitation of judicial review). Or, put differently, a court ruling will not ensure a correct result because lawyers generally lack expertise in the subject matter. The court can only decide whether the agency acted legally correct, namely, in line with a reasonable interpretation of the mandate, the statute, not whether the decision is substantially correct. The normative question of *the rightness of the agency's action* points to a different procedure. Answering the question does not merely require the competence to apply given norms but the competence to validate and justify them as well. This the domain of public reason.

We can only know whether a decision is acceptable when it is justified – when the affected parties or their representatives have a chance to say yes/no to it. In such a debate, the affected parties may ask what the most reasonable outcome is, or why there is no *single correct answer*. The affected parties may not be satisfied with an unfounded, inferior or sub-optimal outcome, with an answer, which is contingent, which could have been different. Stakeholders may, as their notes and comments often testify to, not be satisfied with reasonable outcomes. Alternative reasonable choices may be defended by norms of uneven moral quality and they may have uneven distributive effects. It is also hard to see how decision-makers will justify a policy that is not presumably rational.

When regulation involves burden sharing, when it affects interests and values it raises the question of justice. In that case cost-benefit analysis and the structure of the regulatory regime do not suffice to establish the rightness of the action. The cost-benefit analysis itself is infused with values[18] and the regulatory regime is conferred discretion by the statute. Neither the parliament nor the constitutional court is the exemplar of public reason, but the general public sphere rooted in the civil society – outside the market and the state. Whether normative claims are justified can be tested in free, public debate where there are no limitations with regard to topics, participants, questions, time, or resources. It is only from an impartial point of view, when taking into account all relevant considerations and interests, that definitive answers to the question of agency's actions acceptability and of what principles should guide public decision-making, can be given. As the public speak for all, it has the power to solve normative conflicts. The moral point of view is formed when the matters are viewed from a public perspective. It is in the norm-giving power of public debate that we could find an answer to the normative question that Mashaw (2018: 120) poses, 'Would a reasonable agency make this decision?'

NOMIS operate in democratic societies premised on separation of powers, on judicial review, on mass media and a functioning public sphere in which controversial claims are raised, criticised, vindicated with reference to justice. Normatively speaking, regardless of how the situation for the public sphere pan out, in the face of internet, new social media and fake news, the reason-giving requirement – the right to justification – is an imperative of legitimation. It refers political-normative issues to the norm-testing competence of public reason. Without it we would not know whether a regime deserves recognition.

Publicity both places NOMIS' actions under the public eye and subject them to the scrutiny of public reason. Rightness is, as mentioned, an unconditional validity claim. Hence, incompletely reasoned or morally deficient claims are hard to publicly justify – they would not be mutually acceptable. Opponents may, under conditions of freedom and equality, be able to offer more rational answers to conflictual matters. Moral claims owe their binary coding, either right or wrong, to the consensus-forming functions of a free public debate in which everything that deviates from justice standards, that which cannot meet with the assent of everyone, is discarded. When matters are tried in relation to moral standards, all ungrounded deviations and injustices become problematic.

Clearly, tasks are often of a pragmatic nature and require only cost-benefit balancing. Sometimes, there are unsurmountable obstacles to political agreement because of passion or interests, in which case, the controversies recommend themselves for the bargaining procedure yielding sub-optimal compromises; other times, when uncertainties and value conflicts prevail, working agreements and modi vivendi may have to do (see Eriksen 2009: 49ff).

Moral justificatory discourses are triggered when controversies about what to do occur, when normative issues are raised, when collective-action problems are to be solved and when a regulation which affects interests and identities is called for. Moral discourses, pertaining to impartiality, to what is in the equal interest of all, envision a just society, namely, legitimate interpersonal relationships ensuring equal freedoms for all and equal respect for everyone. They raise obligatory claims, based on the (contra-factual) presumption of one single correct answer to normative disagreements. Would there be civic engagement, a vital public, a knowledge-based administration, constitutional rights, a set of procedures to ensure legitimate and rational decision-making, without the presumption of one single correct answer to moral controversies? In the third-person perspective of an observer, reasonable outcomes may suffice, but in the first-person singular of the participant rational truth-based outcomes would be required. Harold Pinter, in his Nobel Prize Lecture in 2005, alluded to political truth when reflecting on the fact that, as a writer, he had to deal with things that could be both true and false. However, "As citizen I must ask: What is true? What is false?" The performative attitude of the citizen demand that at least the criterion according to which a solution is deemed reasonable/unreasonable be established.[19] The normativity of the democratic *Rechtsstaat* is bound up with the struggle of 'getting it right' as a regulatory ideal, which underscores the political concept of truth.[20]

Alarming the public

In this justificatory account of NOMIS premised on the publicity standard, a specific political, partisan interpretation of ends is not seen as a dictate, but as a premise in a reason-giving process aiming at a cogent answer. NOMIS and expert deliberation are vital for enhancing the quality of policymaking by increasing the reservoir of reasons and the testing of premises for decision-making, while neither constituting nor legitimating power in itself. By improving the reasoning about policy ends in a publicly acceptable manner, NOMIS empower the citizens. When the factual basis has been established correctly and NOMIS have made a decision which can be explained in terms of the statute's goal and procedural criteria for hearing, inclusion and reason giving, when the affected parties are given reasons for decisions affecting their rights and duties, and they are accepted with mutually acceptable argument in a transparent process, there is a justified presumption of a legitimate outcome. In such a process of public deliberation, based on inclusion and equal opportunity, there is the give and take of reasons, which is conducive to a critical evaluation of alternatives, to a rationally motivated *yes* or *no* to policy proposals and to ongoing reflection and learning.[21]

In this reading NOMIS are not merely neutral instruments for implementing statutory law, nor is their reasoning about ends limited to the specification of statutory law; they are epistemic bodies specialised on decision-making and policy advice on the basis of statues and within and sometimes even beyond the constraints of the law. There are rules for conduct as well as a set of rights for officeholders, including freedom of expression and the right to speak 'truth to power', which imply the possibility of challenging the law. The point is not merely that there is 'an ethical or professional commitment to truth-seeking according to the best standards of the expert community' and that they thus 'can speak truth to power' (Schudson 2006: 500); rather, there is an obligation stemming from basic rights and the principles of administrative law,[22] *to alarm* the public about epistemic uncertainty, namely, to report what is at stake in different policy proposals, about the risks, fallacies, and dangers and harms involved. There is an obligation to report about the necessities, alternatives, possibilities and opportunities that exist. Gundersen, in Chapter 9, states that "when assessing the current state of knowledge about climate change, scientific experts are mandated to perform their task in terms of not only epistemic accuracy but also effective communication and moral responsibility". Knowledge obliges. Since Pascal we have known that knowledge is power, but knowledge can also be *counterpower*, that is, communicative power enabling the citizens to act as legislators, as democratic agents.

In this justificatory account, NOMIS are not merely transmission belts or limited to the speciation of statutes but epistemic bodies established to ensure that statues are interpreted correctly, well-grounded and well-reasoned, and can be implemented, sometimes against resistance, often in co-operation with civil society. This entails an obligation to speak truth to power, to the statute's authors, as well as to the citizenry, when ignorance and misconceptions about policies prevail. NOMIS are fact-finding and error-correcting devices; they represent something that authorizes them to speak truth to power as well as to the citizenry at large.[23] NOMIS are, so to speak, on a mission to find out the right thing to do. They can explain and justify policies as well as advocate new undertakings necessary to come to grips with the major challenges currently facing nature, individuals, and society. As they are independent, as they are not seeking re-election or popularity, they can speak truth both to politics and to the citizenry at large. Thus, they have an important role to play in democracies.

Conclusion

The institutionalisation of NOMIS goes to the core of modern democracies, premised on the separation of powers, knowledge-based administration, judicial review, and independent central banks. To understand their democratic role, one must see NOMIS not solely as agents obeying and specifying political directives, but rather as representatives making claims and reasoning on the basis of politically given premises. NOMIS, which prototypically are designed to fulfil technical and efficiency-oriented objectives, need, and, in fact, are assigned, a wide amount of discretion to be able to meet them. Moreover, they have to use extra-scientific support factors when making decisions and resolving conflicts. Experts have to add normative premises in order to reach a viable decision. Establishing valid and expedient knowledge inescapably involves reasoning about ends and a move from 'is' to 'ought'.

Because of their independence, and of the vagueness and indeterminacy of statutes, NOMIS are left with interpretative space, room of manoeuvre and policymaking discretional powers. These circumstances should not be seen as a blunt violation of prescriptions, but rather as a call for different prescriptions; for *a different procedure*. It calls for the public use of reason. Only knowledge-based decisions can be rational, but we cannot know whether knowledge is sound unless it is exposed to the process of critical scrutiny by all the affected parties in free and open public debate. It is the mechanism of *truth-based claims-making* that explains how this can take place on democratic terms. This is due to the very fact that when experts make claims, they direct their nous to others for approval.

However, in order to provide a justificatory account of such a practice, there is need for a shift in basic approach and epistemology. In order to establish the conditions under which unelected bodies can be deemed legitimate, there is need for a revised concept of representation as well as a move beyond decisionism. The fact that also normative questions can be settled rationally makes epistemological space for NOMIS' involvement in rule-making and end-setting. The point made is that experts can be 'representatives', and not 'technocrats', when properly constrained. This approach squares the need for expertise, which positions some in a privileged situation with regard to the truth, with the requirements of democracy, that is, popular authorisation and control through elections, parliamentary, and public debate.

Notes

1 The Charter of Fundamentals Rights (in the Lisbon Treaty) states that there is 'the obligation of the administration to give reasons for its decisions'.
2 'Constituents choose representatives not only to think more carefully than they about ends and means but also to negotiate more perceptively and fight more skilfully than constituents have either the time or the inclination to do'. (Mansbridge 2003: 515).
3 'The source of the concept of objective truth is interpersonal communication. Thought depends on communication. This follows at once if we suppose that language is essential to thought and we agree with Wittgenstein that there cannot be a private language. The central argument against private languages is that, unless a language is shared, there is no way to distinguish between using the language correctly and using it incorrectly, only communication with another can supply an objective check' (Davidson 2001: 209).
4 Experts create a link between facts and norms when they make representative claims. The building of knowledge inescapably involves reasoning about ends, and a move from 'is' to 'ought'. The act of inferring from 'is' to 'ought' entails adding normative premises. Nothing follows from what is the case in the world to what ought – or what ought not – to be done. From the establishment of facts – from descriptive sentences – nothing follows about rightness or wrongness.
5 That is the first person perspective of an actor accomplishing things with words (cp. Austin, 1962).
6 On the problem of emotivist theories, see Gaus (1996:8 ff).
7 A position that populists hold when they 'speak and act as if the people could develop a singular judgment, a singular will, and hence a singular, unambiguous mandate' (Müller 2016: 77).
8 See Cohen (2009: 21–22; Habermas 1989: 53); see also Scanlon (2014: 56 ff).
9 Given the role Rawls assigns to comprehensive worldviews in *Political Liberalism* (1993).
10 In contrast to correspondence, consensus, and coherence theories of truth.
11 The law requires 'the right of each person to equal liberties', not merely the right to liberties in general (Habermas 1996: 120).
12 Only when the norm violators are sanctioned can people abide norms without being 'suckers'.
13 We see the questioning of scientific authority in most policy controversies. The rise of 'populism' has made the normative problem of expert knowledge acute. In times of crisis and upheaval, the world is not only one of calculable risks but also one of *uncertainty and ambiguity*, making rational appraisal and forecasting difficult.
14 Rightness is a normative metric connected to specific qualities of linguistic communication. The validity of moral norms 'does not refer beyond the boundaries of discourses to something that might "exist" independently of having been determined to be worthy of recognition' (Habermas 2003: 258). See also Habermas 2019: 760ff.
15 However, David Estlund (1993: 77), among others, has objected to Habermas's treatment of normative validity, namely, of conceiving of moral claims as only analogues to scientific truth claims. What is wrong with saying that this moral norm is true? Truth is a semantic concept that does not cover the meaning of the validity of moral and legal norms, which are right because they are justified, because they deserve recognition.
16 'All actions relating to the rights of others are wrong if their maxim is incompatible with publicity' (Kant [1795]1996: 347).
17 To establish what is a reasonable outcome can be derived from statute, but as the statute is often ambiguous it difficult to give a definitive answer (Mashaw 2018: 121, see also pages 18, 120, 196).

18 The norm is that

> we should identify and choose the most "cost-effective" option available. Stakeholders are told, explicitly or implicitly, that it would be "wasteful" for society to spend more money than needed to achieve a given level of benefit. But this claim contains a significant value judgment. It presupposes that we should be satisfied with that particular level of benefit and not ask if still more benefit is possible for marginally greater cost.
>
> Finkel (2008: 21)

19 Without this, why would people participate and why would they be able approve of decisions?
20 In the words of the German Federal Constitutional Court,

> [the] institutional and functional differentiation and separation of powers serves the distribution of political authority [politischer Macht] and responsibility as well as the control of those in power. It pursues the aim that, as much as possible, *decisions are right*. This means that they be taken by those institutions, which, according to their organization, composition, function, and procedure, are best suited for taking them.
>
> Bundesverfassungsgericht (BVerfG) I, 86; 98 BVerfG 218, 251–252 (emphasis added)

21 This notwithstanding the dangerous side effect of public discussion that already Tocqueville identified, about the information overload and the 'sort of ignorance which result from extreme publicity. [...] Rather than increasing the rationality of decisions, publicity forces citizens into making choices on wholly arbitrary grounds' (Holmes 1993: 28). These problems are only exacerbated by internet and the new social media; all the more it is important to underline the procedural constraints of a rational discourse, which underpin the public reason approach.
22 That is, the principles of participation, transparency, reason giving, and review.
23 On this point, see Douglas (2009), Schudson (2006) and Wildavsky (1979).

References

Apel, K.O. (1976) *Towards a Transformation of Philosophy*. London: Routledge & Kegan Paul.
Austin, J.L. (1962) *How to Do Things with Words*. Oxford: Clarendon Press.
Brown, M.B. (2009) *Science in Democracy*. Cambridge: The MIT Press.
Cohen, J. (2009) 'Truth and Public Reason', *Philosophy and Public Affairs*, 37(1): 2–42.
Davidson, D. (2001) *Subjective, Intersubjective, Objective*. Oxford: Oxford University Press
Dewey, J. (1927) *The Public and its Problems*. New York: Holt Publishers.
Douglas, H.E. (2009) *Science, Policy, and the Value-Free Ideal*. Pittsburg, PA: University of Pittsburg Press.
Dryzek, J. and Niemeyer, S. (2008) 'Discursive Representation', *American Political Science Review*, 102(4): 481–493.
Estlund, D. (1993) 'Making Truth Safe for Democracy', in D. Copp, J. Hampton and J.E. Roemer (eds.) *The Ide of Democracy* (pp. 77–100). Cambridge: Cambridge University Press.
Eriksen, A. (2020) 'Political Values in Independent Agencies', *Regulation & Governance*, online first. https://doi.org/10.1111/rego.12299
Eriksen, E.O. (2009) *The Unfinished Democratization of Europe*. Oxford: Oxford University Press.
Eriksen, E.O. and Molander, A. (2008) 'Profesjon, Rett og Politikk', in A. Molander and L.I. Terum (eds.) *Profesjonsstudier* (pp. 161–176). Oslo: Universitetsforlaget.

Finkel, A.M. (2018) 'Demystifying Evidence-Based Policy Analysis by Revealing Hidden Value-Laden Constraints', *Hastings Center Report*, 48(S1): 21–49.
Forst, R. (2012) *The Right to Justification: Elements of a Constructivist Theory of Justice* [Trans. J. Flynn]. New York: Columbia University Press.
Galston, W.A. (2012) 'Introduction: The Argument in Brief', in J. Elkins and A. Norris (eds.) *Truth and Democracy: Theme and Variations*. Philadelphia: University of Pennsylvania Press.
Gundersen, T. (2020) 'Value-Free yet Policy-Relevant? The Normative Views of Climate Scientists', *Perspectives on Science*, 28(1): 89–118.
Gaus, G. F. (1996) *Justificatory Liberalism*. New York: Oxford University Press.
Habermas, J. (1984) *The Theory of Communicative Action*, Vol. 1. Boston, MA: Beacon Press.
Habermas, J. (1989) *The Structural Transformation of the Public Sphere*. Cambridge: MIT Press.
Habermas, J. (1996) *Between Facts and Norms*. Cambridge: MIT Press.
Habermas, J. (2003) *Truth and Justification*. Cambridge: MIT Press.
Habermas, J. (2019) *Auch eine Geschichte der Philosophie: Vernünftige Freiheit. Spuren des Diskurses über Glauben und Wissen*, vol. 2. Berlin Suhrkamp.
Holmes, S. (1993) 'Toqueville and Democracy', in J. Hampton, and J.E. Roemer (eds.) *The Idea of Democracy* (pp. 23–63). Cambridge: Cambridge University Press.
Kant, I. ([1795]1996) 'Toward Perpetual Peace', in M. Gregor (ed.) *Practical Philosophy* (pp. 311–352). Cambridge: Cambridge University Press.
Kitcher, P. (2011) *Science in a Democratic Society*. New York: Prometheus Books.
Mansbridge, J. (2003) 'Rethinking Representation', *American Political Science Review*, 97(4): 515–528.
Mansbridge, J. (2011) 'Clarifying the Concept of Representation', *American Political Science Review*, 105(3): 621–630.
Mashaw, J.L. (2018) *Reasoned Administration and Democratic Legitimacy*. Cambridge: Cambridge University Press.
Müller, J.W. (2016) *What is Populism?*. Philadelphia: University of Pennsylvania Press.
Parsons, T. (1951) *The Social System*. New York: The Free Press.
Peirce, C. (1958) *Selected Writings*. New York: Dover Publications.
Pitkin, H. (1967) *The Concept of Representation*. Los Angeles: University of California Press.
Popper, K. (2012) *The Open Society and Its Enemies*. London: Routledge.
Rawls, J. (1971) *Theory of Justice*. Cambridge, MA: Belknap Press.
Rawls, J. (1993) *Political Liberalism*. New York: Columbia University Press.
Richardson, H.S. (2002) *Democratic Autonomy: Public Reasoning about the Ends of Policy*. Oxford: Oxford University Press.
Saward, M. (2010) *The Representative Claim*. Oxford: Oxford University Press.
Scanlon, T.M. (2014) *Being Realistic about Reasons*. Oxford: Oxford University Press.
Schmitt, C. (1932) *The Concept of the Political* [reprint, 1996]. Chicago, IL: University of Chicago Press.
Schudson, M. (2006) 'The Trouble with Experts – and Why Democracies Need Them', *Theory and Society*, 35(5/6): 491–506.
Soper, P. (2002) *The Ethics of Deterrence: Learning from Law's Moral*. Cambridge: Cambridge University Press.
Sunstein, C.R. (1997) *Free Markets and Social Justice*. Oxford: Oxford University Press.
Urbinati, N. and Warren, M.E. (2008) 'The Concept of Representation in Contemporary Democratic Theory', *Annual Review of Political Science*, 11(1): 387–412.
Vieira, M.B. and Runciman, D. (2008) *Representation*. Cambridge: Polity Press.
Wildavsky, A.B. (1979) *Speaking the Truth to Power: The Art and Craft of Policy Analysis*. Boston, MA: Little, Brown & Co.

INDEX

Note: Page numbers followed by "n" refer to notes.

accountability 2, 3; beyond control 119–134; and inter institutional respect 99–115; manifest responses to trustworthiness 108–109; overload 10, 83, 100; for performance 107–111; recognition model of 176; in the regulatory state 82–87; through affirmation 108; through recognition of distinct sphere of action 110–111
active *vs.* passive interaction 123–124
administrative state 4, 16, 38
Administrative Procedure Act of 1946 (APA) 35, 38–42; § 551(12) 47; § 555(e) 45, 47
affirmation: accountability through 108; as intentional act 109–110
agencies 7; drift 26; instrumentalism 23; regulatory *see* regulatory agencies
AIR *see* arguments from inductive risk (AIR)
American administrative law: right to reasons in 38–43
Amtenbrink, F. 69
Anderson, E. 101, 102, 115n3
APA *see* Administrative Procedure Act of 1946 (APA)
arbitrary rule 2–4, 6, 9, 15, 141, 173, 188; *see also* dominance
arguments from inductive risk (AIR) 162–165, 170–171n6, 171n7

authority: of connection 125–126; kinds of 120–122; measuring modes of 122–125
autonomy 8, 9, 14, 24–26, 61, 62, 66, 82, 84, 86–88, 95, 105, 106, 140, 167, 175, 187, 188
autonomy, democratic. private, public 9

Bach, T. 85, 86
Beauchamp, T.L. 168
Beetham, D. 70
Behn, R. 108
BNetzA *see* Federal Network Agency (BNetzA)
bodies, unelected 1–3, 6–9, 11, 16, 19, 20, 25, 40, 139, 142, 155–158, 161, 162, 167, 169, 170, 170n1, 173, 175, 192
Bohman, J. 29n13
Boon, J. 89
Brown, M.B. 12n2, 29n6, 170n5
Bundesbank 61, 64, 74
Bundesverfassungsgericht (BVerfG) 29n5
bureaucratic reputation theory 10, 81, 82, 84, 85, 96
Busuioc, M. 113
BVerfG *see* Bundesverfassungsgericht (BVerfG)

Carpenter, D.P. 86, 89
Charter of Fundamental Rights 193n1; article 41, 34; article II-101, 34

Childress, J.F. 168
Christiano, T. 23–24, 29n9
claims-making: representative 177, 178; truth-based 11, 174, 178–179, 187, 192
Clausing, J. 115n9
Clean Air Act 18; Section 109(b)(1) 19
COG *see* Committee of Central Bank Governors (COG)
Cohen, J. 29n13, 181, 193n8
Committee of Central Bank Governors (COG) 61, 64, 65
common will, formation of 176–177
complexity 1, 4, 17, 20, 104, 111, 144
conferral, principle of 12n12, 19, 29n5
conflict resolution 1, 185
Council of Ministers 68
cybersquatting 115n9

Darwall, S. 104, 110
decisionism 8, 11, 174, 179–181, 192
decision making 5, 11, 21, 80, 81, 85, 86, 88, 122, 144, 151, 170n1, 182, 187, 189, 191; administrative 3, 7, 17, 45; agency 2, 3, 7, 9, 22, 87; democratic 159, 167; depoliticised 3, 4, 15, 20, 23, 28; institutional 44; knowledge-based 173; non-arbitrariness of 6, 22, 23; non-partisan 1–2; political 24, 137–139, 146–148, 150; public participation in 84; rational 25–26, 190; reasoned 44, 48; transparency in 37
deliberation 11, 27, 28, 77, 119, 120, 123, 131, 134, 137–140, 144, 146, 147, 149, 151, 152, 173, 177, 182, 187, 188, 191
democracy 1–11, 14, 15, 21, 22, 26–28, 46, 47, 50, 53n24, 56–60, 62, 67, 69, 71, 75, 76, 121, 141, 145, 147, 149, 152n5, 159, 173, 179–181, 186; and knowledge, internal relation between 187–188; member state 63; neo-republican democracy, revisionist ideal of 138–140; technocratic conception of 170n4
democratic agents 7–9
democratic equality 149–151
democratic republicanism 11, 137–153; expert bodies in 141–145
democratic responsiveness hypothesis 87
democratic self-legislation and political expertise, tensions between 145–149
Demortain, D. 96n1
depolitizisation 3, 4, 7, 15, 16, 20, 23, 27, 138–140, 145
discourse theory 182
discretionary powers 3, 6, 9, 14, 18, 22, 26, 27, 52n21, 67, 72, 173, 174, 176

division of labour 70, 119, 134, 137, 186
dominance 4, 6, 15, 16, 26–28; *see also* arbitrary rule
Douglas, H.E. 163, 165, 194n23
Draghi, M. 68
Dryzek, J. 29n13
Due Process Clauses of the US Constitution 35, 38, 39, 47
Dyson, K. 61, 66
Dyzenhaus, D. 52n22

EBA *see* European Banking Authority (EBA)
ECB *see* European Central Bank (ECB)
ECGAB *see* European Code of Good Administrative Behaviour ('ECGAB')
Economic and Monetary Affairs Committee (ECON) 11, 120, 126, 127
Economic and Monetary Affairs Committee of the Parliament (EMAC) 70
Economic and Monetary Union 16
ECON *see* Economic and Monetary Affairs Committee (ECON)
EEA *see* European Environment Agency (EEA)
EFCA *see* European Fisheries Control Agency (EFCA)
efficient market hypothesis (EMH) 73, 74
EFSA *see* European Food Safety Authority (EFSA)
Egeberg, M. 12n3
EIOPA *see* European Insurance and Occupational Pensions Authority (EIOPA)
Elliott, K.C. 166
EMAC *see* Economic and Monetary Affairs Committee of the Parliament (EMAC)
EMH *see* efficient market hypothesis (EMH)
empirical objection against value-free ideal 160–161
EMS *see* European Monetary System (EMS)
EMU *see* Europe's Monetary Union (EMU)
Environmental Protection Agency (EPA) 18–19
EPA *see* Environmental Protection Agency (EPA)
epistemic asymmetry 11, 137, 138, 149–152, 164
epistemic community 64–65
epistocracy 26, 60, 68–70, 76

epistocratic orders, legitimacy deficits of 16–22; contestation and protest 19–20; new doctrine 18–19; new risk agenda 20–22; statutory regulation 16–17
EP *see* European Parliament (EP)
Eriksen, A. 12n2
Eriksen, E.O. 29n13
ERM *see* exchange rate mechanism (ERM)
ESMA *see* European Securities and Markets Authority (ESMA)
Estlund, D.M. 29n8, 65, 193n15
EU Commission 17
Euro: money, power and knowledge in creation of 58–64
European Banking Authority (EBA) 18, 129
European Central Bank (ECB) 5, 10, 14, 16–17, 56–77, 176; elusiveness of 71–75; Governing Council 74; institutional design 65–67; responsibility 67–71
European Code of Good Administrative Behaviour ('ECGAB') 43, 49; article 18, 49
European Environment Agency (EEA) 157
European Fisheries Control Agency (EFCA) 157
European Food Safety Authority (EFSA) 157
European Insurance and Occupational Pensions Authority (EIOPA) 18, 129
European Monetary System (EMS) 61, 65
European Parliament (EP) 68–71, 127, 130
European Securities and Markets Authority (ESMA) 11, 18, 120, 129, 130, 170n2, 176
European Union (EU) 4, 17, 34, 36, 60, 108, 174
European Union Law 4, 43–45
Europe's Monetary Union (EMU) 60, 61
Eurozone 5, 10, 14
EU *see* European Union (EU)
evidence-based strategy 15, 23–24
exchange rate mechanism (ERM) 61, 62, 65
expertise 137–153; political and democratic self-legislation, tensions between 145–149
experts 173–194; beyond decisionism 179–181; beyond delegation 175–176; bodies, in democratic republicanism 141–145; common will, formation of 176–177; facts and values, representing 177–179; getting things right 181–182; practical reason, dimensions of 183–184; pragmatic concept of truth 185–186;

public, alarming 190–192; reasonable or rational outcomes 188–190; reasoning, values in 155–171; pragmatic view of 11, 165–169; value-free ideal *see* value-free ideal; warranting correctness 186–187; world reference 184–185

FDA *see* Food and Drug Administration (FDA)
Featherstone, K. 61
Federal Network Agency (BNetzA) 87, 88, 91, 93, 95
Federal Tort Claims Act 35
Finkel, A.M. 183–184
FinTech 129
First World War 16
Fischer, F. 29n6
Food and Drug Administration (FDA) 86
forward-looking *vs.* backward-looking 124–125
Foucault, M. 21
Frankfurter Allgemeine Zeitung 82, 88
Freedom of Information Act of 2000 35
French Revolution 59
Friendly, H. 39
Frontex 170n2
Froomkin, M. 53n36

Gardner, J. 37, 38, 53n25
Gaus, G. 57
Gaus, G.F. 193n6
Gelfert, A. 153n11
Gérard, N. 53n30
GMO *see* Government Accountability Office (GMO)
good administration 34, 35
Goodhart, C. 71
Government Accountability Office (GMO) 49, 183
de Grauwe, P. 72
Great Depression 16

Habermas, J. 50, 57, 58, 182, 185
Hacking, I. 12n2, 29n6
Harfst, D.L. 51n15
Harmonised Index of Consumer Prices (HICP) 16
Hegel, G.W.F. 106–107
Herzog, L. 115n6
HICP *see* Harmonised Index of Consumer Prices (HICP)
hierarchy *vs.* reciprocity 123
Hobbes, T. 8, 64, 179–180
Holst, C. 147, 153n8
Honneth, A. 104, 115n4

ICANN *see* Internet Corporation for Assigned Names and Numbers (ICANN)
institutional design 65–67
institutional respect 101–104
instrumental agency model 6, 7, 23, 28, 188
Intemann, K. 158, 161, 171n7
intentional goal 106
Intergovernmental Panel on Climate Change (IPCC) 156, 164
International Monetary Fund 16
Internet Corporation for Assigned Names and Numbers (ICANN) 113, 114, 115n9
IPCC *see* Intergovernmental Panel on Climate Change (IPCC)
Issing, O. 62

Jasanoff, S. 29n6

Kanska, K. 51n4, 51n16, 52n18, 52n22
Kant, I. 141, 150, 153n11, 153n13
knowledge and democracy, internal relation between 187–188
knowledge claims 24, 74, 183, 188
Kohl, H. (Chancellor) 64
Koppell, J. 113, 114
Krause, G.A. 89
Krick, E. 153n8

Laden, A.S. 123
Lamfalussy, A. 73, 74
de Lange, F. 53n23
Latour, B. 21, 29n6
League of Nations 16
legislator-command strategy 15, 24–26
legitimacy deficits, strategies for repairing 14–29; epistocratic orders 16–22; evidence-based strategy 23–24; legislator-command strategy 24–26; participatory strategy 26–28; squaring the circle on NOMIS 22–23
Lisbon Treaty 193n1
Locke, J. 18
Lodge, M. 113
Lord, C. 8

Maastricht European Council 64
Maastricht Treaty 6
Majone, G. 99
mandate 5, 12n5, 20, 25, 46, 61, 66–69, 71–74, 76, 100, 104–106, 108–114, 119, 121, 126, 142, 144, 146, 147, 157, 160, 165, 170, 176, 177, 187, 189, 193n7; multidirectional 10; political objection against value-free ideal 161–162

manifest expression 105–106
Mansbridge, J. 68
Maor, M. 85, 86
Mashaw, J.L. 51n15, 103–104, 188, 189
McCormick, J. 138–139
McCubbins, M.D. 51n8
de Melo-Martín, I. 158, 161, 171n7
member state democracy 63
Mendes, J. 16–17
Meroni doctrine 17
Meroni-Romano doctrine 18
MiFID II 129
Mill, J.S. 57, 58
Mitterrand, François (President) 64
Molander, A. 147
moral 7, 8, 10, 11, 21, 24, 38, 45, 46, 50, 58, 73, 85, 89, 91, 93, 95, 100, 112, 143–145, 151, 155, 156, 158, 159, 163, 166–168, 170, 174, 178–180, 182–187, 189–191, 193n14, 193n15
Moravcsik, A. 60–61
multidirectional mandate 10
multiple accountability disorder 100

neo-republican democracy, revisionist ideal of 138–140
new risk agenda 20–22
NOMIS *see* non-majoritarian institutions (NOMIS)
non-majoritarian institutions (NOMIS) 3–8, 11, 14, 15, 19, 20, 173–176, 179, 183, 184, 187–192; squaring the circle on 22–23

O'Neill, O. 103

Padoa-Schioppa, T. 62
parliamentary hearings 119–135, 122–125; analysis 128–130; authority of connection 125–126; implications 133–134; interaction 130–131; and measuring modes of authority 122–125; orientation 132–133; relationship 131–132; research design 126–128
participation 6, 7, 15, 21, 22, 26–27, 42, 50, 70, 84, 148, 151, 175, 188; participatory strategy 15, 26–28
Peterson, J. 153n13
Pettit, P. 138–141, 152n4
Pildes, R. 101, 102, 115n3
Pinter, H. 190
Plato 29n8, 56
pluralism 1, 8, 181
Pöhl, K.-O. 61
political conception of truth 175, 180–183

political equality 137, 150, 153
political mandate objection against value-free ideal 161–162
Ponce, J. 52n17
positive affirmation 105
practical reason, dimensions of 183–184
pragmatic concept of truth 185–186
pragmatism 171n8, 181
price stability 16
principal–agent theories 7
problem-solving 1, 20, 22, 27
public, alarming 190–192
public reason model 173

Radin, B. 103, 111
rationality 9, 20, 38, 43, 45, 73, 112, 175, 176, 183, 188, 194n21
Rawls, J. 73, 180, 193n9
reasonable or rational outcomes 188–190
reasoned administration 34–53
reason giving 3, 7–10, 28, 108, 120, 131, 174, 179–181, 183, 185, 187, 189, 191; in American administrative law 38–43; in law of the European Union 43–45; revisionist account of 45–50; as social practice 35–39
reciprocal independence 143
recognition model 104–107; of accountability 176; intentional goal 106; manifest expression 105–106; positive affirmation 105; species of 106–107
recognition respect *versus* appraisal respect 104
RegTP see *Regulierungsbehorde fur Telekommunikation und Post* (*RegTP*)
regulatory agencies 99–115; communicative responses of 82–87; in Germany 87–88
Regulierungsbehorde fur Telekommunikation und Post (*RegTP*) 87, 88
reputational profile hypothesis 86
reputational threats 82–87, 96n2
reputation model 113–114
reputation theory 94; bureaucratic 10, 81, 82, 84, 85, 96
Resnik, D.B. 166
restraint model 112–113
revisionist account of reason giving 45–50
Richardson, H.S. 188
rightness 184–185, 193n14
right to good administration 34–36
right to justification 174
right to reasons 173–174
Rodrik, D. 62
Rossi, J. 53n37

Roth, A.S. 115n2
Rousseau, J.J. 141
Rubin, E.L. 53n24
Rudner, R. 162–164, 169

Sabel, C. 29n13
Scanlon, T.M. 115n7, 193n8
Scharpf, F. 67
Schmitt, C. 179
Scholten, M. 17
Schudson, M. 194n23
Schwarze, J. 52n21
science 3, 11, 21, 22, 24, 27, 83, 107, 111, 121, 155, 157–167, 169, 170n2, 171n7, 175, 177, 180, 186, 188
science and technology studies (STS) 21, 107
science, deconstruction of 22
Shapiro, I. 53n38
Shapiro, M. 52n19
Skorupski, J. 104
sovereignty 11, 62, 102, 138, 141, 142, 145, 149, 151
stakeholder engagement 109–110
statutory regulation 16–17
Steele, K. 164, 165
STS *see* science and technology studies (STS)
Sunstein, C.R. 170n4

Taggart, M. 52n22
Talisse, R. 57, 58
technocracy 4, 7, 27, 56, 64, 84, 146, 148, 159–160, 169, 170n4
technocrats 7–9
Tilly, C. 35–36, 38, 51n7
time inconsistency problems 10
transactionism 11, 155, 156, 160, 165–167, 170, 171n7
transactionist arguments against value-free ideal: arguments from inductive risk 162–165, 170–171n6, 171n7; empirical objection 160–161; political mandate objection 161–162
Treaty Establishing a Constitution for Europe 34; article II-101, 51n4
Treaty Establishing the European Community ('EC Treaty'), article 253, 43–45
Trichet, J.-C. 72
Trondal, J. 12n3
trustworthiness, manifest responses to 108–109
Tucker Act of 2000 35
Tucker, P. 74
Turner, S. 138, 149

unelected bodies 1–3, 6–9, 11, 16, 19, 20, 25, 40, 139, 142, 155–158, 161, 162, 167, 169, 170, 170n1, 173, 175, 192

validation 7, 178, 185

value-free ideal (VFI) 11, 155–170, 170n3, 170n4, 171n7; democratic argument for 159–160; epistemic argument for 158–159; for scientific experts in unelected bodies 156–160, 167; transactionist arguments against 160–165, 170–171n6, 171n7

values, in expert reasoning 155–171; pragmatic view of 11, 165–169; value-free ideal *see* value-free ideal

Venzke, I. 16–17
Vesterdorf, B. 51n16, 52n18, 52n22
VFI *see* value-free ideal (VFI)
Viehoff, D. 152n3

Weber, A. 68
Weber, M. 23, 46, 179
Weingart, P. 29n6
wicked problems 20, 27, 175
Wildavsky, A.B. 194n23
Wilholt, T. 158
Wilson, J.Q. 3, 29n3
Woolgar, S. 29n6
World Bank 16

Zweifel, T.D. 53n24

Printed in the United States
by Baker & Taylor Publisher Services